THE GRENADIER GUARDS
IN THE GREAT WAR OF
1914–1918

MACMILLAN AND CO., LIMITED
LONDON · BOMBAY · CALCUTTA · MADRAS
MELBOURNE

THE MACMILLAN COMPANY
NEW YORK · BOSTON · CHICAGO
DALLAS · SAN FRANCISCO

THE MACMILLAN CO. OF CANADA, LTD.
TORONTO

Field Marshal H.R.H. The Duke of Connaught
K.G., G.C.B. &c.

Colonel of the Regiment

THE
GRENADIER GUARDS
IN THE GREAT WAR OF
1914-1918

BY

LIEUT.-COLONEL
THE RIGHT HON. SIR FREDERICK PONSONBY
(LATE GRENADIER GUARDS)

WITH AN INTRODUCTION BY
LIEUT.-GENERAL THE EARL OF CAVAN

MAPS BY MR. EMERY WALKER

IN THREE VOLUMES
VOL. II

MACMILLAN AND CO., LIMITED
ST. MARTIN'S STREET, LONDON
1920

COPYRIGHT

Printed and bound by Antony Rowe Ltd, Eastbourne

CONTENTS

CHAPTER XVIII
JANUARY 1 TO SEPTEMBER 1, 1916 (3RD AND 4TH BATTS.) — 1

CHAPTER XIX
THE BATTLE OF THE SOMME (1ST, 2ND, 3RD, AND 4TH BATTS.) — 27

CHAPTER XX
OCTOBER, NOVEMBER, DECEMBER 1916 (1ST, 2ND, 3RD, AND 4TH BATTALIONS) 148

CHAPTER XXI
JANUARY, FEBRUARY, MARCH 1917 (1ST, 2ND, 3RD, AND 4TH BATTALIONS) 160

CHAPTER XXII
APRIL, MAY, JUNE, JULY 1917 (1ST, 2ND, 3RD, AND 4TH BATTALIONS) 174

CHAPTER XXIII
BOESINGHE (1ST, 2ND, 3RD, AND 4TH BATTALIONS). . 199

CHAPTER XXIV

August, September 1917 (1st, 2nd, 3rd, and 4th Batts.)   235

CHAPTER XXV

The Crossing of the Broembeek (1st, 2nd, 3rd, and 4th Battalions) 246

CHAPTER XXVI

Cambrai and Gouzeaucourt (1st, 2nd, 3rd, and 4th Battalions) 266

CHAPTER XXVII

January, February, March 1918 (1st, 2nd, 3rd, and 4th Battalions) 349

ILLUSTRATIONS

Field-Marshal H.R.H. The Duke of Connaught, K.G., G.C.B., etc., Colonel of the Regiment	*Frontispiece*
	FACING PAGE
Lieutenant-General The Earl of Cavan, K.P., K.C.B.	48
Major-General G. D. Jeffreys, C.M.G.	80
Brigadier-General C. E. Corkran, C.M.G.	112
Inspection of the Guards Division by Field-Marshal H.R.H. the Duke of Connaught, K.G., November 1, 1916	150
The Grenadier Guards marching in Fours past their Colonel, Field-Marshal H.R.H. the Duke of Connaught, K.G., November 1, 1916	159
Brigadier-General G. F. Trotter, C.B., C.M.G., D.S.O.	198

MAPS

Battle of the Somme, the evening of September 15, 1916	118
Battle of the Somme, the night of September 25, 1916	138
Boesinghe, July 31, 1917	200
Broembeek, October 10, 1917	246
Attack on Fontaine, November 27, 1917	306
Attack on Gonnelieu and Gauche Wood, December 1, 1917	332

CHAPTER XVIII

JANUARY TO SEPTEMBER 1916

THE 3RD BATTALION

At the beginning of 1916 the officers of the 3rd Battalion were:

Colonel N. A. L. Corry, D.S.O.	Commanding Officer.
Maj. M. E. Makgill-Crichton-Maitland	Second in Command.
Capt. O. Lyttelton	Adjutant.
Lieut. E. H. J. Wynne	Transport.
2nd Lieut. L. St. L. Hermon-Hodge	Bombing Officer.
Hon. Lieut. G. H. Wall	Quartermaster.
Capt. R. Wolrige-Gordon	No. 1 Company.
Lieut. the Hon. H. E. Eaton	,, ,,
Lieut. G. P. Bowes-Lyon	,, ,,
Capt. the Hon. R. P. Stanhope	No. 2 Company.
2nd Lieut. E. R. M. Fryer	,, ,,
2nd Lieut. J. F. Worsley	,, ,,
2nd Lieut. W. Parker	,, ,,
Capt. G. G. Gunnis	No. 3 Company.
Lieut. the Hon. F. O. H. Eaton	,, ,,
Lieut. F. J. V. B. Hopley	,, ,,
Capt. E. N. E. M. Vaughan	No. 4 Company.
Lieut. the Hon. A. E. F. Yorke	,, ,,
Lieut. R. Asquith	,, ,,
2nd Lieut. R. W. Parker	,, ,,
Lieut. A. T. Logan, R.A.M.C.	Medical Officer.

On the 1st the 3rd Battalion marched from Merville to Laventie, and went into billets vacated

CHAPTER XVIII.
3rd Batt.
Jan. 1916.

by the 2nd Battalion Scots Guards. On the 3rd it took over the left sector from the 1st Battalion Scots Guards, with the Battalion Headquarters at Wangerie Farm. Forty-eight hours in the trenches followed by forty-eight hours' rest was the regular routine for the next fortnight. The trenches in this sector were in a very good state, and it was possible, therefore, to go in for refinements and erect splinter-proof shelters; but the enemy's artillery was very active, and expended a great deal of ammunition on the reserve trenches and communications. During this fortnight a troop of Wiltshire Yeomanry was attached to the Battalion for instruction, and did very well although it was quite new to trench warfare. On the 12th Colonel Corry relinquished command of the Battalion, and on the 14th Lieut.-Colonel Jeffreys took charge of it temporarily, pending the arrival of Major Sergison-Brooke.

On the 14th the Battalion marched back to La Gorgue, where it remained in billets for ten days, after which it returned to Laventie. Great activity was noticeable behind the enemy's lines, and as this might be the prelude to an attack every precaution was taken. There seemed some possibility of a gas attack, and special warnings were conveyed to each company, but although the enemy's artillery shelled the strong points in our line, Elgin Post, Fauquissart Cross Roads, and Hougoumont Post, no infantry attack was made by the enemy.

Feb.

On February 1 the 3rd Battalion proceeded to Merville, where it remained until the 7th, when it marched to Riez Bailleul. The usual routine of two days in and two days out of the trenches was observed until the 16th, when it was relieved by the 9th Battalion Royal Welsh Fusiliers, and marched back to La Gorgue. The only incident worth recording during this tour of duty in the trenches was an unfortunate accident that happened to Lieutenant R. W. Parker. He was returning with a patrol early in the morning, and as he came in over the parapet he slipped, and fell on a bayonet which penetrated his leg below the knee. On the 17th Lieutenant W. Champneys and Second Lieutenant G. D. Jackson arrived, and on the 19th the Battalion marched to Eecke. The following day it proceeded to Wormhoudt, where it remained for two days, and then marched to Poperinghe.

Chapter XVIII.
3rd Batt.
Feb. 1916.

Major-General G. Feilding gave a lecture to the officers on March 1, and impressed on them the importance of making the line north of Hooge strong and defensible, since it was the left flank of the whole British line. This could be done only by ingenious concealment of any new work and by unremitting efforts of all ranks. He added that, if the enemy concentrated opposite the Ypres salient, a withdrawal would be made to the Canal line. Any ground that could not be held against the enemy's artillery fire would be defended by strong points and machine-guns concealed in natural features, and placed apart from entrenchments and other works.

March.

On the 5th the 3rd Battalion proceeded to Calais, and marched to Camp Beaumarais, where it remained until the 18th. Here a most unfortunate bombing accident occurred. No. 4

CHAPTER XVIII.

3rd Batt. March 1916.

Company bombers were practising under Lieutenant L. Hermon-Hodge behind a thick sandbag wall, when a bomb exploded prematurely on leaving the thrower's hand. Five men were killed and sixteen wounded in addition to Lieutenant Hermon-Hodge himself, who received fragments of the bomb in his right arm. On the 18th the 3rd Battalion left Calais, and went by train to Cassel, where it detrained and marched to Oudezeele.

On the 26th it reached the Ypres salient, and went into the support trenches. Lieut.-Colonel Sergison-Brooke was on leave, and the Battalion was commanded by Major Maitland. Special precautions with regard to gas were taken, and on the wind becoming favourable it was arranged that the Brigade would send the message "Gas alert," when all sentries would be doubled, and men would be placed at the entrance of each dugout to give the alarm. Warnings were also issued with regard to the aeroplanes, which required careful watching, since the enemy in that sector was very active, and if any movement was seen on the Canal bank or in the town shelling immediately began. During the sixteen days the Battalion spent at Ypres there were a certain number of casualties, and the number of sick increased slightly.

On the 30th the 3rd Battalion had to relieve the Scots Guards under very trying conditions, for not only was the front line being shelled, but the communication trenches were also included in the bombardment. The three leading companies succeeded in reaching the front line without casualties, but No. 2, under Captain

JANUARY TO SEPTEMBER 1916

Stanhope, came under shrapnel fire as it passed through Potidje, and had seven casualties. Communication between the Battalion Headquarters and the companies was cut, and there was considerable difficulty in transmitting the orders. The leading companies, which were ordered to hold from Duke Street to Roulers railway, found the front trenches devastated and swept by shrapnel fired both frontally and obliquely from Pilkem and Belleward ridge. The 1st Battalion Scots Guards had suffered considerably and was in great difficulties, as communication along the front line was impossible under cover. Men were cut off from the remainder of their company and were covered with mud and debris, some even being buried. Relieving a battalion under such conditions required time, and it was not till 4 A.M. that the relief was complete.

In view of the probability of an attack while the relief was being carried out, three batteries of 18-pounder guns were ordered to put down a barrage on the German front line. This proved to be a great help, and no doubt prevented the 3rd Battalion from suffering as heavy losses as the Scots Guards. There were in all five men killed and sixteen wounded, in addition to Captain R. Wolrige-Gordon, whose leg was grazed by a bullet. The front line was wrecked, but by placing men in the wreckage under what cover there was the trench was made defensible. The enemy, however, showed no signs of life, and the following days were quiet. Meanwhile it was found difficult to drain the trenches, which were in a very dilapidated condition after the

6   THE GRENADIER GUARDS

CHAPTER XVIII.

3rd Batt. March 1916.

April.

bombardment. The whole ground was cut up, and water stood in the shell-holes, while the wooden revetments had been torn to pieces and buried beneath the parapets and parados. The work of clearing away the debris was necessarily slow, and the water could not be got rid of in spite of the good fall in the ground towards Belleward Beer. At first it was impossible to go down the front line for more than a few yards, but after two days' hard work the trench was so far improved that men could crawl along it, although not without difficulty. On April 3, instead of returning to Ypres, the 3rd Battalion went into camp just west of Vlamertinghe.

The officers of the 3rd Battalion at that time were :

Lieut.-Colonel B. N. Sergison-Brooke	Commanding Officer.
Maj. M. E. Makgill-Crichton-Maitland	Second in Command.
Capt. O. Lyttelton	Adjutant.
Lieut. E. H. J. Wynne	Transport Officer.
Lieut. G. H. Wall	Quartermaster.
Lieut. the Hon. H. E. Eaton	No. 1 Company.
Lieut. G. P. Bowes-Lyon	,, ,,
Captain the Hon. R. P. Stanhope	No. 2 Company.
Lieut. J. F. Worsley	,, ,,
Lieut. E. R. M. Fryer	,, ,,
2nd Lieut. R. W. Parker	,, ,,
Capt. E. S. Ward	No. 3 Company.
Lieut. F. J. V. B. Hopley	,, ,,
Lieut. the Hon. F. O. H. Eaton	,, ,,
Lieut. W. Champneys	,, ,,
Capt. E. N. E. M. Vaughan	No. 4 Company.
2nd Lieut. G. D. Jackson	,, ,,
Capt. G. G. Gunnis	Bombing Officer.
Lieut. the Hon. A. E. F. Yorke	Lewis Gun Officer.
Monsieur Minne	Belgian Interpreter.

Attached—Capt. A. T. Logan, R.A.M.C.

JANUARY TO SEPTEMBER 1916

After four days' rest the 3rd Battalion returned to the same line of trenches it had occupied before, and found them worse than ever. The Scots Guards who had been there had again been subjected to a severe bombardment, and all the work that had been done was now obliterated. On the 4th Lieutenant Worsley left to take up his appointment as Trench Mortar Officer. The four days spent in the trenches proved to be very quiet, as the Germans seemed to have expended all their shells on the Scots Guards, and nothing of any interest occurred. On the 11th the Battalion moved to Poperinghe, where most unfortunately four men were killed and two wounded whilst unloading the officers' kits. On the 12th Captain Wolrige-Gordon rejoined, his wound not having proved very serious, and Second Lieutenant M. Thrupp arrived. Two days later Captain A. K. Mackenzie, Captain W. A. L. Stewart, and Second Lieutenant F. J. Heasman joined the Battalion.

The system of reliefs was changed at this time in order to avoid the inconvenience of two brigades relieving on the same night. The tour of duty was divided as follows: five days at Ypres, five days in the front line, three days at Camp B, three days in the front line. On the 18th the 3rd Battalion moved up into Ypres, and went into support trenches. The men were provided with steel helmets, and left their service caps with the transport and their unnecessary kit in sandbags at the prison. On the 24th they relieved the 1st Battalion Scots Guards in the front line, where the trenches proved to be fairly good,

8   THE GRENADIER GUARDS

CHAPTER XVIII.
3rd Batt.
April 1916.

although there was still a lot of water standing everywhere. As the ground was so much cut up, the draining of the trenches was not easy; and since any movement during the day was impossible, all the work had to be done at night. Lieutenant Thrupp was knocked down by a shell during these operations, but was fortunately unhurt, and there were a few casualties every day. On the 29th the 3rd Battalion was relieved by the 1st Battalion Scots Guards, and retired to B Camp near Vlamertinghe.

May.

On May 1 Second Lieutenant M. Duquenoy arrived, and was appointed Transport Officer. The Battalion returned to the trenches on the 2nd, when the relief was carried out in most favourable circumstances. The three days in the front line were uneventful, although the patrols reported great activity in the enemy's lines, and the time was spent in draining operations and in wiring and repairing the parapet. A good many high-explosive shells were sent over by the enemy's artillery, which became fairly active during the third day, but the casualties were few. On the 5th the Battalion was relieved, and went by train to Poperinghe where it went into billets, but it was by no means free from shell-fire, as the German artillery periodically bombarded the town.

After a week's rest it returned to Ypres, and was employed on nightly fatigues, carrying wood for mining parties and wiring the support lines. On the night of the 16th it returned to the trenches from Duke Street to Roulers railway, and came in for a good deal of shelling, chiefly behind the lines. The usual work was continued, but forty yards of the line had been completely blown in, and accordingly the trench had to be re-dug. On the 21st the Battalion returned to Poperinghe after having been relieved by the 10th Battalion Rifle Brigade, and marched to Camp N, where it remained till the end of the month.

On June 1 the 2nd Guards Brigade proceeded to Volckerinchove, where it marched past Lieut.-General Lord Cavan, the Corps Commander, and Major-General G. Feilding, the Divisional Commander. In order to try a new method of attack, a complete representation to scale of the German trenches revetted with sand-bags was constructed, while the British line was also roughly indicated. The assault on the German trenches was then practised on the following lines: the assault was to take place in five waves, the fifth wave being a carrying company, provided by a battalion other than the actual assaulting battalion. The two leading companies were to assault in two waves, the second following about fifty yards in rear of the first. These two waves were to cross the German front-line trench without getting into it, and push on to the objective, roughly speaking, the German third line. The third wave was to pass over the German front line and take the German second line, which was to be consolidated. The fourth wave was to take and consolidate the German front line. Strong bombing parties were to be placed on both flanks of all companies, with centre bombing parties dispersed roughly opposite the German communication trenches. Bombing parties of the two leading waves were to establish blocks in the German communication trenches, while the bombing parties of the rear waves were to clear the communication trenches forward and get into touch with the two leading waves. All the men were to carry two Mills grenades and four sand-bags, tucked through the web equipment in front, and every third man was to carry a shovel slung. The R.E. material and trench-mortar ammunition was to be carried by the fifth wave. At night the men were to carry Roman candles to show the position of the waves. All the battalions in the Brigade carried out this form of attack, and when they had mastered the new features it was practised by the Brigade.

On the 14th the 3rd Battalion moved to Vlamertinghe in motor lorries to relieve the 9th Canadian Battalion, which had suffered heavy losses, and remained there for three days, with one company at Ypres and three companies at the west end of Zillebeke Lake. On the night of the 18th it took over from the 1st Battalion Scots Guards the front trenches in Sanctuary Wood, and found the whole ground much cut about by shell-fire. The wire, which the Germans had put up whilst in occupation of the old British front line, combined with the natural obstacles, such as fallen trees and debris, made any approach on the part of the enemy very difficult. Reconnaissance proved that the Germans had withdrawn to their original front line, leaving the old British line full of dead, equipment, and ammunition. Over 350 rifles and a large quantity

JANUARY TO SEPTEMBER 1916

of ammunition were thus collected. Both on the 19th and 20th the Battalion was subjected to heavy shelling, and even during the relief suffered casualties, among whom was Lieut. the Hon. H. E. Eaton who was wounded. After a week's rest in Camp D, the Battalion took over the left reserve sub-sector, at the junction of the British and French armies on the Yser Canal, where it remained for three days, and on the night of the 30th it went up again into the front line.

CHAPTER XVIII.
3rd Batt.
June 1916.

During the three days the Battalion was in these trenches there was a great deal of activity on the part of the artillery on both sides. Preparation was being made on our side for an attack by the Welsh Guards on Morteloje Estaminet, while the enemy replied by laying down a heavy barrage over our communication trenches; but as the men had been withdrawn from the first trench the casualties of the 3rd Battalion were not heavy. On the 3rd the Battalion withdrew into support by the Canal bank, and returned again to the front line on the 8th. On the 7th Major Maitland left to take command of the 1st Battalion, and on the 9th Second Lieutenant W. W. S. C. Neville arrived. On the 12th the Battalion retired to the Canal bank, and three days later proceeded to Camp E, where it remained for ten days. On the 25th it proceeded to Volckerinchove, and left the Ypres area. On the 31st it moved down to Le Souich, where it was employed for a week in digging for another Division.

July.

On August 3 Lieutenant G. F. R. Hirst and Lieutenant W. A. Stainton joined the Battalion,

Aug.

12 THE GRENADIER GUARDS

<small>CHAPTER XVIII.
3rd Batt.
Aug. 1916.</small>

and on the 6th Second Lieutenant A. H. Penfold and Second Lieutenant H. St J. Williams arrived. On the 9th His Majesty the King paid an informal visit to the 2nd Brigade, but there was no actual inspection or parade. On the 13th the Battalion went up into the trenches in front of Bertrancourt, and beyond the usual amount of shelling nothing of interest occurred. On the 15th Lieutenant C. G. Gardner and Second Lieutenant G. M. Cornish joined the Battalion. Two days later the Battalion went into camp at Sailly-au-Bois, where it was packed rather closely together; and when the enemy began shelling that locality it had to be taken out of the camp and placed in artillery formation in the fields in rear. The remainder of the month was spent in training, during which the Battalion was encamped at Bus-les-Artois, Amplier Naours, and finally Morlancourt.

THE 4TH BATTALION

<small>4th Batt. Jan. 1.</small>

The officers of the 4th Battalion on January 1, 1916, were:

Lieut.-Colonel Lord Henry Seymour	Commanding Officer.
Capt. J. A. Morrison	Second in Command.
Capt. R. S. Lambert	Adjutant.
2nd Lieut. H. H. Sloane-Stanley	Bombing Officer.
2nd Lieut. M. Chapman	Lewis Guns.
Lieut. I. H. Ingleby	Transport Officer.
Lieut. E. Ludlow	Quartermaster.
Capt. C. L. Blundell-Hollinshead-Blundell	No. 1 Company.
2nd Lieut. F. G. Bonham-Carter	,, ,,
2nd Lieut. B. Burman	,, ,,
Capt. C. R. Britten	No. 2 Company.
Lieut. F. C. Lyon	,, ,,

JANUARY TO SEPTEMBER 1916

CHAPTER XVIII.

4th Batt. Jan. 1916.

2nd Lieut. C. G. Keith . . .	No. 2 Company.	
Capt. Sir R. Filmer, Bart. . .	No. 3 Company.	
Lieut. B. C. Layton . . .	,,	,,
2nd Lieut. G. C. Sloane-Stanley .	,,	,,
2nd Lieut. E. W. Nairn . .	,,	,,
Capt. F. O. S. Sitwell . . .	No. 4 Company.	
Lieut. the Hon. E. W. Tennant .	,,	,,
2nd Lieut. D. O. Constable . .	,,	,,

Attached—Capt. W. Hilton-Parry, R.A.M.C.

The 4th Battalion began the new year in billets at Merville, where it remained till the 13th, doing steady drill, route marching, Lewis gun and bombing practice. On the 1st, Second Lieutenant B. Burman, Second Lieutenant C. G. Keith, and Second Lieutenant D. O. Constable joined the Battalion.

On the 13th it moved up to the trenches in front of Laventie, and relieved the 2nd Battalion Irish Guards. There it remained for a fortnight, spending two days in the trenches, followed by two days in support billets. In the line it occupied were certain strong points, A 1 Redoubt, Flank Post, and Firework Post, and these were subjected daily to a systematic shelling from the German artillery. Beyond a few casualties, nothing of importance occurred until the 25th, when Captain Sir Robert Filmer was mortally wounded. He had just left the trenches when he found he had lost his glasses. Being very short-sighted, he determined to go back and look for them, although he was warned that the road was being heavily shelled at the time. With that supreme contempt for all shells that had characterised his whole conduct since he came out, he rode back when a shell burst close to him,

14   THE GRENADIER GUARDS

Chapter XVIII.

4th Batt. Jan. 1916. Feb.

killing his horse and wounding him so severely that he died the next day.

On the 27th the 4th Battalion returned to billets at Merville for four days, and on the 1st of February took over the Red House line at Laventie, where it remained until the 15th, retiring into support billets every two days. Numerous patrols lay out each night in the hopes of capturing prisoners, but these ventures were not attended with any success, and no prisoners were secured. Heavy shelling of the front line of trenches continued daily, but although considerable damage was done to the parapet the casualties were few. On the 12th the enemy shelled Dead End Post, and burnt it to the ground. There were fortunately no men killed or wounded, but all the rifles, S.A.A., bombs, and rations were destroyed. The same night Captain Layton sent out one N.C.O. and four men, with two R.E. men carrying a Bangalore torpedo, which was placed under the German wire, with its nose against the enemy's parapet. After the party had returned in safety the torpedo was successfully exploded by means of an electric cable, and our patrols later reported extensive damage to the enemy's parapet.

On the 15th the 4th Battalion returned to billets at Merville, and the next day entrained at Lestrem for Calais. On arrival at Calais it marched to a camp at Le Beaumarais, where the Y.M.C.A. had hot drinks and cakes ready. The sea air for which the men had come was somewhat powerful when they arrived, as it was blowing a gale, and most of the tents were

JANUARY TO SEPTEMBER 1916

laid flat. In fact, the whole time they were there the weather was bad, with heavy snow and hail storms, which made camp life unpleasant. On the 23rd forty-three officers of the 1st and 4th Battalions dined together, and invited General Heyworth to join them. On the 26th the Battalion went by train to Cassel, where it detrained and marched to Herzeele. A great deal of snow had fallen, and the roads were in a very bad state, which made it difficult for the transport to move with any rapidity. The men were billeted in farms round about, and, although very much scattered, the billets were good.

A new system of parchments, in recognition of good work done by N.C.O.'s and men in the Division, was instituted. These were signed by the Major-General commanding the Division and issued to the men, but as there was every danger of their being lost if carried about, they were re-collected, and sent through the Regimental Orderly Room to the men's relatives. The infinitesimal number of decorations allotted to each battalion necessitated some other means of recognising conspicuous services, and although it could hardly be said that these parchments in any way compensated for the lack of decoration, they at least gave the man the satisfaction of knowing that his services had been brought to the notice of the Major-General.

After spending a fortnight at Herzeele the 4th Battalion moved to a camp of huts and tents near Poperinghe on March 6. A digging party 250 strong, under Captain Blundell, was sent on to work at Ypres, and remained there for

CHAPTER XVIII.

4th Batt. March 1916.

three days. On the 15th the whole battalion went by train to Ypres, where it went into dug-outs, and on the following day took over the line of trenches with its right 200 yards north of the Menin road, and its left on the Roulers railway by Railway Wood. There it remained until the 27th, retiring every four days into dug-outs at Ypres, and although it became a mere target for the German artillery, it had only nineteen casualties in its first four days in the trenches.

On the 23rd the following officers joined the Battalion: Lieutenant C. G. Goschen, Second Lieutenant A. F. Newey, Lieutenant M. F. H. Payne-Gallwey, and Second Lieutenant J. P. Bibby. On the 24th Second Lieutenant B. G. H. Maclear rendered a very good patrol report, and on the information he gained a further reconnaissance under his guidance was sent out the next day, to be followed, if successful, by a bombing raid. The patrol was unfortunately seen by the enemy, and a hot fire was opened on them all down the line. This completely precluded all possibility of surprise, and consequently the enterprise was abandoned. That evening the German artillery heavily shelled the Canadian trenches on the right, and inflicted considerable damage. On the 27th the Battalion returned to Poperinghe, where the men washed in the Corps baths, and received clean underclothing.

The officers of the 4th Battalion at that time were:

April. Lieut.-Colonel Lord Henry Seymour   Commanding Officer.
Major J. A. Morrison . . . Second in Command.

JANUARY TO SEPTEMBER 1916

Capt. R. S. Lambert	. . .	Adjutant.
Lieut. H. H. Sloane-Stanley	. .	Bombing Officer.
Lieut. M. Chapman	. . .	Lewis Gun Officer.
Lieut. I. H. Ingleby	. . .	Transport Officer.
Lieut. E. Ludlow	. . . .	Quartermaster.
Capt. C. L. Blundell-Hollinshead-Blundell	. . . .	No. 1 Company.
2nd Lieut. B. Burman	. . .	,, ,,
2nd Lieut. A. F. Newey	. .	,, ,,
Lieut. C. G. Goschen	. . .	No. 2 Company.
2nd Lieut. C. G. Keith	. . .	,, ,,
2nd Lieut. B. G. H. Maclear	. .	,, ,,
Capt. B. C. Layton	. . .	No. 3 Company.
Lieut. G. C. Sloane-Stanley	. .	,, ,,
Lieut. M. F. H. Payne-Gallwey	.	,, ,,
Lieut. E. W. Nairn	. . .	,, ,,
Capt. F. O. S. Sitwell	. . .	No. 4 Company.
Lieut. the Hon. E. W. Tennant	.	,, ,,
2nd Lieut. D. O. Constable	. .	,, ,,
2nd Lieut. J. P. Bibby	. . .	,, ,,

CHAPTER XVIII.

4th Batt. April 1916.

On April 3 the 4th Battalion moved to Camp B at Vlamertinghe by companies, and on the 8th returned to the trenches, relieving the 1st Battalion Grenadiers as right battalion of the left sector of the Division. There it remained until the 20th, placing two companies at a time in the front line. There was a great deal of work to be done in strengthening and heightening the parapet, which in some parts was in a lamentable condition. On the 17th Second Lieutenant M. H. Ponsonby and Second Lieutenant R. A. Gault arrived. The enemy was very active in this sector, and frequent raids occurred. On the 19th the German artillery began a systematic bombardment of our first and second lines by way of a barrage, while they launched an attack somewhat to the left of the line occupied by the 4th Battalion. At first this attack hardly seemed to affect Nos. 2 and 3 Companies, which were at that time in the front trenches, but when a message arrived from the Brigade-Major to the effect that the enemy had occupied Wieltje in front of the 2nd Battalion Scots Guards, which had held it lightly, it was clear that something had to be done. It afterwards turned out that the enemy had made a determined attack on the Sixth Division, and had taken 600 yards of trench, while a raiding party had got down the trench occupied by the Scots Guards. Lieutenant C. G. Goschen, who was an old hand at this type of fighting, at once sent a strong patrol, under Second Lieutenant Maclear, up the trench to the left to clear up the situation, and if necessary support the Scots Guards. This manœuvre proved eminently successful, and, in spite of the bombs which rained on them the party of Grenadiers carried all before them. In the meantime the Scots Guards ejected all the Germans who had succeeded in penetrating into their trench. There was necessarily some very stiff fighting, but although there were 3 men killed and 24 wounded, of whom 3 died later, the party returned with no men missing. Lieut.-Colonel Lord Henry Seymour afterwards attributed the success of the operation to the coolness and resource displayed by Second Lieutenant Maclear, Lieutenant Goschen, and Captain Blundell. He also praised the marked ability shown by Second Lieutenant Keith and Second Lieutenant Constable in the control of their men under very difficult circumstances.

JANUARY TO SEPTEMBER 1916

One particularly gallant act was performed that night by Private James Grundy, who was on duty with his telephone under very heavy fire, when he suddenly discovered that the wire had been cut by a shell. He at once went out in the open to mend the wire, although he was only 120 yards from the enemy, and had hardly returned when the wire was cut a second time. Again, without a moment's hesitation, he went out to find where the wire was broken. This time, however, he was severely wounded as he was engaged in repairing the line, and when rescued was found still working away in spite of his wounds. Even then he refused to be taken out of the trench until he had handed over the secret code to an officer. Shells, bullets, wounds made no difference to him: he had his duty to do, and he meant to do it. For this act of bravery he was awarded the D.C.M.

On the 20th the 4th Battalion returned to Vlamertinghe, where it remained resting for a week, after which it moved up to Ypres, and took over the right of the right sector at Rifle Farm on the 27th for four days.

The Battalion remained at Ypres until the 15th, taking over various portions of the line every four days. Nothing of interest occurred until the night of the 3rd, when it was found that the enemy had undermined our front line. In order to destroy the enemy's shaft, our miners exploded a mine fifteen yards in front of our trenches. The shock of the explosion was very great, and the crater that was formed was roughly 200 feet in diameter and 80 to 100

Chapter XVIII.

4th Batt.
April 1916.

May.

CHAPTER XVIII.
4th Batt.
May 1916.

feet deep. The far edge of the crater was about seventy yards from the enemy's trenches. Immediately after the explosion Lieutenant Payne-Gallwey dashed over with a N.C.O. and ten men, and occupied the far edge of the crater to form a covering party, while Lieutenant Nairn, with a similar party, occupied the near edge of the crater, and commenced placing previously-filled sand-bags in position to form some cover while digging. Each of these parties took with them long ropes, which proved of the greatest assistance in keeping the men together and showing the line along which they were to dig. One man shot in the chest fell half-way down the crater, and was pulled up with this rope.

While the consolidation of the crater was in progress, Captain Layton determined to link up the wire entanglements and bring them round in front of the crater. He despatched another party from his company for this purpose, and ordered them to report themselves to Lieutenant Payne-Gallwey, but as the enemy was clearly visible, when the lights went up, the erection of barbed-wire entanglements within seventy yards of their line was perilous work. The wiring of the crater, however, was successfully accomplished, although the enemy threw a quantity of bombs. Fortunately most of them pitched short, but seven casualties occurred from splinters. Meanwhile Lieutenant H. H. Sloane-Stanley on the right sent out similar wiring and digging parties from No. 2 Company to join up with No. 3 Company, and the two parties had got within thirty yards of each other when they were discovered by the

JANUARY TO SEPTEMBER 1916

Germans, and a storm of bullets from the enemy's machine-guns put an end to the work. The trench between the two companies had, however, been finished, and as there was no immediate hurry about the wire, the parties were withdrawn.

General Heyworth the next day, in a letter reporting the incident, wrote:

> I personally inspected the crater this morning and was enabled to walk through the trench which was dug, and which now connects H.17 to H.19. The work done last night reflects the greatest credit on those officers and men who took part in it, more especially on the wiring party, who for some time had to work under the most trying circumstances, as the Germans turned a machine-gun on them. It was in this party that all the casualties occurred. The Officer Commanding the 4th Battalion Grenadier Guards must also be congratulated on the excellent arrangements made. The defence of this sub-sector has been considerably strengthened by this trench.

This was the last time General Heyworth saw the 4th Battalion, for he was killed on the 9th whilst going round the trenches of the 1st Battalion Grenadiers.[1]

On the 18th the 4th Battalion retired to Poperinghe by train, and on the 19th marched to Wormhoudt, and remained there till the end of the month, going into the trenches in various parts of the line, where it was continually under shell-fire, but nothing of interest appears to have happened.

On June 1 the 4th Battalion moved to Pope-

[1] See 1st Battalion account.

CHAPTER XVIII.
4th Batt.
June 1916.

ringhe again, and was employed on fatigues and digging. On the 5th Second Lieutenant J. B. M. Burke and Second Lieutenant C. S. Nash arrived, and on the 7th the Battalion marched to Honbeghem. The next day after a march of fifteen miles, it moved to Tatinghem, and on the 17th returned to Poperinghe. These were two long, hot marches, but no man fell out on the line of march either day. On the 18th the Battalion moved up to the Canal Bank at Ypres, and then back into the trenches on the right of R sector, with the Battalion Headquarters at Irish Farm. The line was very much disconnected, and consisted chiefly of a chain of posts, most of which were in bad order, while what trenches there were, were mostly derelict, and required a good deal of work. On the 28th Lieutenant H. H. Sloane-Stanley took out a patrol with the object of capturing an enemy post, but it was surprised by one of the enemy's patrols, which opened fire on it, wounding every man in the left party of the patrol. One wounded man was left behind when the party retired, and although Lieutenant Sloane-Stanley, Lance-Corporal Holland, and Private Heap returned and searched for him, he was never found.

July.

After four very wet days in the trenches the 4th Battalion retired to Ypres for four days' rest, and on the 4th returned for two nights to the trenches. The days spent in the trenches proved uneventful, but on the 7th a raid was made on a part of the enemy's line known as the Canadian Dug-outs. A party under Lieutenant H. H. Sloane-Stanley and Second Lieutenant

D. O. Constable was sent out, and crawled up quite close to the enemy's position. Unfortunately the ground was very wet and muddy, and this made a noiseless advance a matter of some difficulty. There seems no doubt that the enemy heard it, and took precautions. The barrage was timed to commence at 1.5 A.M., and this was to be the signal for the assault. At 1 A.M. the Battery covering the Twentieth Division on the right opened fire, and the raiding party mistook this for their barrage. Immediately Lieutenant Sloane-Stanley and Second Lieutenant D. O. Constable sprang to their feet, and were about to lead the assault when they found themselves confronted at fifteen paces by a party of the enemy who opened a sharp fire on them. Fortunately the shooting was very wild, and only four men were wounded. The fighting then resolved itself into a bombing and Lewis-gun contest, but the Grenadiers were well hidden and suffered no loss. Lieutenant Sloane-Stanley's orders were not to assault unless it could be done by surprise, and he therefore decided to withdraw his party four at a time, covered by the Lewis gunners, who behaved with great coolness. So successfully did they cover the retreat that the whole party returned without loss. This raid alarmed the enemy, who opened a heavy bombardment on our line, during which 4 men were killed and 18 wounded, in addition to Captain M. Chapman, who was struck by splinters of a shell in the leg and hand.

On the 8th the Battalion retired to Poperinghe, and on the 10th Second Lieutenant L. R. Abel-

Smith joined the Battalion. The first anniversary of the formation of the Battalion was celebrated on the 15th in a befitting manner, and a programme suitable for the occasion was carried out. At the men's dinners at 12.30 free beer and extra vegetables were issued. In the afternoon there was a football match between the right half and left half battalions, followed at 5 P.M. by a sergeants' and corporals' dinner, At 6.15 there was a Battalion concert, after which the officers had a dinner. Lord Cavan, who attended the football match, gave away the prizes, and afterwards addressed the Battalion. He visited the N.C.O.'s at dinner, and made them a short speech on the work done by the Division, giving especial praise to the Battalion for its initiative in raids and patrols. Major-General G. Feilding and Brigadier-General C. Corkran attended the officers' dinner.

That night the 4th Battalion moved up again into the line, and became the right reserve Battalion, Nos. 1 and 2 Companies going into dug-outs on the canal bank, and Nos. 3 and 4 remaining at Château Elverdinghe, which was a large and comfortable house with a park and gardens. The shelling was continuous, and even back at the Château the shells fell at times in large numbers. On the 19th "a dummy raid" was carried out with the object of surprising the enemy with artillery fire when he expected an infantry attack. All the usual preparations for an attack were gone through, and at 12.30 A.M. our guns, assisted by the Belgian artillery, opened an intense bombardment for three minutes on a

JANUARY TO SEPTEMBER 1916

selected portion of the enemy's front line, while the infantry indulged in a rapid fire supplemented by Lewis guns. After three minutes the fire was lifted on the enemy's second and third lines, following the procedure observed when an infantry attack was about to be launched. It was then hoped that the Germans would come out of their dug-outs and man their trenches in order to repel the attack. The artillery at once shortened their range, and gave the front German trenches a sound shelling. The result of this manœuvre was of course unknown, but judging by the very feeble reply made by the enemy, the ruse must have been fairly successful.

CHAPTER XVIII.

4th Batt. July 1916.

Second Lieutenant G. H. T. Paton joined the Battalion on the 23rd, and Second Lieutenant A. C. Flower on the 24th. Nothing of interest occurred during the days the Battalion was in the trenches until the 26th, when a party of the enemy raided No. 2 Company trench. About half-a-dozen Germans suddenly got in over the parapet and bombed a working party, which was completely taken by surprise. Second Lieutenant Maclear, hearing the bombing, rushed to the spot, and was instantly killed by a bomb thrown at close quarters. But the German occupation of the trench was only momentary, for bombing parties soon arrived from the right and left, and ejected the raiders, who did not wait but made their escape as fast as they could in the darkness. Second Lieutenant Maclear was an officer who could be ill spared, as he had proved himself to be absolutely fearless and self-reliant, and his loss was felt by every one

CHAPTER XVIII.
4th Batt.
July 1916.

in the Battalion. Captain Layton was hit in the foot during the repulse of the enemy's raid, and Sergeant Aiers, senior sergeant of the Battalion, was wounded for the third time.

The Guards Division now left the Ypres area and moved down farther south by easy stages. Having been relieved by the 1st Battalion Hampshire Regiment, the 4th Battalion Grenadiers marched to Poperinghe, where they entrained for

Aug.

Bollezeele and then marched to Millain. During the first fortnight in August they moved *via* Bollezeele, Millain, Arqueves, Mailly-Mallet to the line of trenches at Beaumont-Hamel. On the 7th Lieutenant J. F. J. Joicey-Cecil and Second Lieutenant R. Y. T. Kendall arrived, and on the 18th Captain C. Mitchell, Lieutenant R. Farquhar, and Second Lieutenant J. W. F. Selby-Lowndes joined the Battalion. The four days spent in the trenches at Beaumont-Hamel proved uneventful, although there was a good deal of shelling in addition to the Minenwerfers. On the 19th the Battalion started off for the Somme area, but this necessitated going a long way round by Vauchelles, Gezaincourt, Vignacourt to Ville. Here it rested for ten days, and on September 8 moved to Carnoy. On August 31 Captain E. G. Spencer-Churchill joined the Battalion.

CHAPTER XIX

THE BATTLE OF THE SOMME

A NEW stage, and a very distinct and important stage, in the Allied operations in the West was marked by the battle of the Somme.

It was at last understood, in the summer of 1916, that spasmodic attacks on the German trenches did little to gain any real and comprehensive success, and that, in order to prevent the enemy moving his reserves from one front to another, a simultaneous assault by all the Allies was necessary.

In accord with this view the Allies at the beginning of the year accepted the principle of an offensive campaign, and as the objective for the British and French advance Sir Douglas Haig and General Joffre selected the Somme area. All idea of "breaking through" had by now been abandoned. Such a thing was no longer regarded as possible in the West, and the plan adopted was one more suited to modern conditions of war and more economical of human life. The objects of the offensive were to relieve Verdun, to prevent the transfer of German troops elsewhere, and to wear down the resistance of the enemy on the Western front.

CHAPTER XIX
1916.

Conditions had changed, too, in other ways. The British Army had been slowly gaining strength, and the old Army had given place to the new. There were now fifty divisions in the field. At the same time, the supply of ammunition had been steadily increasing, and, thanks to the patriotism of the trade unions and the splendid performances of the workers, immense quantities of guns and shells were pouring into France. Consequently there was no reason why a general attack should not be made on the Western front, although, as Sir Douglas Haig pointed out in his despatch, he considered it advisable to postpone it as long as possible.

During the gigantic battle, which began on July 1 and lasted till November 18, the fighting was continuous. The German positions were amazingly strong. First came a network of trenches, well provided with bomb-proof shelters and protected in front by wire entanglements, many of which were in two belts forty yards broad and built of iron stakes, interlaced with barbed wire, often as thick as a man's finger. Behind these lines the enemy's strongholds had been reinforced with every device of military ingenuity—woods and villages turned into fortresses, cellars filled with machine-guns and trench mortars, dug-outs connected by elaborate passages. The enormous power of modern weapons of defence had been used to the utmost. In fact, the whole line was as nearly impregnable as Nature, art, and the unstinted labour of close on two years could make it. And undoubtedly the Germans believed it impregnable.

THE BATTLE OF THE SOMME 29

The first phase of the battle took place at the beginning of July, and although the attacks in the northern sector were unsuccessful, the armour was pierced; while in the south our troops secured Mametz, Montauban, Fricourt, Contalmaison, and Trônes Wood. On July 14 and the three following days, the capture of the enemy's second line on a front of three miles gave us possession of the main plateau between Delville Wood and Bazentin-le-Petit.

The long and severe struggle, which was the second phase, began on July 18 and culminated on September 15 with the fall of Ginchy, after Pozières, Delville Wood, Guillemont, Falfemont Farm, and Leuze Wood had been taken in succession. But although the main ridge from Delville Wood to the road above Mouquet Farm was secured, Morval on the right and Thiepval on the left remained in German hands.

In the third phase Flers, High Wood, Martinpuich, Courcelette, and the Quadrilateral came into our hands one after another, and on September 25 Morval, Lesbœufs, and Gueudecourt were secured by the British Army, while the French took Combles. During October Thiepval was taken, and also Eaucourt l'Abbaye and Le Sars, while in November, as the outcome of an advance on both sides of the Ancre, we captured St. Pierre Divion, Beaucourt, and Beaumont-Hamel.

Thus all our principal objects were achieved, in spite of the fact that the Germans were able to mass more than half their army upon this part of their front. The British Army took 38,000 prisoners, including over 800 officers; also

Chapter XIX.
1916.

29 heavy guns, 96 field-guns and field-howitzers, 136 trench mortars, and 514 machine-guns.

The battle was marked by the sudden appearance of the Tanks. So well had their secret been kept that until they came upon the battlefield the Germans had no idea of their existence. "The Machine-gun Corps, Heavy Section" was the official title of these heavy armoured cars which could move anywhere, over trenches and through wire entanglements, pushing down walls and even houses; they contained a garrison of six men with machine-guns and 6-pdr. guns. So many legends had grown up of their supernatural powers that their actual début caused a certain disappointment. But although in some parts of the battlefield they failed us, some of them did wonders, and many of the strongholds in the German line could never have been taken without their help.

The net result of the battle was a brilliant victory for the British Army, for not only was a large tract of ground captured from the enemy, but the three objects which we had set out to gain were fully attained. Verdun was relieved of pressure, the main portion of the German Army was detained on the Western front, and a crippling blow was struck at the enemy forces. It was clearly shown that, on anything like equal terms, the British could drive back the German Army, sheltered even by the strongest entrenchments.

As the area and duration of modern battles are immense, a long time naturally elapses before their effects are felt by the losing side.

THE BATTLE OF THE SOMME 31

Formerly battles lasted only a few days, and their results were seen immediately in the retirement of the beaten army. After the battle of the Somme, however, nothing happened at first, and it was not until six months later that the Germans found that their positions had become untenable, and a general retirement was advisable.

CHAPTER XIX.

1916.

THE GUARDS DIVISION AT THE SOMME

Nothing has ever been done by battalions of the Guards finer than the part they took in the battle of the Somme. It was not until the beginning of September that the Guards Division arrived in the Somme area, so it was not present at the first two phases of the battle. But in the attacks of September 15 and 25 the men covered themselves with glory; their discipline and coolness under fire were magnificent, and they captured lines which had up to then been considered impregnable. The final assault of Lesbœufs was one of the most successful operations of the war.

Sept.

Not only were the staff arrangements admirable, but the co-operation between infantry and artillery proved in every way perfect. Against the unflinching attack of the Division nothing could stand; the mass of shells poured over by the German artillery, the hail of bullets from their machine-guns, and the rifle-fire of their infantry in the trenches, were all powerless to check it. The men were splendid: it made not a scrap of difference whether they had officers or not, whether they were with their own units or mixed up with other regiments. Nothing could stop them. When the 3rd Brigade went up, the battle had already been raging for over two months; and the Germans were then busily but vainly carrying out counter-attacks, in the hope of re-taking some of the ground that had been wrested from them. Consequently the two battalions sent forward came in for some very stiff fighting, especially the Welsh Guards, who went through some anxious moments owing to the advanced position they were occupying. They were fiercely attacked by large bodies of the enemy, but, with the help of one company of the 1st Battalion Grenadiers, managed to hold their own. Meanwhile the 4th Battalion Grenadiers—the other battalion sent up from the 3rd Brigade—held an uncomfortable position near the Quadrilateral, to the right and in rear of the Welsh Guards.

Parts of the line had also to be straightened, and "pockets" of Germans to be cleared away before the general attack of the 15th; and for this task were detailed those battalions from the 1st and 2nd Brigades which would not be in the front line on the 15th. There were some closely-contested bombing fights, supported by artillery, in the parts of the line that needed straightening, and these operations were all successfully carried out.

On the 12th Major-General G. Feilding issued the following orders :

THE GUARDS DIVISION ORDER, No. 76

1. The Fourth Army will attack the enemy's defences between Combles Ravine and Martinpuich on Z day

THE BATTLE OF THE SOMME

with the object of seizing Morval, Lesbœufs, Gueudecourt, and Flers, and to break through the enemy's system of defence.

The French are undertaking an offensive simultaneously on the South and the Reserve Army on the North.

2. The attack will be pushed with the utmost vigour all along the line until the most distant objectives are reached. The failure of one unit on the flank is not to prevent other units pushing on to their final objective, as it is by such means that those units who have failed will be assisted to advance.

3. *Preliminary Bombardment.*—(a) Commencing on the 12th September a bombardment and wire-cutting on the hostile defensive system will take place from 6 A.M. to 6.30 daily.

(b) The preliminary bombardment on the day of the attack will be similar to that of previous days, there being no further increase of fire previous to zero.

(c) At 6.30 each evening from the 12th September inclusive night firing will commence, and continue till 6 A.M., lethal shells being used.

4. (a) The Sixth Division is to attack on the right and the Fourteenth Division on the left.

(b) The 2nd Guards Brigade will attack on the right of the Division, the 1st Guards Brigade on the left. The 3rd Guards Brigade will be in Divisional Reserve.

5. *Forming-up Areas.*—Forming-up areas are shown on attached maps. The 1st and 2nd Guards Brigades will allot a forming-up area for the 75th and 76th Field Companies R.E. respectively in their forming-up areas.

Instructions as to movements of troops to their forming-up areas will be issued separately.

6. The objectives allotted to the Guards Division and neighbouring divisions are shown on attached map.

First objective is marked Green.
Second   ,,   ,,   Brown.
Third   ,,   ,,   Blue.
Fourth   ,,   ,,   Red.

7. (*a*) 50 per cent Field Artillery covering the Division will be used for creeping barrage, and 50 per cent for stationary barrage.

(*b*) Details of the stationary barrages will be issued later. In all cases the stationary barrage will lift back when the creeping barrage reaches it.

(*c*) At zero the creeping barrage will open 100 yards in front of our front trenches, and will advance at the rate of 50 yards per minute until it is 200 yards beyond the first objective, when it will become stationary. At zero + 1 hour the creeping barrage will become intense on the line 200 yards in front of first objective, and will creep forward at the rate of 50 yards per minute in front of that portion of the 1st Guards Brigade which is to advance to the second objective.

(*d*) At zero + 1 hour and 10 minutes the creeping barrage will become intense on a line 200 yards in front of the first objective as far north as T.86.4.6, thence on a line 200 yards in front of the second objective, and will advance at the rate of 30 yards per minute until it has passed 200 yards beyond the third objective, when it will become stationary.

This barrage is to cover the advance of the tanks. There will be no creeping barrage in front of infantry during their advance to third objective, which commences at zero + 2 hours.

(*e*) At zero + 3 hours and 30 minutes the creeping barrage will become intense on a line 200 yards in front of third objective, and will advance at the rate of 30 yards per minute until it has passed 200 yards beyond fourth objective, when it will become stationary. This barrage is to cover the advance of the tanks. There will be no creeping barrage in front of the infantry during the advance on the fourth objective, which commences at zero + 4 hours and 30 minutes.

(*f*) In the attack on the first and second objectives gaps of 100 yards wide will be left in the creeping barrage for the routes of the tanks.

8. The flow of troops to the 2nd Guards Brigade and 1st Guards Brigade must be maintained so as to ensure a strong attack being pressed against each successive objective. Sufficient men will be left in each line captured to clear it of the enemy. No troops of the 2nd and 1st Guards Brigades will be detailed to remain behind in objectives after they have been passed for purposes of consolidation.

The task of the two leading Brigades is to press the attack through to their ultimate objectives with every means at their disposal.

9. The 3rd Guards Brigade will advance at zero + 1 hour and 30 minutes until its leading troops reach the south-western outskirts of Ginchy, when the Brigade will halt and await orders.

Special instructions as to action of Reserve Brigade will be issued.

10. Tanks will be employed to operate with the attack; instructions as to their movements are attached.

(Remainder of orders related to R.E., R.A., Aircraft and Transport.)

C. HEYWOOD, Lieut.-Col.,
General Staff, Guards Division.

September 12, 1916.

So great was the danger of battalions being practically annihilated in an attack that orders had been issued for a certain nucleus of officers and N.C.O.'s to be left with the Transport, whenever a battalion went into action, so as to make sure of a sufficient number surviving to carry on the work. Accordingly on this occasion the Second in Command, the junior Captains of companies, the Battalion and Company Sergeant-Majors and Quartermaster-Sergeants in each battalion were left behind.

At 6.20 on the morning of the 15th the artillery

bombardment ceased, and the Guards Division advanced, preceded by a creeping barrage, with Pereira's Brigade on the left and Ponsonby's Brigade on the right, while Corkran's Brigade remained in reserve. In the front line were the 1st, 2nd, and 3rd Battalions of the Coldstream and the 3rd Battalion Grenadiers. The advance of the three Coldstream battalions was a wonderful sight, and they carried everything before them, but in their eagerness to reach the enemy lost direction and went too far to the left. Meanwhile the 3rd Battalion Grenadiers on the right kept straight on, so there was a considerable gap between it and the three battalions of Coldstream. Coming up through the German barrage, the 2nd Battalion Grenadiers, which was in support of the 2nd Coldstream, completely lost sight of the Coldstream battalions. In accordance with its orders it advanced with its right on the Ginchy — Lesbœufs road, but on reaching the first objective it found it occupied by the enemy instead of by the Coldstream, as it expected, and suffered heavy loss. Under the impression that it was following in the wake of the 2nd Battalion Coldstream, it was advancing in artillery formation, and had to form line when within a few yards of the enemy's trench, which was untouched, as the Coldstream battalions had passed farther to the left.

When the first objective was secured, the order from right to left was as follows: the 3rd Battalion Grenadiers, the 2nd Battalion Grenadiers, the 1st, 2nd, and 3rd Battalion Coldstream. Between the first two objectives there were

THE BATTLE OF THE SOMME 37

several intermediate lines of trenches, all of which were most confusing for the battalions in front. The Coldstream battalions mistook these intermediate lines for objectives, and thought that they had reached the third objective when they were really between the first and second objectives. Their real position, however, was correctly reported by the air scouts.

Meantime the Quadrilateral—a powerful system of redoubts—on the right had made any advance by the Sixth Division impossible, and on the left also the Fourteenth Division had been held up by some strong points in the enemy's line. The result was that the Guards Division had both flanks in the air, and was subjected to a withering fire almost from the start. The 3rd Battalion Grenadiers on the right and the 3rd Battalion Coldstream on the left were obliged to throw out protective flanks, and so had some difficulty in keeping pace with the battalions in the centre.

It was some time before the two brigades were firmly established in the first objective, as there were parts of the line in which some Germans had been left, more especially in the space reserved for the tanks, which unfortunately never arrived. However, the 1st and 2nd Battalions Coldstream in the centre pushed on and gained the second objective, while the battalions right and left threw back protective flanks. The second objective was a trench running into the first objective, and only concerned the Coldstream battalions on the left.

On the next day, the 16th, Corkran's Brigade was ordered to advance through the leading

CHAPTER XIX.

Sept. 1916.

brigades and continue the attack. But it did not start till the middle of the day, and after having gone some distance was held up by machine-gun fire and the men were told to dig themselves in where they were.

The whole Division was taken out of the line on the night of the 18th and remained resting in bivouacs until the 20th, when each brigade sent battalions into the front line to dig assembly trenches and straighten parts of the line. On the 22nd Major-General G. Feilding issued the following orders :

Guards Division Order, No. 82

1. (*a*) The Fourth Army will renew the attack on Z day in combination with attacks by the French to the South and the Reserve Army to the North.

(*b*) The objectives of the Fourteenth Corps include Morval and Lesbœufs, and those of the Fifteenth Corps Gueudecourt.

(*c*) The attack of the Fourteenth Corps will be carried out by the Fifth Division on the right, the Sixth Division in the centre, and the Guards Division on the left. The Fifty-eighth Division will form a defensive flank to the south of the Fifth Division. The Twenty-first Division will be attacking on our left.

2. The 1st Guards Brigade will attack on the right and the 3rd Guards Brigade on the left.

The 2nd Guards Brigade (less one Battalion) will be in Divisional Reserve.

1st Battalion 2nd Guards Brigade will be in Corps Reserve ; 2nd Guards Brigade will notify Divisional Headquarters the name of the Battalion detailed.

3. *Preliminary Bombardment.*—A steady bombardment of hostile positions will be commenced at 7 A.M. on Z day, and will be continued to 6.30 P.M.; it will recommence at 6.30 A.M. on Z day.

THE BATTLE OF THE SOMME 39

The ground in front and rear of the German trenches which are being bombarded will be searched occasionally with 18-pdr. shrapnel and H.E. shell.

CHAPTER XIX.

Sept. 1916.

There will be no intensive fire previous to the hour of zero. Night firing will be carried out nightly between the hours of 6.30 P.M. and 6.30 A.M.

4. Forming-up areas are shown on the attached map. The 1st and 3rd Guards Brigades will allot forming-up areas to the 75th and 55th Field Companies R.E. respectively, within their areas.

Instructions for movements to forming-up areas will be issued separately.

5. Objectives allotted to the Guards Brigades and neighbouring Divisions, also the dividing lines, are shown on attached map.

> First objective is marked Green.
> Second   ,,   ,,   Brown.
> Third   ,,   ,,   Blue.

6. The infantry will advance to the attack on the Green line at zero ; to the attack on the Brown line at zero + 1 hour, and to the attack on the Blue line at zero + 2 hours.

7. *Barrages*—

(*a*) 50 per cent of the Field Artillery covering the Division will be used for the creeping barrage and 50 per cent for stationary barrage.

(*b*) In all cases the stationary barrage will lift when the creeping barrage meets it.

8. (*a*) At zero the creeping barrage will commence 100 yards in front of our front trenches. It will advance at the rate of 50 yards per minute until it is 200 yards beyond the Green line, when it will become stationary.

(*b*) At zero + 1 hour the creeping barrage will commence 200 yards in front of the Green line and will advance at the rate of 50 yards per minute until it has passed 200 yards beyond the Brown line, when it will become stationary.

(c) At zero + 2 hours the creeping barrage will commence 200 yards in front of the Brown line, and will advance at the rate of 50 yards per minute until it has passed 200 yards beyond the Blue line, when it will become stationary.

9. (a) The task of the two leading Guards Brigades is to press the attack through to the Blue line. A sufficient flow of troops must be maintained by the 1st and 2nd Guards Brigades from zero onwards to ensure that the attack made from the Brown line is strong and well supported.

(b) Special arrangements must be made to deal with resistance in Lesbœufs and thus prevent any possibility of the enemy getting round our troops who have gained the Blue line.

(c) The 1st and 3rd Guards Brigades will garrison and consolidate the Brown line with a portion of their reserves when the attack goes forward to the Blue line.

(d) On gaining the Blue line, Battalions will be sent forward to any ground from which observation can be gained; such points will be consolidated and eventually joined up with our line.

On the 24th the Battalions that were to lead the attack took their place in the line ready for the next day. The order of attack was for the Fifty-sixth Division to form the right flank guarding Combles, the Fifth Division to capture Morval, the Sixth Division to occupy the southern end of Lesbœufs, and the Guards Division to take Lesbœufs.

In Pereira's Brigade, which attacked on the right, the 2nd Battalion Grenadiers and 1st Battalion Irish Guards were in the front line, and were supported by the 2nd and 3rd Battalions Coldstream. In Corkran's Brigade on the left the 4th Battalion Grenadiers and 2nd Battalion

THE BATTLE OF THE SOMME 41

Scots Guards led, supported by the 1st Battalion Grenadiers and 1st Battalion Welsh Guards. The orders of the two brigades differed. In the 1st Guards Brigade the leading battalions were to take all the objectives, and when they passed on the battalions in support were to consolidate each line. In the 3rd Brigade the two leading battalions were to take the first two objectives and then throw out a defensive flank; the battalions in support were then to advance through them and secure the third objective, one of these again throwing out a defensive flank.

CHAPTER XIX.

Sept. 1916.

At 12.35 P.M. on the 25th the attack started, and in spite of the wire, in some places intact, the first objective was secured. At 1.30 the advance to the second objective began. The battalions in front suffered heavily, especially in officers, but by 1.45 the second objective was in our hands. All this time the Twenty-first Division on the left had been held up, and the left flank of the Guards Division was consequently in the air. The 4th Grenadiers had therefore to throw out a defensive flank to the left, which eventually became so long that not only that battalion but also the Welsh Guards were employed to guard it. Major-General Feilding regarded this defensive flank as of the utmost importance, since it was from this quarter that a counter-attack was expected. In some parts of the line the wire was uncut, and the advance was retarded, but this did not prevent the objectives being secured by the times specified in the orders.

As soon as we had gained the second objective, the 1st Battalion Grenadiers and 1st Battalion

Chapter XIX.
Sept. 1916.

Welsh Guards passed through the leading battalions of Corkran's Brigade and attacked Lesbœufs, while the 2nd Battalion Grenadiers and 1st Battalion Irish Guards continued their advance.

Thus with the 4th Battalion Grenadiers on the defensive flank there were three Grenadier battalions engaged in the attack on the third objective. The capture of Lesbœufs itself fell to the lot of the 1st Battalion, and news was at once sent back that all the objectives had been secured. The battalions in front appear to have been so elated by their success that they asked for the cavalry to be allowed to go through. But Lord Cavan, the Corps Commander, realised that it would be madness to employ cavalry on such a limited front, and gave orders that the leading battalions were to consolidate their position.

The 2nd Battalion

2nd Batt.

Detached from the 1st Guards Brigade on August 31 the 2nd Battalion Grenadiers had been sent up to Carnoy to dig in rear of the Twentieth Division. It returned on September 3rd to Méaulte, where it underwent a thorough course of training, something in the nature of a dress rehearsal. Expert bombing officers gave instruction to every company in the Brigade, so that each man had an opportunity of learning the latest developments in bombing. All the battalions practised deploying in artillery formation, attacking an imaginary line of trenches, and then moving on immediately to a second objective. A great deal was learned in the way of signalling, and trials were made of a system of organising a single main trunk line, as central as possible, so as to avoid having a number of defective lines to each unit. This line was to consist of telephone or visual or relay posts—or, if possible, of all three. Careful consideration was given to the difficult task of getting the men across No Man's Land, and every detail was rehearsed. Later the whole Brigade was practised in the attack, and in maintaining constant communication during an advance.

Chapter XIX. 2nd Batt. Sept. 1916.

After a week the 1st Brigade received orders to proceed to Carnoy, and all surplus kit and equipment were left behind in store. The 2nd Battalion Grenadiers marched to Carnoy, and bivouacked not far from the place where it had been at the beginning of the month.

Sept. 9.

On the 11th orders were received for the 1st Brigade to relieve the left half of the 3rd Guards Brigade, while the 2nd Guards Brigade was to take the place of the other half. These orders (given below) were communicated to commanding officers at a conference held at Brigade Headquarters.

Sept. 11.

Brigadier-General Pereira issued the following orders :

1st Guards Brigade Order, No. 73

1. The Fourth Army will attack the enemy's defences between Combles Ravine and Martinpuich on Z day with the object of seizing Morval, Lesbœufs, Gueudecourt, and Flers, breaking through the enemy's system of defence.

The French are undertaking an offensive simultaneously on the south and the Reserve Army on the north.

2. The attack will be pushed with the utmost vigour, all along the line, until the most distant objectives are reached.

The failure of a unit on a flank is not to prevent other units pushing on to their final objectives, as it is by such means that these units, which have failed, will be assisted to advance.

3. *Preliminary Bombardment.*—(*a*) Commencing on the 12th September bombardment and wire-cutting on hostile defensive system will take place from 6 A.M. to 6.30 P.M. daily.

(*b*) The preliminary bombardment on the day of the attack will be similar to that on previous days, there being no increase of fire previous to zero.

(*c*) At 6.30 P.M. each evening from the 12th September inclusive, night firing will commence and continue till 6 A.M. Lethal shells will be used.

4. (*a*) The 2nd Guards Brigade will attack on the right of the Division—the 1st Guards Brigade the left, and the 3rd Guards Brigade will be in divisional reserve.

(*b*) The 4th Brigade of the Fourteenth Division will attack on the left of the 1st Guards Brigade.

(*c*) Boundaries are shown on attached map.

5. *Forming-up Areas.*—Forming-up areas are shown on attached maps.

Instructions as to movement of troops to their forming-up areas will be issued separately.

6. Objectives allotted to Guards Brigades and neighbouring Divisions are shown on attached map.

First objective is marked Green.
Second ,, ,, Brown.
Third ,, ,, Blue.
Fourth ,, ,, Red.

7. The infantry will advance to the attack of the Green line at zero.

THE BATTLE OF THE SOMME 45

To the attack of the Brown line at zero + 1 hour.
To the attack of the Blue line at zero + 2 hours.
To the attack of the Red line at zero + 4 hours and 30 minutes.

CHAPTER XIX.

2nd Batt. Sept. 1916.

8. *Artillery Barrages*—

(*a*) 50 per cent of Field Artillery covering the Division will be used for creeping barrage, and 50 per cent for stationary barrage.

(*b*) Details of stationary barrages will be issued later. In all cases the stationary barrages will lift back when the creeping barrage reaches it.

(*c*) At zero the creeping barrage will open 100 yards in front of our trenches, and will advance at rate of 50 yards per minute until it is 200 yards beyond the first objective, when it will become stationary.

At zero + 1 hour the creeping barrage will become intense on a line 200 yards in front of the first objective, and will creep forward at rate of 50 yards per minute in front of that portion of the 1st Guards Brigade which is to advance to the second objective.

(*d*) At zero + 1 hour and 10 minutes the creeping barrage will become intense on a line 200 yards in front of the first objective as far north as T.8.b.4.6, thence on a line 200 yards in front of second objective, and will advance at rate of 30 yards per minute until it has passed 200 yards beyond the third objective—when it will become stationary.

This barrage is to cover the advance of the tanks.

There will be no creeping barrage in front of the infantry during their advance to third objective, which commences at zero + 2 hours.

(*e*) At zero + 3 hours 30 minutes, the creeping barrage will become intense on a line 200 yards in front of the third objective—and will advance at rate of 30 yards per minute until it has passed 200 yards beyond fourth objective, when it will become stationary. This barrage is to cover the advance of the tanks.

There will be no creeping barrage in front of the

infantry during the advance to the fourth objective, which commences at zero + 4 hours 30 minutes.

(*f*) In the attack on first and second objectives gaps of 100 yards wide will be left in the creeping barrage for the routes of the tanks.

9. The attack will be carried out as follows:

(*a*) The 2nd and 3rd Battalions Coldstream Guards will attack and capture the first, second, and third objectives. The dividing line between these battalions is shown on attached maps.

(*b*) The 2nd Battalion Grenadier Guards will move in rear of the 2nd and 3rd Battalions Coldstream Guards. When the latter advance to the assault of the second objective the 2nd Battalion Grenadier Guards will occupy the first objective until the 1st Battalion Irish Guards have passed through them; they will then follow and support them in their attack on the fourth objective.

The rôle of the 1st Battalion Grenadier Guards is to form a defensive flank, if necessary, and to support the attack of the 1st Battalion Irish Guards in their attack on the fourth objective, with such troops as are not required for a defensive flank.

(*c*) 1st Battalion Irish Guards will attack the fourth objective.

(*d*) Machine-gun Coy. One section will accompany each battalion in the assault, and will be under the orders of the O.C. Battalion.

(*e*) Stokes T.M. Battery. Four guns will accompany the 2nd Battalion Grenadier Guards in case it is necessary to form a defensive flank. They will not go farther than the second objective. They will act under the orders of the O.C. Battalion.

The remaining four guns will be in the trench in which advanced Brigade Headquarters is situated, S.24.b.6.2.

(*f*) The 75th Field Coy. and the four work platoons will remain in their forming-up area until further orders are received.

THE BATTLE OF THE SOMME 47

10. *Formation of Attack.*—The formation for the carrying out of the attack is shown on attached sketch.

The 2nd Battalion Grenadier Guards and 1st Battalion Irish Guards will move into line or small columns according as to whether they are under rifle-fire or not.

11. The flow of troops will be continuous. This is to ensure a strong attack being pressed against each successive objective.

Officers commanding battalions will call for support, if necessary, from the battalions immediately in rear of them. If necessary, men will be left in each line captured to clear it of the enemy, but troops will not be detailed to remain behind in objectives for purposes of consolidation, except that the 2nd and 3rd Battalions Coldstream Guards will remain in the third objective ready to support the troops attacking the fourth objective.

The task of the Brigade is to press the attack through to their ultimate objectives with every means at our disposal.

12. Tanks will be employed to co-operate with the attack. Instructions as to their employment are attached.

Instructions will be issued as to movement of tanks to their departure positions, and as to time of their advance to the various objectives.

13. *Royal Flying Corps—*

(*a*) 9th Squadron, Royal Flying Corps will have one Contact aeroplane in the air from zero to dark on Z day, and again from 6.30 A.M. to 9 A.M. on Z + 1 days.

(*b*) Flares will be lit as follows :
    (1) On obtaining each objective.
    (2) At 12 noon and 5 P.M. on Z day by leading troops.
    (3) At 6.30 A.M. on Z + 1 day by leading troops.

Red flares will be used by infantry, Green flares by Cavalry.

Chapter XIX.

2nd Batt. Sept. 1916.

48 THE GRENADIER GUARDS

Chapter XIX
2nd Batt.
Sept. 1916.

14. An orderly with a watch will visit all Battalion H.Q. about 1 P.M. and 7 P.M. on Y day, so that time may be checked.

15. Special instructions will be issued on the following subjects :
   (*a*) Medical arrangement.
   (*b*) Supply of rations, water, S.A.A., Light T.M. ammunition and hand grenades.
   (*c*) Communications.

16. All transport will be packed up and ready to move forward at one hour's notice after zero + 4 hours.

The Brigade Transport officer will remain at Divisional Headquarters, Minden Post, from zero + 2 hours onwards.

On Y day after 7.30 P.M. the road running north from cross-roads S.28.d.4.2 will be clear of all wheeled traffic.

17. As soon as the final objectives have been captured by the infantry the cavalry will advance and seize the high ground Rocquigny—Villers-au-Flos—Riencourt-les-Bapaume—Bapaume.

The Fourteenth Corps will be prepared to support the cavalry on the above line at the earliest possible moment.

18. Prisoners will be sent *via* Brigade Headquarters to Divisional Collecting Station at Crater Post A.8.a.6.3, where they will be taken over and searched under A.P.M. arrangements.

Receipts will be given for prisoners and escorts will return to their units.

All captured documents should be sent with prisoners to Divisional Collecting Station, whence they will be forwarded under Divisional arrangements.

19. *Dumps.*—R.E. dumps of sand-bags and wire have been established along the Guillemont—Waterlot Farm road in the Brigade area. A water dump is being established at Advanced Brigade Headquarters at S.24.b.6.1½.

Dumps of bombs and S.A.A. are also being estab-

Lieutenant-General The Earl of Cavan, K.P., K.C.B.

THE BATTLE OF THE SOMME

lished along the Guillemont—Waterlot Farm road in the Brigade area.

20. Brigade Headquarters will be established at S.24.b.6.1½ from 9 P.M. to-night.

M. B. SMITH, Captain,
Brigade-Major, 1st Guards Brigade.

September 13, 1916.

By September 12 the whole Brigade was fully equipped. To every battalion had been issued bombs, sand-bags, distinguishing arm-bands, rockets, flares, wire-cutters, etc., and all that remained to be done was to fix the hour and the day of attack.

The 2nd Battalion Grenadiers took over the left half of the line occupied by the 3rd Guards Brigade on the night of the 12th, while the 1st Battalion Irish Guards moved up in support to Trônes Wood and Bernafay Wood. The 2nd and 3rd Battalions Coldstream, which were to carry out the assault, remained resting at Carnoy till the last moment, and the Brigade Headquarters moved up to a dummy trench between Trônes and Bernafay Woods.

The following message from Lieut.-General Lord Cavan was circulated:

The Corps Commander knows that there are difficulties to be cleared up on the left and in front of the 1st Guards Brigade, and on the right of the 2nd Guards Brigade, but the Commander-in-Chief is of opinion that the general situation is so favourable that every effort must be made to take advantage of it and that tanks should carry out a special programme before zero to deal with these unsatisfactory positions. The Commander-in-Chief states that there were only two German divisions in reserve on a large front, and that one of

CHAPTER XIX.
2nd Batt.
Sept. 1916.

them had recently had enormous casualties, and the other heavy casualties.

The French operations yesterday have been most successful, and they have captured Bouchavesnes, which was their objective.

Sept. 13.

Next night the 2nd Battalion Grenadiers, which was holding the northern sector of the Ginchy line, was instructed to go out and straighten the line, so that the battalions which were to attack on the following day should not be held up at the very start. Lieut.-Colonel C. de Crespigny issued these orders:

1. In order to have a good "jumping-off" place for X day it is essential to gain ground forward and dig a trench running from T.13.b.4.9. to T.14.a.2½.2½. It will be necessary to establish a post at the top of the cutting at T.13.b.4.9 and to drive the Germans from the trench T.13.b.6.4. point of orchard T.14.a.5.5.

2. No. 4 will carry this out to-night. Time given later.

3. Two Stokes guns and one Lewis gun will report to you about 9 P.M. to-night. The Stokes gun will be used previous to the attack. If possible a position will be chosen by O.C. No. 4 in readiness.

4. No. 3 Company will be in readiness to move up to No. 4 Company's present position, and the route should be reconnoitred by daylight if possible. No. 2 Company will watch the left flank of No. 4.

5. No. 3 Company will detail small parties after dark to carry up fifty boxes of bombs from H.Q. to No. 4. A party will also be required to carry up S.A.A., but this will be called for when S.A.A. is available.

6. No. 2 Company will be prepared to dig through the sunken road and join up with the new left of No. 4.

7. O.C. No. 2 Company will send up one Lewis gun after dark to report to O.C. No. 4.

8. All companies will detail two men to report at H.Q. as guides for ration parties after dark.

9. O.C. Nos. 2 and 3 Companies will meet C.O. at H.Q. of No. 4 Company at 8.0. P.M.

W. R. BAILEY, Captain and Adjutant,
2nd Battalion Grenadier Guards.

As it was known that the enemy held the point of the Ginchy orchard, and that they had machine-guns in the Ginchy—Flers sunken road, about four hundred yards north of that village, Captain G. Harcourt-Vernon, who commanded No. 4 Company, detailed two platoons under Second Lieutenant T. W. Minchin for the operation, while No. 2 was to protect their left flank and keep touch with them. Lieutenant M. H. Macmillan was ordered to bring up two platoons from No. 3 Company to support No. 4 Company and take over the line evacuated by Lieutenant Minchin's platoons.

The enterprise was difficult, as the left flank had to advance farther than the right in order to form a line facing north-east. By way of artillery preparation, thirty or forty shrapnel shells were fired at the German trench just north of the orchard, but this had the effect only of putting the enemy on his guard. Unfortunately, too, it was a bright moonlight night, and the attacking party showed up distinctly.

The two platoons under Second Lieutenant Minchin advanced, and cleared the orchard of all Germans, in spite of a heavy rifle and machine-gun fire, which caused several casualties. Not content with this, they tried to push on farther, but were fiercely resisted by the Germans, and

52 THE GRENADIER GUARDS

CHAPTER XIX.
2nd Batt. Sept. 1916.

failed to make good any more ground. As it was imperatively necessary to have a trench dug before daylight, Second Lieutenant Minchin decided to hold a line on the edge of the orchard, and the trench was completed by the next morning. The task assigned to the party had been carried out, and there seemed no necessity to attempt anything further.

That evening the following confidential message was received:

> Day of attack (Z day) will be 15th Sept. Zero hours will probably be in the early morning.

Sept. 14.

All next day the 2nd Battalion remained in the front trenches, where it was very heavily shelled. One shell pitched on the headquarters of No. 1 Company; Company Sergeant-Major Percival was mortally wounded and died later, and Captain A. F. R. Wiggins was so severely shaken that he retired suffering from shell shock. Company Sergeant-Major Gudgeon of No. 3 Company was buried by another shell, and had to be sent back. These losses were particularly regrettable, just as the Battalion was going into action.

The Battalion was relieved in the evening by the 2nd and 3rd Battalions Coldstream, and went into bivouac just behind Ginchy, where rations and rum were served out. The men had been three days in the trenches, and Lieut.-Colonel de Crespigny and the Adjutant, Captain Bailey, hardly had a moment's sleep during that time. It was bitterly cold at night, and the men, who had no greatcoats, suffered very much.

The time appointed for the attack was re-

THE BATTLE OF THE SOMME 53

vealed during the afternoon, in this message : "Zero hour to-morrow, September 15, will be at 6.20 A.M." As shown in the above orders, four successive objectives had been allotted to the Brigade. The first was about 1200 yards distant, and the second 1500—but this concerned only the left battalion of the Brigade. The third was 2500 yards off, while the fourth or final objective, which included the northern outskirts of Lesbœufs, was no less than 3500 yards away. The infantry were to advance to attack the first objective at 6.20 A.M., to the second at 7.20, the third at 8.20, and the final objective at 10.50. The front allotted to the Brigade was 500 yards.

The 2nd and 3rd Battalions Coldstream were to assault the first, second, and third objectives. The 2nd Battalion Grenadiers was to follow them, and form a defensive flank to either side, if required. On reaching the first objective the 2nd Battalion Grenadiers was to remain there until the Irish Guards passed through them, and if the flanks were all secure was to follow on and support them. The 1st Battalion Irish Guards was to pass through the 2nd and 3rd Battalions Coldstream at the third objective, and take and consolidate the fourth objective.

Each battalion had a section of machine-guns attached to it, and was told to place two guns on the flanks of the battalion and two at the Battalion Headquarters. The 2nd Battalion Grenadiers had four Stokes guns, while four more were kept in reserve. Three tanks were to start on the left outside the Brigade area, and were to

CHAPTER XIX.

2nd Batt. Sept. 1916.

pass into it north of the cutting, which was known to be a troublesome place, on the left flank.

Detailed instructions for the attack were issued in the following operation orders by Lieut.-Colonel C. R. C. de Crespigny, Commanding 2nd Battalion Grenadier Guards:

1. The Battalion will be relieved to-night by the 2nd and 3rd Battalions Coldstream Guards and part of the 41st Brigade on the left, and will form up on the assembly area S.W. of Ginchy.

2. Companies will detail guides as follows to be at H.Q. at 7.30 P.M.:

    No. 1 Company, 4 guides.
    No. 2   ,,   4 ,,
    No. 4   ,,   8 ,,

No. 3 Company will not wait to be relieved, but will move off to place of assembly east of the Waterlot—Guillemont road. On relief, Nos. 1, 2, and 4 Companies will march to H.Q. of No. 3 Company, where they will draw rations and water. They will then move on to their positions in assembly area, where fresh meat, sandwiches, and rum will be issued.

3. The assembly march will be carried out in absolute silence, and there must be no smoking, and no lights shown. Between dawn and zero (about 6 A.M.) there will be no movement.

4. Companies will each detail one N.C.O. to report at H.Q. of No. 3 Company at 6 P.M. to get rations ready for issue, also one officer to be at H.Q. No. 3 Company at 4 P.M. to be shown forming-up positions. Companies are responsible for reconnoitring the route to H.Q. No. 3 from their present positions.

5. *Dress.*—All men will carry two bandoliers S.A.A. and two Mills bombs. This must be made up before leaving the trenches. Every third man will carry a shovel, every fourth man a pick. Two days' rations will be carried.

THE BATTLE OF THE SOMME

6. *Forming-up.*—Companies will form up as under on the assembly:

350 Yards Frontage

No. 1 Coy.		No. 2 Coy. . . A.
	100 yards.	
No. 3 Coy.		No. 4 Coy. . . B.

Line of platoons at forty yards' intervals. G.G lines are A and B. Lateral pegs on the company frontage at ten yards apart. Forward direction time boards are five yards apart, one central line and two on tanks.

7. The Brigade will attack at zero on the morning of 15th on the left of the Division. Six tanks will co-operate on this Divisional front.

>First objective T.8.a.2.5—T.8.d.3.7.
>Second objective T.2.a.9.4—T.8.b.2.3.
>Third objective T.3.a.5.9—T.3.L.2.6.
>Fourth objective N.3.a.0.9—N.34.C.9.0.

8. Infantry will advance to the attack of—
>The first objective at zero.
>The second objective at zero + 1 hour.
>The third objective at zero + 2 hours.
>The fourth objective at zero + 4 hours 30 minutes.

9. The attack will be carried out as follows:
The 2nd and 3rd Battalions Coldstream will attack and capture the first, second, and third objectives. The 2nd Battalion Grenadier Guards will move in rear of the two Coldstream battalions. When the latter advance to the assault of the second objective this battalion will occupy the first objective until the 1st Battalion Irish Guards has passed through them. They will then follow and support the Irish Guards in their attack on the fourth objective. The rôle of this Battalion is to form a defensive flank, if necessary, and to support the attack of the Irish Guards. The Irish Guards will attack the fourth objective.

10. The Battalion will advance in the same formation as it forms up (two lines at 100 yards' distance of two

56 THE GRENADIER GUARDS

CHAPTER XIX.
2nd Batt.
Sept. 1916.

companies each in lines of platoons at 40 yards' interval). If it comes under rifle or machine-gun fire it will deploy into extended order.

11. When the Coldstream have captured the first objective the Battalion will halt until zero + 1 hour, probably in the old British front line.

12. Battalion Headquarters will move about the centre of the two rear companies. A dressing-station will probably be established in the old British front line.

13. As soon as the final objectives have been captured by the infantry, the cavalry will advance and seize the high ground ahead.

14. The first line transport will be packed up and ready to move forward at one hour's notice after zero + 4 hours.

W. R. BAILEY, Capt. Adjt.,
2nd Battalion Grenadier Guards.

September 14, 1916.

The officers of the 2nd Battalion who took part in the operations from September 15 to 17 were :

Lieut.-Colonel C. R. C. de Crespigny, D.S.O.	Commanding Officer.
Capt. Viscount Lascelles	Second in Command.
Capt. the Hon. W. R. Bailey	Adjutant.
Capt. C. N. Newton	No. 1 Company.
Lieut. P. M. Walker	,, ,,
Lieut. A. T. A. Ritchie, M.C.	,, ,,
2nd Lieut. C. C. Cubitt	,, ,,
Capt. A. K. S. Cunninghame	No. 2 Company.
Capt. M. K. A. Lloyd	,, ,,
Lieut. T. Parker Jervis (Pioneer Platoon)	,, ,,
Lieut. N. McK. Jesper	,, ,,
Capt. W. H. Beaumont-Nesbitt	No. 3 Company.
Lieut. H. F. C. Crookshank (Lewis Guns)	,, ,,
Lieut. M. H. Macmillan	,, ,,

2nd Lieut. J. Arbuthnott	. .	No. 3 Company.
2nd Lieut. A. Hasler	. . .	,, ,,
Capt. G. C. FitzH. Harcourt-Vernon		No. 4 Company.
2nd Lieut. T. W. Minchin	. .	,, ,,
2nd Lieut. D. Harvey	. . .	,, ,,
Capt. J. Andrews, R.A.M.C. .	.	Medical Officer.

CHAPTER XIX.
2nd Batt. Sept. 1916.

At 5 A.M. on the 15th the tanks were seen moving slowly forward on the left flank of the Brigade, but they apparently aroused no suspicion, and did not attract any fire. Punctually at 6.20, the zero hour, the two Coldstream battalions started off, and immediately came under a terrific fire from the enemy's machine-guns. The unevenness of the "jumping-off line," and the total absence of any recognisable landmarks in that desert of shell-holes, made a certain loss of direction inevitable. The leaders of the assault were mown down, but the remainder, undeterred by losses, pushed on until they were within twenty yards of the sunken road. It was a red-letter day in the history of the Coldstream, for with the 1st Battalion Coldstream from the 2nd Brigade there were three battalions of Coldstream all in line.

Sept. 15.

When they reached the sunken road there was a momentary check, as the leading companies had lost a large number of officers or non-commissioned officers. Lieut.-Colonel J. Campbell saw that to pause for a moment in the attack would mean failure, and dashed forward. Knowing that in the infernal roar of rifle and machine-gun fire no commands could possibly be heard, he had provided himself with a hunting-horn, which he now blew. The familiar sound, piercing the din,

CHAPTER XIX.

2nd Batt.
Sept.
1916.

instantly arrested the attention of the men, and they at once followed their Colonel. Straight into the midst of the enemy they went with an irresistible rush, and got to work with the bayonet.

Large numbers of Germans were killed or taken prisoner, and four machine-guns were captured, in addition to a number of trench mortars. The casualties in the 2nd Battalion were considerably increased by the fact that the tank, which should have passed over the place where the machine-guns were posted, never reached its objective, and consequently a gap of 100 yards was left where it should have gone.

On reaching the road the Coldstream battalions did not halt, but swept on down the valley, where they found another entirely unexpected German line. Their losses had been very heavy, especially among the officers; in the 2nd Battalion Coldstream there were only two officers left besides the Commanding Officer. Yet so splendid were the rank and file that they " carried on " as if they still had officers at their head. The fact that the whole Coldstream Regiment was in line leading the Guards Division undoubtedly lent an additional impetus to the whole attack. When they reached what they thought the third objective, Lieut.-Colonel Campbell reported their position to General Feilding, but Lord Cavan, who had received reports from aeroplanes, discovered that it was not the third but the first objective that the Coldstream were occupying, and sent back at once to say so.

Again the three Coldstream battalions had to go forward in the face of a withering fire, and

THE BATTLE OF THE SOMME 59

were joined soon after they started by No. 2 Company 2nd Battalion Grenadiers under Captain Cunninghame and parties from the Irish Guards. But with a heavy barrage from the enemy's artillery, in addition to the machine-gun and rifle fire, an advance was no easy matter. It was asking a great deal even of a regiment like the Coldstream to face such a terrible ordeal a second time, but when they were clear of the German barrage the note of the hunting-horn once more rang out and warned them that Lieut.-Colonel Campbell was in front, calling upon them to follow. Without hesitation the line again swept forward, and the second objective was reached.

Meanwhile, the 2nd Battalion Grenadiers started off, moving forward by platoons in artillery formation some 350 yards in rear of the Coldstream. With it came Lieut.-Colonel de Crespigny, who was easily distinguished as he marched along, for he wore a forage cap in place of a helmet. When the Battalion reached Ginchy a heavy German barrage came down on the men, who were almost blinded by the shells. Fortunately, the bulk of the barrage was chiefly on the south side of the village, but huge shells, bursting at the appalling rate of one a second, were shooting up showers of mud in every direction, and the noise was deafening. All this in addition to a fierce rifle fire, which came from the right rear. Though the softness of the ground prevented many shells from exploding, there were naturally a considerable number of casualties. Captain M. K. A. Lloyd was killed as he came along with his half company through the barrage,

CHAPTER XIX.

2nd Batt. Sept. 1916.

60　THE GRENADIER GUARDS

CHAPTER XIX.
2nd Batt.
Sept. 1916.

and Lieutenant Macmillan was slightly wounded in the knee, but was able to go on. Lieutenant Hasler, who was severely wounded in the stomach, never recovered from his wound, and about the same time Second Lieutenant J. Arbuthnott was also fatally wounded.

Twenty minutes later Lieut.-Colonel de Crespigny decided to push on, and the Battalion emerged from the barrage with its right on the Ginchy—Lesbœufs road, but nothing could be seen of the two Coldstream battalions. It turned out afterwards that the leading battalions of the 2nd Guards Brigade, which were on the right, had started off in the wrong direction, and had consequently pushed the Coldstream battalions in the 1st Guards Brigade too far to the left, so that they were no longer in front of their support. The orders given to the Grenadiers were to keep their right on the Ginchy—Lesbœufs road, and this they had managed to do in spite of the barrage. Lieut.-Colonel de Crespigny knew he was in his right place, but was totally unable to understand what had happened to the Coldstream battalions.

He sent a message to General Pereira and received the following reply:

Your pigeon message timed 7.45 A.M. not quite clear. Irish Guards reported their Headquarters in Green line (first objective) and in touch with 41st Brigade on left at 8.45 A.M. You state no signs of Coldstream. Presume they are pushing on to next objective. Am sending bombs up.

Throughout the day it appears to have been assumed that the 2nd Battalion Grenadiers was in touch with the two Coldstream battalions, but

THE BATTLE OF THE SOMME 61

although the Coldstream were fully aware of the position of the Grenadiers, the Grenadiers had no knowledge of the whereabouts of the Coldstream.

CHAPTER XIX.

2nd Batt. Sept. 1916.

Almost immediately after the 2nd Battalion Grenadiers cleared the barrage it came under machine-gun fire from the left front and rifle fire from the right rear. Instead of finding itself, as it expected, in rear of the Coldstream, it was suddenly confronted by a trench full of the enemy. This was the first objective, which the men naturally imagined had been taken by the Coldstream. Here they were in artillery formation instead of in line, marching forward under the impression that the two battalions of Coldstream were in front of them. To approach the trench with any prospect of success it was necessary to deploy into line, and in doing this they lost very heavily. Our creeping barrage had, so to speak, run away, and there was now no artillery support of any kind.

The companies on the right pushed on into the Green line, the first objective, and there gained touch with the 3rd Battalion Grenadiers in Ponsonby's Brigade, which was attempting to stop the Germans turning its right flank. Here Lieutenant Jesper was wounded, and Lieutenant Macmillan, who had gone on in spite of the wound in his knee, was struck a second time in the left thigh. The attack of the Division on the right had failed, with the result that the right flank of the Guards Division was dangerously in the air. On the left there was a considerable gap, which caused great trouble, as it happened to be opposite one of the enemy's strong points. Lieutenant

CHAPTER XIX.
2nd Batt.
Sept. 1916.

A. T. A. Ritchie was wounded as he was trying to deal with this difficult situation, and Sergeant Lyon, who took charge of his platoon, was soon afterwards shot through the head.

One platoon of No. 1 Company with a machine-gun went out and succeeded in forming a defensive flank, thus preventing the Germans, who were in considerable strength, from working behind us. The greater part of the casualties in the 2nd Battalion occurred about this time. Although three of our machine-guns reached the first objective, two were instantly required on the right flank, as the Sixth Division had failed to take the Quadrilateral; this left only one to deal with the Germans on the left. The centre of the Battalion then rushed a part of the Green line and bayoneted all the Germans who did not surrender, making prisoners of the rest. One German soldier who was taken in this way thought it too dangerous to wait for an escort and ran off towards our supports, holding up his hands as he went.

Meanwhile the left of the Battalion was still held up outside the wire of the first objective, as the two Coldstream battalions had apparently passed still farther to the left. As soon as the companies in the centre entered the trench which was the first objective, the enemy started bombing down it from the left. The Grenadier bombers ran short of bombs and were powerless to stop the rush. The situation looked ugly, when Company Sergeant-Major J. Norton, who was lying outside the wire, gathered some men together and led a bayonet attack against the German bombers. This momentarily relieved the situation.

THE BATTLE OF THE SOMME 63

All available bombs were then collected, and a party began to work up the trench, but on reaching the enemy they were driven back with great loss. The situation again became critical, as the Germans were slowly driving our men back. Captain Harcourt-Vernon, finding that the supply of bombs had given out, determined not to waste any more men's lives in what must necessarily be a one-sided contest, and organised a bayonet charge over the top.

Calling on the Adjutant, Captain Bailey, to come with him, he led the charge and took the German bombers completely by surprise. Many of them were killed before they realised what had happened, and forty to fifty more in rear all surrendered. Captain Harcourt-Vernon himself, on arrival at the enemy's trench, was confronted by a stalwart German who immediately held up both hands and was made a prisoner, but Captain Bailey's man proved a fighter although, happily, a bad shot. Captain Bailey missed him with the first three shots of his automatic pistol, but despatched him with the fourth.

The Grenadier bombers, having managed to find some more bombs, now worked along the trench to the left, and the Germans who had escaped from Captain Harcourt-Vernon's bayonet attack broke and ran across the open to their support trench. Having cleared the line for some distance, the Grenadiers began to consolidate. Two small parties of the enemy tried to return but were dealt with by Lewis guns. Lieutenant Crookshank, who was in charge of these guns, was wounded by a H.E. shell which exploded a few

Chapter XIX.

2nd Batt. Sept. 1916.

CHAPTER XIX.
2nd Batt.
Sept. 1916.

yards in front of him, and Captain Lord Lascelles, who was explaining to Captain Beaumont-Nesbitt what he wanted him to do, and had just sent for a runner, was hit by a bullet and had his arm broken.

Meanwhile No. 2 Company under Captain Cunninghame had pushed forward, and got into line with the 3rd Coldstream, some 500 yards to the left front of the remainder of the Grenadiers, who were in the first objective, with the 3rd Grenadiers on their right and a mixture of men from the Guards Division on their left. The Irish Guards had followed the Coldstream, and had been able to send up some platoons to support them.

When the aeroplanes reported that the two Coldstream battalions were not at the third but between the first and second objectives, General Feilding despatched the 2nd Battalion Scots Guards from the 3rd Brigade, which was in reserve, to support them. But their position was not accurately known, and only one company with two Lewis guns reached them.

During the afternoon Lord Cavan had issued orders for the third objective to be bombarded by heavy artillery. On hearing this, General Pereira strongly protested, as he believed that two of his battalions were already occupying that position. But Lord Cavan was so well satisfied that the aeroplane reports were correct that he overruled the protests, and the bombardment took place.

Further and costly attempts to retake the lost ground were made by the enemy during the

THE BATTLE OF THE SOMME 65

evening, but all their counter-attacks were easily repulsed. The position in the evening was this: the remnants of the 2nd and 3rd Battalions Coldstream and the Irish Guards, with one company of the 2nd Battalion Grenadiers and one company of the 2nd Battalion Scots Guards, were holding the second objective. The 2nd Battalion Grenadiers was holding the first objective to the right, with its right flank on the Ginchy—Lesbœufs road and in touch with the 3rd Battalion Grenadiers.

Nothing of importance happened during the night of the 15th, and the 1st Guards Brigade remained in the same position throughout the 16th, when it was subjected to a terrific shelling. That evening the troops in the first objective were relieved by the 59th Brigade, and those in the second objective by the 62nd Brigade. The 2nd Battalion Grenadiers was relieved by the 15th King's Royal Rifles and retired about five miles to bivouacs, where it arrived dead-beat, having had practically no sleep for five days. It slept through the whole day on the 17th.

The casualties throughout the 13th, 14th, and 15th were: killed and died of wounds 108, 235 wounded, and 12 missing—total 365, excluding officers. Amongst the officers, Captain M. K. A. Lloyd was killed, and Lieutenant H. Hasler and Second Lieutenant J. Arbuthnott were seriously wounded and died a few days later, while the following were wounded: Captain Lord Lascelles, Lieutenant T. Parker Jervis, Lieutenant M. H. Macmillan, Lieutenant A. T. A. Ritchie, Lieutenant H. F. C. Crookshank, Second Lieutenant

66 THE GRENADIER GUARDS

Chapter XIX.
2nd Batt.
Sept. 1916.

T. W. Minchin, Second Lieutenant N. McK. Jesper, Second Lieutenant D. Harvey, and Second Lieutenant C. C. Cubitt.

Captain J. Andrews, R.A.M.C., was also wounded, but insisted on remaining at duty. His gallant conduct throughout these three days elicited much praise from the Commanding Officer.

General Pereira addressed the following message to the 2nd Battalion:

2ND BATTALION GRENADIER GUARDS.

As your Brigadier I wish to say in a few words how deeply I appreciate the gallant work done by you in the recent operations at Ginchy.

On the 12th September you took over Ginchy trenches, and the following night you drove the German out of Ginchy Orchard; this work caused you one hundred casualties, but by your fine work you cleared the ground for the advance on September 15, and ensured that it would not be held up at the very beginning.

On September 15 your first advance was through a heavy artillery barrage, but owing to the splendid discipline of your Regiment, you went through it as if on parade.

Your opportunity came later on when you cleared trenches at the point of the bayonet, having run out of bombs, and when you charged a trench strongly held and in the face of machine-gun fire.

You have shown the Germans what they have to expect when they meet the pick of the British Army.

In the near future you may be called upon to do as much again, and I know that you will not fail.

C. E. PEREIRA, Brigadier-General,
Commanding 1st Guards Brigade.

IN THE FIELD,
September 18, 1916.

THE BATTLE OF THE SOMME 67

The 2nd Battalion remained at the Citadel from September 17 to 20 with the rest of Pereira's Brigade. The weather was wet and cold, and the Brigade was busily employed in absorbing drafts. On the 19th a conference of Commanding Officers was held at Brigade Headquarters, when the frontage and objectives for the attack which was to take place on the 25th were outlined. As the front allotted to the Brigade was 700 yards, it was decided to attack with three battalions in front and one in support; but when this scheme was subsequently changed, and the frontage decreased to 500 yards, it was proposed to entrust the next attack to the 2nd Battalion Grenadiers and 1st Battalion Irish Guards, with the 2nd and 3rd Battalions Coldstream in support.

On the 20th the Brigade began moving in companies from the Citadel to relieve the 61st Brigade. It was still very wet, and the roads were blocked by transport in a sea of mud. The weather had now broken, and owing to the cold nights the men took their greatcoats with them, though the rest of their spare equipment was stored as before.

The two Coldstream battalions remained in the front line from the 20th to the 24th, while the 2nd Battalion Grenadiers and 1st Battalion Irish Guards, who were to undertake the attack, were bivouacked in Bernafay and Trônes Woods. The 3rd Guards Brigade was employed in digging an assembly trench about 150 yards in rear of our front line. The fact that the trench was completed only the night before the attack accounted for the Germans being, apparently, ignorant of its exact situation, for although they shelled all the other trenches this one escaped their notice. The 2nd Battalion Grenadiers was put on to salvage work and carrying during the days that preceded the attack.

On the 21st the following orders were issued by Brigadier-General Pereira:

SECRET.

1ST GUARDS BRIGADE ORDER, No. 77

21st September 1916.

1. The Fourth Army will renew the attack on Z day, in combination with the attacks by the French to the south and Reserve Army to the north.

2. (*a*) The Guards Division will form part of the attack of the Fourteenth Corps.

(*b*) 1st Guards Brigade will attack on the right and 3rd Guards Brigade on left of Guards Division.

(*c*) 18th Infantry Brigade of Sixth Division will be attacking on the right of 1st Guards Brigade.

Attacking Troops—

3. The attack of 1st Guards Brigade will be carried out by 2nd Bn. Grenadier Guards on the right and 1st Bn. Irish Guards on the left.

The 2nd Bn. Coldstream Guards will be in support on the right and 3rd Bn. Coldstream Guards in support on the left.

Preliminary Bombardment—

4. A steady bombardment of hostile positions will begin at 7 A.M. on Y day and will be continued to 6.30 P.M. It will begin again at 6.30 A.M. on Z day.

Night firing will be carried out nightly from 6.30 P.M. to 6.30 A.M.

There will be no intensive fire previous to zero hour.

Forming-up Areas—

5. Forming-up areas, boundaries, and objectives are shown on the attached map.

THE BATTLE OF THE SOMME 69

The first objective is marked Green.
The second objective is marked Brown.
The third objective is marked Blue.

CHAPTER XIX.

2nd Batt.
Sept.
1916.

Formation for Attack—

6. The 2nd Bn. Grenadier Guards and 1st Bn. Irish Guards will form up in two lines—one in the firing line and one in the support line.

The 2nd Bn. Coldstream Guards will form up in the communication trench from T.8.a.9.4 to T.3.c.3.8.

The 3rd Bn. Coldstream Guards will form up in the trench from T.8.a.9.4 to T.8.d.5.5.

The 1st Guards Brigade Machine-gun Coy. will assemble with one section at the head of 2nd Bn. Coldstream Guards—one section in rear of 2nd Bn. Coldstream Guards and one section on right of 3rd Bn. Coldstream Guards.

The 1st Guards Brigade Trench Mortar Battery will form up with two guns on right of front line and two guns on right of support line.

The 75th Field R.E. and work platoons will form up in trenches T.8.d.

7. The infantry will advance to the attack of the Green line at zero—to the attack of the Brown line at zero + 1 hour. To the attack of the Blue line at zero + 2 hours.

Barrages—

8. (*a*) 50 per cent of Field Artillery barrage will be used for creeping barrage, and 50 per cent for stationary barrage.

(*b*) In all cases the stationary barrage will lift back when the creeping barrage meets it.

9. (*a*) At zero the creeping barrage will start 100 yards in front of our front-line trenches. It will advance at the rate of 50 yards a minute until it is 200 yards beyond the Green line, when it will become stationary.

(*b*) At zero + 1 hour, the creeping barrage will start 200 yards in front of the Green line, and will advance at the rate of 50 yards a minute until it has passed

200 yards beyond the Brown line, when it will become stationary.

(c) At zero + 2 hours the creeping barrage will start 100 yards in front of the Brown line, and will advance at the rate of 50 yards a minute until it has passed 100 yards beyond the Blue line, when it will become stationary.

(d) Other permanent barrages are being arranged along certain sunken roads.

Tasks—

10. (a) The task of the Division is to press the attack through to the Blue line. A sufficient flow of troops will be maintained from zero onwards to ensure that the Brown line is strong and well supported.

(b) The attack on all objectives will be carried out by 2nd Bn. Grenadier Guards on the right and 1st Bn. Irish Guards on the left.

The 2nd and 3rd Bns. Coldstream Guards will be in support under command of Lieut.-Colonel J. V. Campbell, D.S.O.

Method of Assault—

11. The assault will be carried out by leading battalions in two waves of 75 yards' distance.

Action of Support Battalions—

12. As soon as the front and support lines are vacated by 2nd Bn. Grenadier Guards and 1st Bn. Irish Guards the 2nd Bn. Coldstream Guards and 3rd Bn. Coldstream Guards will occupy them.

All movement to these lines by supporting units should be by the communication trench from T.8.a.9.4 to T.8.c.3.8.

Similarly 2nd and 3rd Bns. Coldstream Guards will occupy the Green and Brown lines as soon as they are vacated by 2nd Bn. Grenadier Guards and 1st Bn. Irish Guards.

As soon as the 2nd Bn. Grenadier Guards and 1st Bn. Irish Guards have gained the Brown line, 2nd and

THE BATTLE OF THE SOMME 71

3rd Bns. Coldstream Guards will each send a company as clearing-up parties in Lesbœufs. These two companies must shelter in shell-holes behind the Brown line during the pause on that line. They must on no account be mixed up with 2nd Bn. Grenadier Guards and 1st Bn. Irish Guards. They will carry a special supply of P. bombs and Mills grenades for dealing with cellars.

The 2nd and 3rd Bns. Coldstream Guards are responsible for making good each objective as captured, and for guarding either flank if threatened, paying special attention to the right flank.

Lieut.-Colonel J. V. Campbell, D.S.O., commanding supporting battalions, will be prepared to give such additional support as may be required to carry out the attack on the final objective—bearing in mind the necessity for holding positions already captured.

Machine-guns—

13. (a) At the first favourable opportunity after the Green line has been captured, O.C. Machine-gun Coy. will send one section forward to it. In this line and in his subsequent move to the Brown line two guns will always be on the right flank, ready to assist in the formation of a defensive flank.

(b) Similarly, when the Brown and Blue lines have been captured, one section will be sent forward to help in the consolidation of each of these lines.

Thus when the final objective has been captured there should be four guns in the Blue line and eight in reserve in the Brown line.

Stokes T.M.—

14. (a) Previous to the assault two guns will be established on the right of the Brigade area. These two guns will move forward at the first favourable opportunity and establish themselves on the right of the Green line.

(b) Two other guns will be in reserve in the front line, and will only move forward to the Green line if ordered

Chapter XIX.

2nd Batt. Sept. 1916.

to do so by Lieut.-Colonel J. V. Campbell, D.S.O., or by the Brigadier.

R.E. and Work Platoons—

15. 75th Field Coy. R.E. and Work Platoons will move forward from their assembly area to the trench about T.8.b.3.0, as soon as this trench is clear of 3rd Bn. Coldstream Guards. They will be ready to move forward on receipt of orders from Brigade H.Q. and consolidate ground gained. O.C. 75th Field Coy. R.E. will detail one officer and three orderlies in liaison with O.C. supporting battalions.

Patrols—

16. When the Blue line has been gained, patrols will be sent forward, and any ground from which good observation can be gained will be occupied.

Such points will be consolidated and eventually joined up with our line.

Contact Patrol and Flares—

17. One contact aeroplane will be in the air from zero till 6.30 P.M. on Z day. Flares will be lit by leading infantry lines on obtaining each objective and also at 6 P.M. on Z day.

18. Watches will be synchronised at 7 P.M. on Y day and at 9 A.M. on Z day.

First Line Transport—

19. Ammunition portions of first line Transport will be collected on the south-west side of Bernafay Wood to the south of the Guillemont—Montauban Road, and remainder of first line Transport in the neighbourhood of Minden Post by 12 noon on Z day.

Brigade Transport Officer will detail an orderly to be in waiting at Advanced Divisional H.Q. Bernafay Wood, and will himself be at Minden Post from 12 noon on Z day to receive instructions.

Prisoners—

20. Prisoners will be sent back to the Corps Cage at the Craters A.8.a under escort. In future correspondence

THE BATTLE OF THE SOMME

will not be taken off prisoners except off officers. Officers' documents will be removed as soon as they are captured and sent to the Corps Cage with their escort.

Dumps—

21. An advanced Brigade Dump of bombs—S.A.A.—Stokes mortar ammunition—R.E. material and rations has been established about T.8.c central.

Equipment—

22. The equipment to be carried by assaulting troops will be the same as that laid down for the attack on September 15.

23. Arrangements have been made for the Brigade on our right to open enfilade machine-gun and trench-mortar fire on the Green line from about T.9.d.3.9 at zero. This fire will be continued until the creeping barrage passes beyond the Green line.

Medical Arrangements—

24. Medical arrangements will be notified later.

Brigade Headquarters—

25. Brigade Headquarters will be at T.19.a.$\frac{1}{2}$.3$\frac{1}{2}$. An advanced Brigade Report Centre will be established in the communication trench T.8.b—T.3.c on September 22.

Pigeons will be supplied to the battalions on Z day as follows :

    3 to 2nd Bn. Grenadier Guards.
    3 to 1st Bn. Irish Guards.
    6 to 3rd Bn. Coldstream Guards.

As soon as all pigeons have been released pigeon men must return at once to Brigade Headquarters.

26. Z day will be September 23. Zero hour will be notified later. It will probably be in the afternoon.

Acknowledge.

      M. B. SMITH, Captain,
    Brigade-Major, 1st Guards Brigade.

CHAPTER XIX.

2nd Batt.
Sept.
1916.

A Memorandum from the Brigade-Major on the lie of the land followed.

1ST GUARDS BRIGADE, No. 262

2ND BATT. GRENADIER GUARDS—

The forthcoming attack differs from the last in that the whole scheme is not such an ambitious one. The distance to the first objective is about 300 yards, to the second objective 800 yards, and to the last objective about 1300 yards. In each case the objective is a clearly defined one, and not merely a line drawn across the map.

Between our present front line and the first objective there is only "No Man's Land." During the next two nights this should be actively patrolled to ensure that our attack is not taken by surprise by some unknown trench, and in order that Officers and N.C.O.'s may have a knowledge of the ground.

It would also be of great assistance to the Artillery if reports as to the actual distance to the Green line were sent in.

The ground slopes down to Lesbœufs, beyond which there is a distinct hollow with a plateau the same level as Lesbœufs beyond. On reaching the final objective Officers and N.C.O.'s should understand the necessity for pushing patrols out to command this hollow and give warning or prevent counter-attacks forming up here.

Large-scale maps of Lesbœufs have been sent to all battalions. These should be carefully studied by all Officers and N.C.O.'s, and especially by those of the companies detailed for the cleaning up of Lesbœufs.

All runners and signallers should know the position of the advanced Brigade Report Centre, and that the best means of approach to it will probably be down the communication trench T.3.c and T.8.b.

Finally, it cannot be too much impressed on assaulting troops the necessity for clinging to our own barrage.

THE BATTLE OF THE SOMME

It will be an attack in which this should be comparatively easy and on which the success of the whole operation may depend.

M. B. SMITH, Captain,
Brigade-Major, 1st Guards Brigade.

September 22, 1916.

The Operation Order by Lieut.-Colonel de Crespigny, Commanding 2nd Battalion Grenadier Guards, was as follows :

22/9/16. *Map Ref. 57.c.S.W.*

1. *Intention.*—The Fourth Army will renew the attack on Z day in combination with the attacks by the French to the south and Reserve Army to the north.

> 1st Guards Brigade will attack on the right of the Division.
> 3rd Guards Brigade will attack on our left.
> 18th Infantry Brigade will attack on our right.

2. This Battalion will be on the right of the 1st Guards Brigade.

> 1st Bn. Irish Guards will be on the left.
> 2nd Bn. Coldstream Guards will be in support on the right.
> 3rd Bn. Coldstream Guards will be in support on the left.

3. *Formation of Attack.*—The Battalion will form up in two lines, one in the firing line and one in the support line, care being taken that bayonets do not show on the top of the trenches before zero.

> *Front Line.*—No. 1 Coy. on left, No. 2 Coy. on the right.
> *Support Line.*—No. 3 Coy. on left, No. 4 Coy. on the right.

Forming-up areas, boundaries, and objective as shown on map at Headquarters, to be copied in.

4. First objective is marked Green. Second objective Brown. Third objective Blue.

5. *Task.*—To press the attack through to the Blue line, a sufficient flow of troops being maintained to ensure that the Brown line is strong and well supported.

6. (*a*) At zero the creeping barrage will start 100 yards in front of our front-line trenches. It will advance at the rate of 50 yards a minute until it is 200 yards beyond the Green line, when it will become stationary.

At zero Nos. 1 and 2 Coys. will advance to the attack of the Green line, followed at 75 yards' distance by Nos. 3 and 4 Coys., who will not stop at our old front line but will push on into the Green line. On reaching the Green line companies will at once reorganise.

(*b*) At zero + 1 hour the creeping barrage will start 200 yards in front of the Green line, and will advance at the rate of 50 yards a minute until it is 200 yards beyond the Brown line, when it will become stationary. At zero + 1 hour Nos. 3 and 4 Coys. will advance to the attack of the Brown line, followed by Nos. 1 and 2 Coys. at 75 yards' interval.

(*c*) At zero + 2 hours the creeping barrage will start 100 yards in front of the Brown line and will advance at the rate of 50 yards a minute until it has passed 100 yards beyond the Blue line.

At zero + 2 hours Nos. 1 and 2 Coys. will attack the Blue line, followed by Nos. 3 and 4 Coys. at 75 yards' distance. The Battalion will consolidate on the Blue line and hold it at all costs.

(*d*) Other permanent barrages are being arranged along certain sunken roads.

When the Blue line has been gained, patrols will be pushed forward at once to seize and hold any point from which good observation can be obtained.

7. *Lewis Guns.*—Each company will have one Lewis gun: the remainder (four) under Lieut. Knatchbull-Hugessen will move up with the second wave and be prepared to act against hostile machine-guns in the village or forward objectives or against counter-attacks.

THE BATTLE OF THE SOMME 77

They will also be ready to form a defensive flank to the right or left.

8. *Mopping Up.*—The dug-outs in the first and second objectives will be promptly dealt with by Nos. 3 and 4 Coys. As soon as the Battalion has gained the Brown line, the 2nd and 3rd Batts. Coldstream will occupy the Green line, and will each send clearing parties of 1 Coy. to clear the village of Lesbœufs.

9. *Dress and Equipment.*—Greatcoats will not be carried, and arrangements will be made for them to be collected before moving up.

Following will be carried: Per man—three sand-bags, two bandoliers, two Mills bombs, one day's rations, one iron ration. A large percentage of each company will carry slung shovels. Flares will be carried by every officer and platoon sergeant, and the remainder of the flares and rockets will be distributed among the companies. V.P. lights should be distributed among companies, men carrying one or two in their pockets.

Water-bottles must be filled before starting, and men must be very sparing in their drinking.

10. All S.A.A. and bombs to be taken off casualties, whenever possible, and dumped in the nearest objective.

11. One contact aeroplane will be in the air from zero till 6.30 P.M. on Z day. Flares will be lit by leading troops on obtaining each objective, and also at 6 P.M. on Z day.

12. *Communication.*—A party of signallers will accompany the second wave and lay a telephone line from the jumping-off place to the Green line, afterwards extending it to Brown and Blue lines.

Battalion Headquarters will not move from the jumping-off place until the Green line has been captured.

13. *Watches* will be synchronised at 7 P.M. on Y day and at 9 A.M. on Z day.

14. *Prisoners.*—If prisoners are taken they must be sent out of the way, to prevent blockage in the trenches.

The Corps Cage is at the Crater A.8.a.

Chapter XIX.
2nd Batt. Sept. 1916.

In future correspondence will *not* be taken off prisoners except off officers. Officers' documents will be removed as soon as they are captured, and sent to the Corps Cage with their escort.

15. *Dumps.*—An advanced Brigade Dump is at T.8.c central.

16. The Brigade on our right will open enfilade machine-gun and mortar fire on the Green line from about T.9.d.3.9 at zero, and continue until the creeping barrage has passed Green line.

17. Z day and zero will be notified later, but zero will probably be in the afternoon.

18. *Miscellaneous.*—(*a*) Assaulting troops should keep as close behind our creeping barrage as possible.

(*b*) There will be no intense artillery fire before zero.

(*c*) All troops should watch for any messages which aeroplanes may drop.

W. R. BAILEY, Capt. and Adjt.,
2nd Batt. Grenadier Guards.

Sept. 25.

The following officers of the 2nd Battalion took part in the attack on the 25th:

Lieut.-Colonel C. R. C. de Crespigny, D.S.O.	Commanding Officer.
Capt. the Hon. W. R. Bailey.	Adjutant.
Lieut. M. A. Knatchbull-Hugessen.	Lewis Gun Officer.
Lieut. A. F. Irvine	No. 1 Company.
2nd Lieut. G. A. Arbuthnot.	,, ,,
Capt. A. K. S. Cunninghame.	No. 2 Company.
Lieut. H. G. Wiggins.	,, ,,
2nd Lieut. F. H. G. Layland-Barratt	,, ,,
Capt. W. H. Beaumont-Nesbitt.	No. 3 Company.
Lieut. A. McW. Lawson-Johnston.	,, ,,
Capt. G. C. FitzH. Harcourt-Vernon	No. 4 Company.
Lieutenant the Hon. W. A. D. Parnell	,, ,,
Lieut. R. B. B. Wright.	,, ,,
Capt. J. Andrews, R.A.M.C..	Medical Officer.

The remainder of the officers remained with the transport.

THE BATTLE OF THE SOMME 79

Late on the night of the 24th the Brigade was informed that zero hour would be 12.35 P.M. the next day. The 2nd Battalion Grenadiers moved up that night from Bernafay Wood to relieve the 2nd Battalion Coldstream in the trenches preparatory to the attack, with its right on the Ginchy—Lesbœufs road. On arrival at the assembly trench No. 1 Company was placed on the right and No. 2 on the left, with No. 3 and No. 4 in support. The trenches were so narrow that the men were unable to sit or lie down, and had to remain standing all the next morning, shoulder to shoulder.

Punctually at 12.35 P.M. the attack was launched, and immediately the creeping barrage was put down by our artillery with great accuracy 200 yards in front of the attacking force. The necessity of getting men across No Man's Land as promptly as possible after zero had been found from experience to be of paramount importance, and the Grenadier and Irish Guards therefore did not hesitate for a moment, but dashed forward in two waves. The enemy must have had some very accurate information about our intentions, for the attackers had hardly left their trench (it was three-quarters of a minute after zero) when they put down a heavy barrage on our front trenches, as well as on the support and communication trenches.

The leading wave of men was able to get close up under our creeping barrage, and the Irish Guards found no difficulty in capturing the first objective at the point of the bayonet. The 2nd Battalion Grenadiers would have had an equally

80 THE GRENADIER GUARDS

CHAPTER XIX.
2nd Batt.
Sept. 1916.

simple task but for the fact that the wire in front of them, which was in standing crops and therefore hidden, had been very little damaged by our artillery fire. There seemed no possibility of getting through it, with the Germans so close, and for the moment the whole advance of the Grenadiers was held up.

Captain A. Cunninghame, Second Lieutenant G. A. Arbuthnot, Lieutenant W. Parnell, and Lieutenant Irvine at once ordered their men to lie down, and the four gallantly advancing by themselves proceeded with the utmost coolness to cut gaps in the wire. Their one thought seems to have been that the attack must not be checked on any account, and as the task of cutting the wire meant almost certain death, they never thought of sending on any of their men, but decided to do it themselves. Captain Cunninghame, Second Lieutenant G. Arbuthnot, and Lieutenant Parnell were killed, and Lieutenant Irvine was wounded, but sufficient room was made for the men to go through, and the Grenadiers swept forward into the first objective.

Apparently the line was strongly held by the enemy, and a large number were killed and one man taken prisoner, while three machine-guns fell into our hands. Lieutenant H. Wiggins, who was on the extreme right, was trying to creep down the fire-swept sunken road when he was struck by a fragment of a shell which burst near him. Lieutenant Knatchbull-Hugessen brought up the Lewis guns by the sunken road and did great execution with them. He was still directing the fire of his guns, although wounded and covered

Major-General G. D. Jeffreys, C.M.G.

THE BATTLE OF THE SOMME 81

with blood, when a shell pitched on the road near him and killed him.

By 1.30 the first objective was entirely in our hands, and five minutes later the advance to the second objective began, close up under our barrage. This was a complete success, as the barrage kept the enemy in their trenches, and they had not even shown themselves when the Grenadiers and Irish Guards were on them with the bayonet.

After the capture of the first objective there were only two company officers left, Lieutenant A. Lawson-Johnston and Second Lieutenant Layland-Barratt, and the attack on the second objective was practically carried out by the non-commissioned officers. Never have the sergeants of the regiment showed to better advantage. The skill with which they handled their companies or platoons, their quick grasp of an order conveyed to them, and the intelligent way in which they carried out their instructions elicited the warmest praise from the Commanding Officer.

By 1.45 P.M. the second objective was secured, and many of the enemy killed. The dug-outs in the sunken road on the right of the Grenadiers were all searched, and a large number of prisoners taken. The following message was received from Brigade Headquarters:

> Prisoner you sent down states that the rest of his Company are in dug-outs or subterranean passages about 250 yards east of Lesbœufs and south of the sunken road. He appears to think they are anxious to surrender, but gives no reasons. In thinking this he seems to be more talkative than reliable.

Chapter XIX.
2nd Batt.
Sept.
1916.

The prisoner proved to be right, though, by the time the search of these dug-outs started, all their occupants had already run out, holding up their hands. During this second phase of the attack, the enemy appear to have offered little resistance, and many more were captured than killed.

Meanwhile the company of Coldstream under Captain Verelst which had been detailed for clearing Lesbœufs closed up in rear of the Grenadiers, according to the programme, and at 2.35 P.M. the advance on the third objective began. To this also there was little resistance, and soon the Grenadiers and Irish Guards were established in a line 100 yards east of Lesbœufs village. During the whole of their advance the Grenadiers had kept in perfect touch with the Irish Guards on their left and the 1st West Yorks on their right, and the orders were carried out almost to the minute. However, the situation on the left of the 1st Guards Brigade seemed doubtful, and General Pereira therefore sent up a company from the 3rd Battalion Coldstream to strengthen that flank.

Thus Lesbœufs passed into our hands, and these positions, which had been considered quite impregnable, were taken by the combination of the creeping barrage and a simultaneous infantry attack.

It was about this time that the only real hitch in the attack occurred. Arrangements had been made for the artillery barrage to be put down 200 yards east of the final objective, but the position of the trench was marked differently on the artillery and infantry maps,

THE BATTLE OF THE SOMME 83

and the shells fell short. This not only caused a good many casualties amongst the men who were digging in, but also prevented the attacking force from pushing forward patrols and occupying the best ground for observation. A furious message was sent back by Captain Bailey: "Our artillery are blowing us out. Please stop it at once," but whether the messages miscarried or whether the maps were so inaccurate that the orders were not understood, the shelling continued for nearly two hours.

Chapter XIX.
2nd Batt.
Sept. 1916.

Meanwhile the 2nd and 3rd Battalions Coldstream moved up by the new communication trench to the support line and thence across the open to the first objective, where they remained in support.

When the barrage eventually cleared away it was found that there were practically no Germans in front, although a good many of them could be seen running towards Le Transloy without rifles or equipment, and the enemy were not shelling us at all, no doubt because they had been obliged to move their guns. It seemed to Lieut.-Colonel de Crespigny that some advantage should be taken of this situation, and he sent a message back that it was a splendid opportunity for the cavalry to go through. Lord Cavan, however, decided that the circumstances did not permit of such a move, as the front was too narrow.

Lord Cavan sent the following message to General Pereira:

Hearty thanks and sincere congratulations to you all. A very fine achievement, splendidly executed.

84   THE GRENADIER GUARDS

CHAPTER XIX.
2nd Batt.
Sept. 1916.

To which General Pereira replied :

Your old Brigade very proud to be able to present you with Lesbœufs. All ranks most gratified by your kind congratulations.

Later this message was received from General Ponsonby, commanding the 2nd Guards Brigade :

G.O.C. and all ranks wish to congratulate the 1st and 3rd Guards Brigades on their splendid success to-day.

The men were in the highest spirits, and that evening they had a quiet time even in the front trench, so quiet that there was no difficulty in getting supplies up. During the night each battalion was ordered to thin out the front line, as there were far too many men in the trench; this order was carried out, but next morning it was found that still further thinning had to be done.

Sept. 26.   On the 26th the 2nd Battalion Grenadiers and Irish Guards received orders to try and push patrols on to the ridge which ran 800 yards east of Lesbœufs; but, although this might have been possible the night before, it was found to be impracticable now as the Germans had had time to recover, and had established a strong line of posts with machine-guns, so that our patrols were unable to advance more than 300 yards.

That night the 2nd Battalion Grenadiers was relieved by the 2nd Battalion Irish Guards from the 2nd Guards Brigade, and marched back to the Citadel Camp, where it arrived at 4 A.M. on the 27th, after stopping on the way at the south end of Bernafay Wood for hot food provided by the cookers.

The casualties in the Battalion were 108 killed, 222 wounded, and 12 missing, making a total of 342 excluding officers. Considering what had been accomplished this was surprisingly little, but the percentage of officers was very high, the result, no doubt, of the fact that the wire had not been cut at the first objective. Captain A. K. S. Cunninghame, Lieutenant the Hon. W. A. D. Parnell, Lieutenant M. A. Knatchbull-Hugessen, and Lieutenant G. A. Arbuthnot were killed, and Captain Harcourt-Vernon, Captain Beaumont-Nesbitt, Lieutenant A. F. Irvine, Lieutenant H. G. Wiggins, and Lieutenant R. B. B. Wright were wounded.

The following order was issued by General Pereira to the 1st Guards Brigade:

2ND BATT. GRENADIER GUARDS—

You have again maintained the high traditions of the 1st Guards Brigade when called upon a second time in the battle of the Somme. For five days previous to the assault the 2nd and 3rd Battalions Coldstream Guards held the trenches under constant heavy shell-fire and dug many hundred yards of assembly and communication trenches, this work being constantly interrupted by the enemy's artillery. The 2nd Battalion Grenadier Guards and 1st Battalion Irish Guards, though under shell-fire in their bivouacs, were kept clear of the trenches until the evening of 24th September, and were given the task of carrying by assault all the objectives to be carried by this Brigade. Nothing deterred them in this attack, not even the fact that in places the enemy wire was cut in the face of rifle and machine-gun fire, and in spite of all resistance and heavy losses the entire main enemy defensive line was captured.

86 THE GRENADIER GUARDS

Chapter XIX.

2nd Batt. Sept. 1916.

Every battalion in the Brigade carried out its task to the full.

The German Reserve Division, which includes the 238th, 239th, and 240th Regiments, and which opposed you for many weeks at Ypres, left the salient on the 18th September. You have now met them in the open, a worthy foe, but you have filled their trenches with their dead and have driven them before you in headlong flight.

I cannot say how proud I am to have had the honour of commanding the 1st Guards Brigade in this battle, a Brigade which has proved itself to be the finest in the British Army.

The Brigade is now under orders for rest and training, and it must now be our object to keep up the high standard of efficiency, and those who have come to fill our depleted ranks will strive their utmost to fill worthily the place of those gallant officers and men who have laid down their lives for a great cause.

C. E. PEREIRA, Brigadier-General,
Commanding 1st Guards Brigade.

September 28, 1916.

THE 3RD BATTALION

3rd Batt.

At the beginning of September the 3rd Battalion Grenadiers was at Morlancourt, being trained with the rest of the 2nd Guards Brigade. On the 9th the Brigade moved into camp at Happy Valley and on the 12th it marched to Carnoy.

The following officers of the 3rd Battalion took part in the attack of September 15, 1916:

Lieut.-Colonel B. N. Sergison-Brooke,
    D.S.O. . . . . Commanding Officer.
Capt. O. Lyttelton . . . Adjutant.

THE BATTLE OF THE SOMME 87

Capt. G. G. Gunnis	Bombing Officer.	CHAPTER XIX.
Lieut. A. O. Whitehead	Asst. ,, ,,	
Capt. R. Wolrige-Gordon	No. 1 Company.	3rd Batt.
Lieut. C. G. Gardner	,, ,,	Sept. 1916.
Lieut. W. A. Stainton	,, ,,	
Lieut. E. H. J. Wynne	,, ,,	
Capt. the Hon. R. P. Stanhope	No. 2 Company.	
Lieut. G. F. R. Hirst	,, ,,	
2nd Lieut. M. Thrupp	,, ,,	
2nd Lieut. D. W. Cassy	,, ,,	
Capt. F. J. V. B. Hopley	No. 3 Company.	
Lieut. W. Champneys	,, ,,	
2nd Lieut. J. F. Worsley	,, ,,	
2nd Lieut. G. M. Cornish	,, ,,	
Capt. A. K. Mackenzie	No. 4 Company.	
Lieut. R. Asquith	,, ,,	
2nd Lieut. G. D. Jackson	,, ,,	
2nd Lieut. H. St. J. Williams	,, ,,	
Lieut. A. T. Logan, R.A.M.C.	Medical Officer.	

On the night of the 12th the 2nd Guards Brigade was ordered to relieve the right subsection of the 3rd Guards Brigade. In the front line was placed the 2nd Battalion Irish Guards, with the 1st Battalion Scots Guards in support, while the two battalions which were eventually to undertake the attack, the 3rd Battalion Grenadiers and 1st Battalion Coldstream, remained behind in reserve. Orders were given to the 2nd Battalion Irish Guards to clear away isolated posts in front, where it was reported that some Germans were lurking, and this was successfully done; but an attack that was afterwards organised with the 71st and 16th Infantry Brigades was not quite so successful. *Sept. 12-13.*

Up to this point the 3rd Battalion Grenadiers had stayed in reserve. Its packs, greatcoats, and surplus kit were now sent into the Divisional *Sept. 14.*

88 THE GRENADIER GUARDS

Chapter XIX.
3rd Batt. Sept. 1916.

store at Méaulte, and bombs, sand-bags, tools, flares, etc., issued to the men for the attack on the following day. The Battalion marched off by companies at 9 P.M. to take up its position.

The following orders were issued by Brigadier-General J. Ponsonby, commanding the 2nd Guards Brigade :

2ND GUARDS BRIGADE

1. The Fourth Army will attack the enemy's defences between Combles Ravine and Martinpuich on Z day with the object of seizing Morval, Lesbœufs, Gueudecourt, Flers.

The French will attack simultaneously on the right, and the Reserve Army on the left.

The attack is to be pushed with the utmost vigour all along the line until the most distant objectives are reached. The failure of a unit on the flank is not to prevent other units from pushing on to their final objective.

As soon as the final objectives have been captured by the infantry, the cavalry will advance and will seize the high ground Rocquigny—Villers-au-Flos—Riencourt-les-Bapaume—Bapaume.

The Guards Division is to be prepared to support the cavalry on the above line at the earliest possible moment.

2. The objectives allotted to Guards Brigades are marked on the attached map as follows :

    First objective, Green (X line).
    Second ,, Brown (Xa line).
    Third ,, Blue (Y line).
    Fourth ,, Red (Z line).

2nd Guards Brigade will be on the right. 1st Guards Brigade will be on the left. 3rd Guards Brigade will be in reserve. 71st Infantry Brigade will be on the right of 2nd Guards Brigade.

THE BATTLE OF THE SOMME

3. The Brigade will attack with two battalions in front and two battalions in support.

3rd Battalion Grenadier Guards will be right front battalion.

1st Battalion Coldstream Guards will be left front battalion.

1st Battalion Scots Guards will be right support battalion.

2nd Battalion Irish Guards will be left support battalion.

4. Battalions will be formed up on a company front in column of half-companies. Troops will be in single rank. Each battalion will therefore advance in four waves.

5. 2nd Guards Brigade Machine-gun Company will detail guns as follows:

I. Two guns to advance with 3/G.G. and two guns with 1/C.G. These guns will take position in the third wave on the inner flank of the right and left flank platoons respectively.

II. Four guns to advance with 1/S.G., and four guns with 2/I.G. Four of these guns will take position in the sixth wave on the inner flank of the right and left platoons respectively. The other four will take the same position in the eighth wave.

The remaining three guns will advance in the centre of the ninth wave.

6. Four Stokes guns will be detailed to advance on the flanks of the ninth wave.

1/S.G. and 2/I.G. will find carrying parties of one officer and fifty men each to advance with these guns.

Remaining guns will be in Brigade Reserve, with 76th Field Company, R.E.

7. The formation for attack will accordingly be as follows:

	1/C.G.				3/G.G.			
	B Coy.		A Coy.		B Coy.		A Coy.	
First Wave . .	6	5	2	1	6	5	2	1
Second Wave .	8	7	4	3	8	7	4	3

	D Coy.	C Coy.	D Coy.	C Coy.
Third Wave . .	14 13	10 9	14 13	10 9
	2 M.G.'s		2 M.G.'s	
Fourth Wave .	16 15	12 11	16 15	12 11
	2/I.G.		1/S.G.	
	B Coy.	A Coy.	B Coy.	A Coy.
Fifth Wave . .	6 5	2 1	6 5	2 1
Sixth Wave . .	8 7	4 3	8 7	4 3
	2 M.G.'s		2 M.G.'s	
	D Coy.	C Coy.	D Coy.	C Coy.
Seventh Wave .	14 13	10 9	14 13	10 9
Eighth Wave .	16 15	12 11	16 15	12 11
	2 M.G.'s		2 M.G.'s	
Ninth Wave . .	S.G. S.G.	4 M.G.'s	S.G. S.G.	

Carrying Parties.

Sapping platoons will be formed up in rear of Battalion H.Q., which will move in the centre of the fourth and eighth waves. The distance between waves will be 50 yards.

8. Details of artillery barrage are given in Appendix A.

9. Nine tanks will advance from Guards Division front. They will probably start from each successive line well in advance of the attacking troops.

The action of the troops will be entirely independent of the action of the tanks, and will be carried out as ordered, whether the tanks are held up or not.

10. The assaults on successive objectives will be delivered at the following times:

Attack on X line at zero.

Attack on Xa line at zero + 1 hour.

(This second assault is limited to 1st Guards Brigade. 2nd Guards Brigade will not move till time for third assault.)

Attack on Y line at zero + 2 hours.

Attack on Z line at zero + 4 hours and 30 minutes.

THE BATTLE OF THE SOMME 91

11. The action of the waves of attack will be as follows :

CHAPTER XIX.

3rd Batt. Sept. 1916.

(a) First four waves will pass over X line and lie down close in rear of the barrage, which will halt till zero + 1 hour and 10 minutes at X + 200 yards.

Fifth and sixth waves will clear up X line.

Seventh and eighth waves will clear up X line and lie down in rear of fourth wave.

Ninth wave will lie down short of X line.

(b) At zero + 2 hours all waves will advance to the Y line. Seventh and eighth waves will advance in front of fifth and sixth waves. Ninth wave will be in rear as before.

(c) On reaching Y line, first four waves will pass over Y line and lie down close in rear of barrage as before.

Seventh and eighth waves will clear up Y line.

Fifth and sixth waves will pass over Y line and lie down in rear of fourth wave.

Ninth wave will lie down short of Y line.

(d) Half an hour after reaching Y line all Commanding Officers will meet at Battalion Headquarters of 3rd Bn. Grenadier Guards, and will confer on attack on Z line.

Lieutenant-Colonel Brooke, D.S.O., 3rd Bn. Grenadier Guards, if present, will command the attack on the Y line.

In the absence of Lieut.-Colonel Brooke, senior officer present will command.

Stokes Gun Sections will act in accordance with orders of O.C. attack.

12. It is the object of these dispositions to ensure a steady flow of troops so as to press the strongest possible attack against each successive objective.

Rear lines will reinforce leading lines wherever they appear thin.

No troops will be left in any objective when the attack goes on.

The task of the two leading Guards Brigades is to

drive the attack through Lesbœufs to the ultimate objective by every means in their power.

3rd Guards Brigade will be in close reserve to carry out any of the following duties, as may be required:

(a) To pass through Z and press the attack behind the cavalry.
(b) To make a defensive flank, if the attack on our flanks is held up.
(c) To support the attack of the leading Guards Brigades, if held up anywhere.

13. 76th Field Company, R.E., will be in Brigade Reserve. It will be formed up in a place to be notified later, and will await orders from the Brigade.

14. Ninth Squadron, R.F.C., will have two contact aeroplanes in the air from zero to dark on Z day, and again from 6.30 A.M. to 9 A.M. on Z + 1 day.

Flares will be lit as follows:

(i.) On obtaining each objective.
(ii.) At 12 noon and 5 P.M. on Z day.
(iii.) At 6.30 A.M. on Z + 1 day.

Red flares will be used by infantry, Green flares by cavalry.

15. All transport will be packed up and ready to move forward at 1 hour's notice after zero + 4 hours.

Brigade Transport Officer will report at Divisional Headquarters, Minden Post, at zero + 2 hours, and await orders there.

16. Separate orders will be issued regarding—

I. Supply of rations.
,, ,, water.
,, ,, S.A.A.
,, ,, Stokes ammunition.
,, ,, bombs.
II. Disposal of prisoners.
III. Medical arrangements.

17. Watches will be synchronised at 12.30 P.M. and 6.30 P.M. on Y day by telephone from this Office.

18. Brigade Headquarters will close at Bernafay Wood at 5 P.M. to-morrow and open at T.19.a.$\frac{1}{2}$.3$\frac{1}{2}$ at the same hour.

Acknowledge. E. W. M. GRIGG, Captain, Brigade-Major.

13/9/16.

The following orders are supplementary to this Office No. 129/G. The latter will be amended, where required, accordingly.

1. 3/G.G., 1/C.G. will relieve 2/I.G. in the line to-night. 2/I.G. will move back to its assembling area on relief, and remain there till zero hour.

3/G.G. will march off at 9 P.M.
1/C.G. will march off at 9.30 P.M.
1/S.G. will march off at 10.45 P.M.
T.M.B. will march in rear of 1/C.G.

Company guides from 2/I.G. will be at Brigade Headquarters, Bernafay Wood, for relieving battalions at the following hours :

    3/G.G. 9.45 P.M.
    1/C.G. 10.15 P.M.
    1/S.G. 11 P.M.

2. Forming-up will be carried out as follows :

(a) Every battalion is provided with printed boards to mark the waves and the flanks of platoons.

3/G.G., 1/C.G. and 1/S.G. will detail marking parties of 1 officer and 12 O.R. each to put these out before relief to-night. Brigade Signal Officer will provide three guides for this party to be at Brigade Headquarters, Bernafay Wood, at 7 P.M.

(b) In order to avoid the enemy barrage, all battalions will form east of the road from G of Ginchy (1/20,000 Sheet 57 C., S.W.) and the southern end of the Sunken Road in T.14.a. In order to make room, battalions will feel their right in forming up as far as a line running parallel to the direction of the attack through Ginchy Telegraph.

On starting at zero hour, battalions will incline left until the left flank is in touch with the right flank of 1st Guards Brigade.

(c) The direction of the attack is 58 degrees magnetic from the cross-roads in T.14.a.

Marking boards will be put out on a line 148 degrees magnetic from left flank mark, or 328 degrees magnetic from the right flank mark. Right and left flanks have been marked in advance by 2/I.G.

3. The dividing line between battalions in attack on X and Y lines is as follows :

        X line. T.8.d.9.4.
        Y line. Road junction T.3.d.5.2.

4. 2/I.G. will be formed up in two waves. First wave will clear up second German trench in X line.

Second wave will clear up first German trench in X line. Both these waves will clear up Y line.

Officer commanding 1st Bn. Scots Guards will make arrangements for clearing the part of these two trenches in his area.

5. The creeping barrage will open at zero hour on a line at right angles to the direction of the attack through cross-roads in T.14.a.

It will advance and halt thereafter as laid down in Appendix A to this Office No. 129/G.

6. Prisoners will be collected at Battalion Headquarters under Battalion arrangements, and sent back to Divisional Collecting Station, Crater Post, A.8.a.6.3, when possible.

They should be made to carry wounded when practicable.

        (Signed)   E. W. M. GRIGG, Captain,
                                  Brigade-Major.

14/9/16.

The first phase of the attack of the Guards Division was to be carried out with Pereira's Brigade on the left and Ponsonby's Brigade on the right, while Corkran's Brigade would be in reserve. To the 2nd Brigade was allotted a front of 500 yards, north-east of Ginchy, and the attack was to be carried out by the 3rd Battalion Grenadiers on the right with the 1st Battalion Scots Guards in support, and the 1st Battalion Coldstream on the left with the 2nd Battalion Irish Guards in support. In order to evade the heavy barrage which the Germans usually put down along the east of Ginchy and Guillemont villages, it was decided to assemble the whole Brigade east of Ginchy.

This precaution had the advantage that the assembly trench was not shelled, but there were certain disadvantages. In the first place, the assembly ground was not square with the line of attack, so that a change of direction was necessary after the attack had started, and, in the second place, it was by no means easy to keep the 2nd Guards Brigade in immediate touch with the 1st Guards Brigade. It had been intended to align the Brigade on painted boards showing the waves and the flanks of the platoons, but these showed up so bright in the clear moonlight that they were thrown away and men were put out as markers instead.

The 3rd Battalion Grenadiers was formed up in four waves, all the men being in single rank, and companies in columns of half-companies, with fifty yards' distance between platoons. Their distribution was as follows:

No. 4 Company.		No. 3 Company.	
No. 14 Platoon.	No. 13 Platoon.	No. 10 Platoon.	No. 9 Platoon.
„ 16 „	„ 15 „	„ 12 „	„ 11 „

No. 2 Company.		No. 1 Company.	
No. 6 Platoon.	No. 5 Platoon.	No. 2 Platoon.	No. 1 Platoon.
" 8 "	" 7 "	" 4 "	" 3 "

At 4 A.M. the Battalion was in position and everything was ready. Sandwiches and an issue of rum were served out to the men, who then tried to snatch a little sleep. Complete silence reigned, except for the sound of the tanks making their way slowly to their places. At 6 A.M. exactly our heavy guns started, and fired about forty shells apiece in quick succession. This immediately woke up the enemy and brought down their barrage in exactly the place where it was expected, but of course there were no troops there. Orders were passed down at 6.15 to fix bayonets and get ready, and five minutes later the attack started.

The first objective or Green line lay over the ridge about 600 yards away, and it was hoped that this would be reached without any serious opposition. The ground in and around Ginchy was a battered mass of irregular ridges and shell-holes, which overlapped and stretched away into the early morning mist. Direction became a matter of the greatest difficulty, as there were absolutely no landmarks to go by. No one except the Irish Guards had seen the ground before, as it had been found impossible to send officers up during the heavy fighting of the last days. On the map it seemed a simple matter to pick out the Lesbœufs road and the church of Lesbœufs, either of which would have served as a guide, but on the actual ground, which was just a great desert of shell-holes, with our own

THE BATTLE OF THE SOMME

CHAPTER XIX.

3rd Batt. Sept. 1916.

barrage ahead and the enemy's shells falling all round, it was practically impossible to distinguish anything.

Soon after it started off the 3rd Battalion Grenadiers came on unexpected intermediate lines. These were no more than connected shell-holes, but had served to shelter a number of Germans, who fought with the utmost bravery. The guns had not bombarded them, while the creeping barrage had passed over too quickly to do much harm. Though the men holding them were all shot or bayoneted, and the delay thus caused was very slight, it had the effect of breaking the regularity of the formation and telescoping up the men in the rear.

Almost at the outset Captain A. K. Mackenzie was hit and fell, as he led his company to the attack. Though mortally wounded, he got up again and struggled on, still waving his men forward. Once more he fell, and this time was unable to rise, but even then he managed to raise himself on one knee and cheer the company on. Afterwards he was carried down on a stretcher, but never recovered and died in the ambulance on the way. About the same time Lieutenant Raymond Asquith was shot through the chest and killed as he led the first half of No. 4 Company. He had endeared himself to both officers and men in an extraordinary degree since he joined the regiment at the beginning of the war, and his preference of service with his Battalion to the good staff appointment which he had just given up had won the admiration of all ranks. Lieutenant E. H. J. Wynne was mortally wounded by a German officer in one of the intermediate lines, and Lieutenant C. G. Gardner was killed soon afterwards. Captain G. G. Gunnis, Lieutenant A. Whitehead, Second Lieutenant H. Williams, and Second Lieutenant J. Worsley were wounded.

While these intermediate lines were being cleared, an extremely heavy machine-gun fire was opened from the right flank, where the Sixth Division had been held up at the start. The tanks which were to have flattened out the wire and helped the advance never appeared, and so it came about that, from the moment it crossed over the Ginchy ridge and came within view of the enemy's lines, the 2nd Guards Brigade was committed to hard and continuous fighting in a position of much difficulty.

By now the Brigade had got very much mixed up, and, though still all together, continued its advance as a brigade rather than as four battalions. Whenever the leading wave met with any check, those in rear, impatient to get at the enemy, closed in on them, and thus companies and even battalions became intermingled. As an inevitable result of this quick advance the right flank of the Brigade was completely exposed, and Lieut.-Colonel Sergison-Brooke deciding that some protection was essential, threw out a company as a defensive flank to within 200 yards of the enemy's flanking trench, to keep down the fire, while the rest of the 3rd Battalion Grenadiers pressed on to the main assault.

It had been arranged that after the first objective had been captured our artillery should bombard the second objective and prepare it for attack, so when these lines were carried there was some uncertainty as to whether the advance should be continued or not. In spite of the casualties the 3rd Battalion Grenadiers, with the 1st Battalion Scots Guards, continued to push on till it reached the first objective, and was able to secure it according to the specified time, though the task was no easy one. In some parts between the right and left columns of the assault, and also on the extreme right, the wire had been untouched, but as soon as any man gained a foothold in the trench he at once proceeded to clear the way by bombing. Curiously enough, though the Germans had fought with such tenacity in the intermediate lines, the garrison of the first objective offered comparatively little resistance, and surrendered in large numbers.

The men were out of breath, as the pace had been hot, and they were carrying a good weight, so a pause in this first objective was not unwelcome. The prisoners were grouped together, and sent back in batches; in one part of the line the German machine-gunners caught sight of them and turned their guns on them, but the prisoners scurried off and ran as fast as they could back through our lines.

On the right Captain Wolrige-Gordon with No. 1 Company was attempting to keep touch with the Sixth Division, and as the Battalion advanced he started firing down the enemy's trench where the machine-guns were holding it up. At first the Germans were puzzled, but

CHAPTER XIX.

3rd Batt. Sept. 1916.

when they grasped where the fire came from their snipers got to work and accounted for many men before Captain Wolrige-Gordon could join the rest of the Battalion.

In the meantime the three battalions of Coldstream advanced in a splendid manner, carrying all before them. When men in line are going forward with no reliable landmarks to guide them, small incidents, quite insignificant in themselves, will often cause a slight change of direction without their being aware of it. On starting off the 1st Battalion Coldstream met with little resistance, and in its endeavour to rush the foremost German trenches the left flank of the Battalion moved ahead faster than our creeping barrage. Quickly realising what had happened, the men checked the pace and hung back for a little, while the right flank of the Battalion still pressed on. The check was momentary, but caused the whole Battalion to swing slightly to the left. This led the 2nd and 3rd Battalions Coldstream in the 1st Guards Brigade also to ease off slightly to the left, and, as often happens, the slight deviation was exaggerated as the advance continued, and soon all the Coldstream battalions were moving in a northerly instead of a north-easterly direction. A switch trench running at an angle into the German main line gave them the impression that they were going in the right direction, as it seemed square with their advance. The 2nd Battalion Irish Guards swung with the 1st Battalion Coldstream, but the 1st Battalion Scots Guards followed the 3rd Battalion Grenadiers.

THE BATTLE OF THE SOMME 101

While this was happening the 2nd Battalion Grenadiers from the 1st Guards Brigade, having completely lost sight of the 2nd and 3rd Battalions Coldstream as it passed through the enemy's barrage, continued to advance according to its orders, and eventually forced its way to the first objective, where to its surprise it found itself between the 3rd Battalion Grenadiers and the 1st Battalion Irish Guards.

CHAPTER XIX.

3rd Batt. Sept. 1916.

The situation was most complicated, and yet all was well. The Division, as a Division, had swept everything in front of it, although not quite in the order in which it should have moved. But parts of the German trenches remained untouched, and these had to be dealt with before any farther progress could be made. When the 1st Battalion Coldstream began to swing to the left, a gap was made between the two front battalions of the 2nd Guards Brigade, which widened out as the advance progressed. Observing this, Captain Oliver Lyttelton pushed up 100 men of the 3rd Battalion Grenadiers to fill the intermediate space, but as the gap gradually extended, and the smoke and dust made it impossible for them to see where they were going, these hundred men were able to keep touch with the 1st Battalion Coldstream only, and became detached from the rest of the Battalion.

Progress towards the first objective was made very difficult by the failure of the Sixth Division to take the Quadrilateral. As soon as the attacking lines showed themselves they were met by a sweeping fire from the enemy's machine-

Chapter XIX.
3rd Batt.
Sept. 1916.

guns on the right flank, and were mown down. After the first objective had been entered, and Lieut.-Colonel Campbell, Coldstream Guards, was organising an attack upon the second objective, it was discovered that the whole of the first objective was not entirely secured. An attack was immediately made on that portion of the line still occupied by the enemy, and Lieut.-Colonel Guy Baring, who commanded the 1st Battalion Coldstream, in attempting to gain touch with the remainder of the Brigade from which he had, for the moment, been separated, left the trench to advance over the top of the ground when he was struck by a bullet in the head and instantly killed.

Lieut.-Colonel Campbell then ordered Captain Lyttelton to bomb down the trench together with a party of the 2nd Irish Guards under Lieutenant Mylne. But hardly had they started when the Germans came running down the trench, holding up their hands. They were being pursued by another bombing party, composed, not of the 3rd Battalion Grenadiers as might have been expected, but the 2nd Battalion Grenadiers.

Now that the whole of the first objective was in our hands the advance towards the second objective at once took place. On the extreme right no ground could be gained, but farther towards the centre the 3rd Battalion Grenadiers reached a position which it assumed to be the second objective, but was in fact, according to the report from the aeroplanes, half-way between the first and second objectives.

THE BATTLE OF THE SOMME 103

During this last advance Captain Stanhope and Second Lieutenant Jackson were killed. Lieutenant W. Stainton was reported missing, and there were several conflicting stories as to what had happened to him. Second Lieutenants Thrupp and Cassy were wounded, as well as Second Lieutenant Cornish, who behaved with great gallantry and was recommended for a Military Cross.

As to whether it would have been possible to push on at once into Lesbœufs, accounts vary. Certainly those in front thought that had reinforcements come up the town would have fallen into our hands without further opposition. It was not known, however, that the right flank of the Division was absolutely unprotected, and that the farther the Division advanced the more perilous its position was bound to become. Even if Lesbœufs had been taken, it is difficult to believe that it could have been held against counter-attacks with the right flank thus in the air.

The sight of the Germans retiring hastily towards Bapaume and withdrawing their field-guns proved too tempting for some adventurous spirits, and patrols were organised to press on towards Lesbœufs. After consulting their maps, Captain Sir Ian Colquhoun, 1st Battalion Scots Guards, and Captain Lyttelton, 3rd Battalion Grenadiers, determined to keep the Germans in front of them on the move, and they were joined soon after by Major Rocke, Captain Alexander, and Lieutenant Mylne of the Irish Guards. Sir Ian Colquhoun had already won a reputation as the bravest of the brave, and was credited with having killed a large number of Germans in personal combat. The others were very much of the same type—officers who were never content with simply carrying out their orders, but would instantly take advantage of any weakness in the German defence to drive a success home.

Having collected about twenty men, Sir Ian Colquhoun pushed forward to reconnoitre towards Lesbœufs, followed soon after by Major Rocke and Captain Alexander with some men of the Irish Guards. Captain Lyttelton called on the men of the 3rd Battalion Grenadiers who were near, and brought the whole party up to about 120. This party pushed on, and met with no opposition for 800 yards. At this stage they found themselves in an unoccupied trench running along the bottom of a little gully, with standing crops in front of them. They could have pushed on into Lesbœufs, but owing to their small numbers and, as they expressed it, the "draughtiness of their flanks," they decided to hold on where they were and send back for reinforcements. Messages were accordingly despatched to the Brigade Headquarters, and were marked, " To be read by all officers on the way."

This daring attempt to capture more ground from the enemy was quite a feasible operation, but its success undoubtedly depended on whether reinforcements could reach them before the Germans returned. For so small a party to try and do anything more than hold the trench until an adequate force arrived would

THE BATTLE OF THE SOMME

have been madness. Every possible precaution was taken against surprise, and Lewis guns were placed on each flank. From 1 P.M. onwards this gallant little band waited and waited for the reinforcements which never arrived. Meanwhile, finding that the British attack had spent itself, the Germans began returning in small bodies, and soon after 5 P.M. a whole battalion was seen advancing. The position of this party was now becoming serious. Gradually the Germans were moving round each flank, and even getting to their rear.

At 6 P.M. they were still doggedly holding on to their trench, being fired at from all sides, when suddenly a company of the enemy, 250 strong, charged them in front. The surprise was complete, as the standing crops hid the Germans till the last moment. With 250 of the enemy rushing a trench occupied by less than 100 British troops, one might have thought it only a matter of time before our men were all killed or taken prisoners. But the men who had followed Major Rocke, Sir Ian Colquhoun, and Captain Lyttelton were naturally stout fighters, and when the order to retire was given they actually contrived to disengage themselves and get away, after killing a good number of the enemy. Captain Lyttelton, finding himself surrounded, threw his empty revolver at the Germans; thinking it was a Mills bomb, they ducked, and gave him time to scramble out of the trench and escape.

Even then, had the Germans only stayed where they were and fired at the retreating party, they

CHAPTER XIX.
3rd Batt.
Sept.
1916.

might have inflicted considerable losses, but they came running on, firing from the shoulder, and so allowed these gallant men to rejoin the main British line with astonishingly few casualties. When once they were safe, the pursuers were greeted by such a deadly fire from our trenches that numbers of them were killed, and the rest scattered in all directions.

Meanwhile General Ponsonby pressed for the 3rd Guards Brigade to be sent up, but the reports which reached General Feilding from the air showed that the troops in front were not in the positions ascribed to them, and as the situation on both flanks of the Division was unsatisfactory, and the Germans were reported to be massing between Morval and Lesbœufs, he considered that it would be impossible to throw forward all his reserves. However, the 4th Battalion Grenadiers was ordered to reinforce the 2nd Guards Brigade, and told by General Ponsonby to strengthen the right flank.

Sept. 16.

All that night the right flank of the 2nd Guards Brigade was being bombed, and Captain J. Hopley, who behaved with great gallantry, at one time had his men standing back to back and firing both ways. The next day, September 16, the 2nd Guards Brigade was relieved by the 61st Infantry Brigade, who continued the attack, and secured the next objective.

The percentage of officers killed and wounded in the 3rd Battalion Grenadiers was exceptionally high; out of 22 officers who went into action, 17 were killed or wounded. Lieut.-Colonel Sergison-Brooke was wounded almost at the start. Captain

THE BATTLE OF THE SOMME 107

A. K. Mackenzie, Captain the Hon. R. P. Stanhope, Lieutenant E. H. J. Wynne, Lieutenant Raymond Asquith, Lieutenant W. A. Stainton, Lieutenant C. G. Gardner, Second Lieutenant G. D. Jackson were killed; Captain G. G. Gunnis and Second Lieutenant E. G. Worsley were mortally wounded, and subsequently died; Captain F. J. V. B. Hopley, Lieutenant W. Champneys, Lieutenant A. O. Whitehead, Second Lieutenant M. Thrupp, Second Lieutenant D. W. Cassy, Second Lieutenant G. M. Cornish, Second Lieutenant H. St. J. Williams, and Second Lieutenant J. F. Worsley were wounded.

CHAPTER XIX.

3rd Batt. Sept. 1916.

Amongst other ranks the casualties were 395 killed and wounded.

On September 20 the 3rd Battalion moved into bivouacs at Carnoy, where it remained until the second attack of the Guards Division on the 25th. The 2nd Guards Brigade was then, however, in reserve, and, owing to the complete success of the attack, its services were not required. The 3rd Battalion Grenadiers was in Corps Reserve during the attack, but returned to the Brigade in the evening. On the 26th Lieutenant C. C. Carstairs and Second Lieutenant C. F. Johnston joined.

THE 1ST BATTALION

At the end of August the 3rd Guards Brigade went through a period of training which lasted until September 7; during this time it stayed in billets at Ville-sous-Corbie. Captain E. Sheppard joined the 1st Battalion Grenadiers on

1st Batt.

108 THE GRENADIER GUARDS

CHAPTER XIX.
1st Batt.
Sept.
1916.

September 3. On the 8th the Brigade moved up into the line and took over Ginchy, which had just been captured by the Sixteenth Division. The 4th Battalion Grenadiers and 1st Battalion Welsh Guards were placed in the front trenches, while the 1st Battalion Grenadiers and 2nd Battalion Scots Guards were in reserve.

The officers who went up with the 1st Battalion were :

Lieut.-Colonel M. E. Makgill-Crichton-Maitland	Commanding Officer.
Capt. E. H. J. Duberly	Adjutant.
Lieut. R. P. le P. Trench, M.C.	Bombing Officer.
Lieut. A. V. L. Corry, M.C.	Lewis Gun Officer.
Capt. W. D. Drury-Lowe, D.S.O.	King's Company.
Lieut. G. F. Pauling	,, ,,
2nd Lieut. B. G. Samuelson	,, ,,
Capt. A. C. Graham	No. 2 Company.
Lieut. E. B. Shelley	,, ,,
2nd Lieut. E. G. L. King	,, ,,
Capt. E. N. E. M. Vaughan	No. 3 Company.
2nd Lieut. O. F. Stein	,, ,,
2nd Lieut. C. C. T. Sharp	,, ,,
Capt. L. G. Fisher-Rowe	No. 4 Company.
2nd Lieut. R. H. P. J. Stourton	,, ,,
2nd Lieut. W. H. Lovell	,, ,,
2nd Lieut. L. de J. Harvard	Sapping Platoon.

The rest of the officers, as well as the Sergeant-Major, Senior Drill-Sergeant, and Company Sergeant-Majors, remained behind with the Transport.

Sept. 10–11.

At 3.30 A.M. on the 10th the 1st Battalion Welsh Guards reported that it had completed the relief of the 48th Brigade, and was digging in on a line 200 yards east of the south-east corner of Delville Wood to 100 yards north of

THE BATTLE OF THE SOMME 109

Ginchy on the Flers road, and 250 yards east of the Lesbœufs road. Its left was in touch with the 164th Brigade, but its right was in the air. Meanwhile the 4th Battalion Grenadiers was relieving the 47th Brigade between Guillemont and Leuze Wood. But although both these battalions were carrying out their orders correctly, there was a gap of at least 600 yards between them, owing doubtless to the fact that the troops they had to relieve were not quite in the positions they had been reported as occupying. The 47th Brigade had been held up by the Quadrilateral, while the 48th Brigade on its left had advanced some distance.

On learning this, Brigadier-General Corkran decided to employ some companies from the battalions in reserve to fill up the gap, and accordingly instructed Lieut.-Colonel Maitland to send one company to support the 4th Battalion Grenadiers and another company to the Welsh Guards. No. 2 Company, under Captain Graham, was despatched to Arrow Head Copse in support of the 4th Battalion Grenadiers on the right of the Brigade, and while going on ahead to find Lieut.-Colonel Lord Henry Seymour, Lieutenant E. King was hit by a rifle bullet in the leg, and Lieutenant E. B. Shelley and Lieutenant Llewellyn were wounded shortly afterwards. Captain Vaughan, with No. 3 Company, was instructed to place himself under the orders of Lieut.-Colonel W. Murray-Threipland, while the rest of the Battalion remained a little distance behind in case of emergency.

Hardly had the Welsh Guards finished their

CHAPTER XIX.

1st Batt.
Sept. 1916.

relief, when they were attacked, and had to fight hard to maintain their position. Coming on in great force as early as 3 A.M., the Germans began to press back the right of their line from the sunken road. Every available man had been hurried to the front line, where the casualties were thinning out the ranks to an alarming extent, and even the 100 Grenadiers who had been sent up as ammunition carriers had to be put in as supports. The Welsh Guards had lost a good many officers and N.C.O.'s, and matters were beginning to look serious when Captain Vaughan arrived with No. 3 Company of the 1st Battalion Grenadiers, having passed through a barrage of 5·9 shells near Trônes Wood in artillery formation. He was at once sent off by Lieut.-Colonel Murray-Threipland to take over the line on the right of the Welsh Guards and relieve the Munster Fusiliers, who had had some very heavy fighting and were much shaken. Second Lieutenant Stein went on with the leading platoon, and the relief was carried out by sections and completed by noon.

It was anything but a pleasant position, as both flanks were in the air, and the Company was occupying an extended front at right angles to the trench occupied by the Welsh Guards. Captain Vaughan was told that the attack would probably come from the left, and made his dispositions accordingly. He placed two sections in shell-holes in échelon on the left, and established a double block at that end of the trench with a strong bombing section, supported by a Lewis gun; the other Lewis gun he stationed on the right flank. Second Lieutenant Sharp was in charge of the left of the Company and Second Lieutenant Stein of the right.

The day proved quiet and uneventful, the enemy showing no inclination to advance, but at 10 P.M. their attack began. Coming on in four waves, they not only succeeded in getting between No. 3 Company and the Welsh Guards, but even gained a footing in the front trench. The Lewis gun on the left did excellent work, but the men in the bombing post were all knocked out. At the same time the Welsh Guards were heavily attacked all down their line, and Lieut.-Colonel Murray-Threipland sent a message to Captain Vaughan to say that his front line was falling back somewhere to the centre of Ginchy, and asking him to fill up the gap between them until reinforcements could be brought up. Captain Vaughan replied that his left flank was in contact with the enemy, and he could not, therefore, throw back that flank, but that he had double-locked the trench on that side; if reinforcements did not reach him soon, he would endeavour to protect his flanks as best he could.

This Company's situation was now becoming precarious. It had the enemy at each end of a very long trench; enemy in front of it and enemy behind it. It was short of bombs and practically out of ammunition. At one time it had some of the enemy actually in the trench, but fortunately their bayonets were still left to them, and not a German survived to dispute possession with them. Apparently the enemy did not know that this was an advanced trench, thinly held; probably he thought it was his old line 100 yards farther back. In any case he found it a hard nut to crack, in spite of his superior numbers and obvious advantages. The men of No. 3 understood that if they gave way it would go hard with the Welsh Guards, and refused to yield an inch. Sergeant Whittaker showed great courage and skill with the bombing party, and was responsible for killing a large number of Germans, as well as holding up the enemy's attack on the left.

Both Second Lieutenant Sharp and Second Lieutenant Stein were wounded, in addition to many N.C.O.'s, and 56 men in all were killed, but the rest fought on and made it plain to the enemy that they had no intention of retiring. When the ground was afterwards cleared, over 100 Germans were found dead in front of the trench, amongst them being a captain named von Hahen and two other officers. Throughout this difficult operation Captain Vaughan directed the proceedings with great coolness, and his messages were clear, precise, and cheerful. His stubborn defence of his trench undoubtedly saved the Welsh Guards from being surrounded.

General Corkran in the meantime sent up two companies of the 2nd Battalion Scots Guards to the assistance of the Welsh Guards, and they arrived at 3.30 P.M. The remaining companies of the 1st Battalion Grenadiers were despatched to Guillemont, while the rest of the Scots Guards took their place near Bernafay Wood. After continuous fighting the Welsh Guards had managed to straighten their line, and Captain Ashton of that regiment organised

Brigadier-General C. E. Corkran, C.M.G.

THE BATTLE OF THE SOMME 113

some bombing attacks, and regained all the ground lost during the day. About midnight on the 11th the Welsh Guards were relieved by the 2nd Battalion Scots Guards.

CHAPTER XIX.
1st Batt.
Sept. 1916.

Meanwhile the King's Company 1st Battalion Grenadiers, under Captain Drury-Lowe, moved into the line to fill up the gap between the left of No. 3 Company and the 2nd Battalion Scots Guards, which now occupied the line originally held by the Welsh Guards. In carrying out this operation the King's Company captured fifty German prisoners. No. 4 Company, under Captain L. G. Fisher-Rowe, moved into the line on the left of the Scots Guards to fill up another gap there. Second Lieutenant Stourton was wounded in the shoulder while in charge of the carrying party of 100 men that went into the line early that afternoon.

At 2 A.M. No. 2 Company, under Captain A. C. Graham, was ordered to bomb along a trench running east from the right of No. 3 Company along the south side of the Ginchy Telegraph Road, and attack the Quadrilateral. At that time it was not known how strongly this point was held. The formation of the bombing attack was:

Sept. 12.

Bombing party . . .	10 men and	1 N.C.O.
Blocking party . . .	4 ,,	1 ,,
Bombing party . . .	10 ,,	1 ,,
One platoon under a subaltern.		
Bombing party . . .	10 men and	1 N.C.O.
Blocking party . . .	4 ,,	1 ,,
Lewis gun	6 ,,	1 ,,
One platoon.		
The Company Commander.		
Two platoons.		

VOL. II I

Each bombing party was composed as follows :

2 bayonet men carrying 6 bombs each.
1 thrower carrying 6 bombs.
2 carriers carrying 12 bombs each.
1 N.C.O. carrying 6 bombs.
1 Mills adapter firer carrying 6 Mills adapters.
2 Mills adapter carriers carrying 10 Mills adapters.
2 bomb carriers carrying 12 bombs each.

Each blocking party was composed of four privates and one N.C.O., carrying 25 sand-bags and 1 shovel each.

Every man in the Company carried 4 Mills bombs, 4 sand-bags, and 225 rounds S.A.A., while every alternate man carried a shovel. Six men and 1 N.C.O. were left in the old line, with a Lewis gun to cover the right flank, while No. 3 found the Lewis gun to cover the left.

All the ground had been obliterated by shells, and No. 2 Company found its line with some difficulty and advanced to within 100 yards of the Quadrilateral, where it was held up by machine-gun fire. Captain Graham was killed by a shell during the advance, and Captain Fisher-Rowe took his place, but among other ranks the casualties were not heavy. There was nothing more to be done but to block the trench as far as they had got and consolidate the line. At 6 A.M. the whole Battalion made another attack, and attempted to seize the Quadrilateral in conjunction with the Fifty-sixth Division, but the place proved too strong. This time the Battalion lost heavily; Lieutenant A. V. L. Corry was killed, and there was a large number of casualties among the other ranks.

THE BATTLE OF THE SOMME 115

Next day the 1st Battalion Grenadiers was relieved at 2 A.M. by the 2nd Battalion Irish Guards, and went into camp at Happy Valley.

That afternoon there was a conference of Commanding Officers, when General Corkran explained the dispositions for the impending attack. The 1st and 2nd Guards Brigades were to attack on the 15th, while the 3rd Guards Brigade would be in reserve. The orders issued by Brigadier-General Corkran are given below.

3RD GUARDS BRIGADE

Operation Order, No. 59

1. The Fourth Army will attack the enemy's defences between Combles Ravine and Martinpuich on the 15th September, with the object of seizing Morval, Lesbœufs, Gueudecourt, and Flers, and breaking through the enemy's system of defence.

The French are attacking simultaneously on the south and the Reserve Army on the north.

The Eighth Division are attacking on the right of the Guards Division and the Fourteenth on the left. The Division is attacking with the 2nd Guards Brigade on the right and the 1st Guards Brigade on the left. The forming-up areas are shown on the map issued to the C.O.'s. Tanks will be employed to co-operate with the attack. Information regarding their employment is forwarded separately.

2. The 3rd Guards Brigade will be in Divisional Reserve, and will be formed up on the night of the 14/15th Sept. in and east of Trônes Wood as follows :

4th Batt. Grenadier Guards, east of wood between railway and Montauban—Guillemont road.

2nd Batt. Scots Guards, north of railway in S.24.C.

1st Batt. Grenadier Guards, about the trench

running north and south through the centre of the wood.

1st Batt. Welsh Guards and Machine-gun Company, less four guns, along the edge of the wood.

Trench Mortar Battery in the vicinity of Copse S.24.C.50. A separate order is issued regarding the move to these positions.

3. At zero hour plus 1 hour and 30 minutes the Brigade will advance in the following order :

The 4th Batt. Grenadier Guards to T.19.b astride the Guillemont—Ginchy road.
The 2nd Batt. Scots Guards to T.13.c.
These two Battalions will halt when leading troops reach S.W. outskirts of Ginchy.
1st Batt. Grenadier Guards to the vicinity of Guillemont Station.
1st Batt. Welsh Guards to N.W. of 1st Batt. Grenadier Guards with their left on Waterlot Farm.
Brigade H.Q. Company to S.24.a.
Brigade T.M. Battery will not move.
The Battalions will be formed up in depth.

4. (*a*) If the attack is completely successful, the rôle of the Brigade will be to pass through the 1st and 2nd Guards Brigades and support the cavalry beyond the fourth objective. The cavalry will not enter villages.

(*b*) Should the attack be partially successful and the fourth objective reached in the face of determined resistance, the Brigade might be required to relieve the 1st and 2nd Guards Brigades in the line of the fourth objective, and move into position in reserve in T.8.c and T.7.d.

As soon as the situation permits, the O.C. 4th Batt. Grenadiers and 2nd Batt. Scots Guards will send forward officers to reconnoitre these reserve positions and lines of approach to them. Reports from these officers will be at once forwarded to Brigade Headquarters.

(*c*) Should the advance be held up, the Brigade might

THE BATTLE OF THE SOMME 117

be ordered to press home a fresh attack, passing through the 1st and 2nd Brigades.

(*d*) If the attack on either flank be held up, the Brigade might be required to secure the flank of the Division, probably by offensive action.

(*e*) Detailed information regarding artillery support will form part of the orders for any of these movements.

(*f*) The direction of the attack is N.E. Officers must know the compass bearings to prominent points.

[The remainder of the orders referred to artillery and transport, etc.]

E. C. WARNER, Captain,
Brigade-Major, 3rd Guards Brigade.

14/9/16.

On the 14th the 1st Battalion Grenadiers marched to Carnoy and then to Trônes Wood, where it spent the night huddled together in shell-holes. It was so bitterly cold that it was difficult to get any sleep, and next morning every one was chilled to the bone. The " wood " consisted of trunks of trees blackened by shell-fire, the upper parts having been shot away; they were quite leafless, and the splintered branches lay all tangled over the shell craters. Amongst the wreckage were shapeless bodies in khaki and grey; some almost skeletons, and others with the skin stretched over the bones and tanned like leather. Flying about among the bare trees were half-a-dozen magpies, the only occupants of the wood. All was quiet, when suddenly our barrage began, followed by the German one, and soon the noise was terrific.

With the rest of the 3rd Guards Brigade, the 1st Battalion Grenadiers advanced to a position south-west of Ginchy in artillery formation, and

118   THE GRENADIER GUARDS

CHAPTER XIX.
1st Batt.
Sept. 1916.

proceeded to strengthen the line of trenches there. The Brigade was to support the attack of the other two brigades, or to counter any hostile movements against the right flank of the Division, which was in the air, as the Sixth Division had been held up by the Quadrilateral. The 4th Battalion Grenadiers and 2nd Battalion Scots Guards accordingly moved up to a position about half-a-mile north of Ginchy, while the 1st Battalion Grenadiers and 1st Battalion Welsh Guards took their places south-west of that village, and were employed most of the day in supplying carrying parties for the other two brigades.

Second Lieutenant L. G. E. Sim and 100 men of No. 3 Company did particularly good work in carrying up ammunition and materials under fire to the battalions in the front line of trenches.

Lieutenant Samuelson was sent forward that night by Lieut.-Colonel Maitland to ascertain where the leading line had got to, so that he might know exactly the position occupied by the 1st and 2nd Guards Brigades. After stumbling about for three-quarters of an hour he reached the trench indicated by the guides, but it was deserted except for a few wounded. So he had to push on still farther, and eventually found the front trench occupied by a mixed mass of men of the Guards Division.

Sept. 16.

He reported this to Lieut.-Colonel Maitland, who gave orders for the King's Company under Captain Drury-Lowe, and No. 4 Company under Captain Fisher-Rowe, to advance through Ginchy. There were apparently no guides, and after

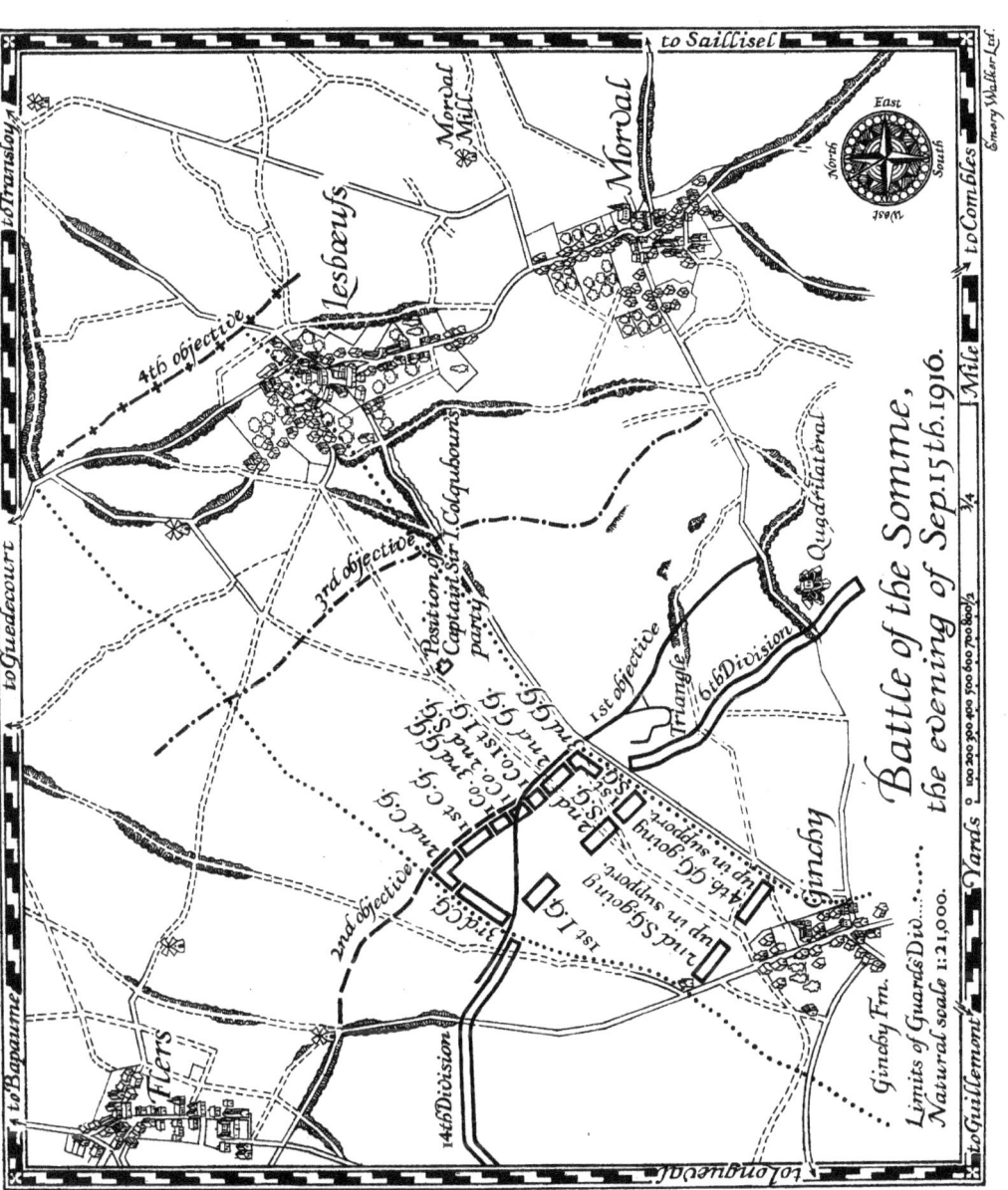

passing south of Ginchy these two companies advanced towards the front line until they met Lieut.-Colonel Murray-Threipland, who told them there were no unoccupied trenches in front. They therefore returned to their original position, having unluckily lost five N.C.O.'s, who were killed or wounded by a single shell that pitched in their midst.

At 9 A.M. the order came for the 1st Battalion to move up so as to be ready to attack with the rest of the 3rd Guards Brigade. Having joined the other battalion, the 1st Battalion Grenadiers reached a position just behind the starting-point at 11.15 A.M. The 3rd Guards Brigade, with the 1st Battalion Grenadiers on the right, the 1st Battalion Welsh Guards on the left, and the 4th Battalion Grenadiers in support, was ordered to pass through the battalions in the front line and attack the previous day's third objective, or Blue line, but all the Commanding Officers raised a protest against an advance unsupported in any way by artillery fire, and General Corkran reported this back to the Divisional Headquarters. The protest was overruled, and the attack was ordered to begin at once. The 1st Battalion Grenadiers reached the high ground west of Lesbœufs, but was met with heavy machine-gun fire, opened on it from the church tower and other strong points. Second Lieutenant Sim was killed, and Second Lieutenant Samuelson wounded, in addition to some casualties among other ranks.

Orders were given to consolidate the position which had been reached, and the 1st Battalion, having been relieved by the 59th Infantry

Brigade, returned to bivouacs in Carnoy. On the 18th Major A. F. A. N. Thorne, D.S.O., left to take command of the 3rd Battalion, and Lieutenant C. H. C. Healy and Lieutenant W. J. Dashwood joined.

On the 20th the 1st Battalion Grenadiers marched to the trenches west of Lesbœufs and remained there till the next day, when it was relieved by the 3rd Battalion Coldstream. Lieutenant Dashwood was wounded while his Company was going into the front line. On the 24th the 1st Battalion left Trônes Wood and marched to the assembly trenches in preparation for the attack next day, for which Brigadier-General Corkran issued the following orders :

3RD GUARDS BRIGADE
Operation Order, No. 66

1. The Fourth Army will renew the attack on the 25th Sept. in combination with the attacks by the French in the south and the Reserve Army in the north. The Guards Division will capture Lesbœufs. The 1st Guards Brigade will attack on the right and the 3rd Guards Brigade on the left. The Fifth Division will attack Morval on the right and the Twenty-first Division (62nd Brigade) will attack Gueudecourt on the left of the Guards Division.

2. *Objectives.*—The objectives, assembly trenches, and dividing line between brigades and divisions are marked on attached map.

        The first objective Green.
        The second objective Brown.
        The third objective Blue.

The 2nd Batt. Scots Guards and the 4th Batt. Grenadiers will capture the first and second objectives,

THE BATTLE OF THE SOMME 121

and will advance in two waves on a front of two companies each. The 2nd Batt. Scots Guards will attack on the right and the 4th Batt. Grenadiers on the left.

The 1st Batt. Grenadiers will pass through the two leading battalions and capture the third objective. The 1st Batt. Welsh Guards, less two companies, will be held in Brigade Reserve in T.8.a.

3. *The Assault.*—The 2nd Batt. Scots Guards and 4th Batt. Grenadiers will be formed up in X and Y trenches, and will advance to the attack of the first objective at zero hour close up to their barrage. There are two hostile lines to cross before the objective is reached, the first being from T.2.b.97 to T.8.b.3.10, and the second in the main German Brown line.

These two battalions will reorganise in the first objective and advance to the attack of the second objective at zero + 1 hour.

The left of the 2nd Batt. Scots Guards will direct. The 1st Batt. Grenadiers will be formed up in Z trench and will advance so as to reach the first objective at zero hour + 1 hour. The Battalion will advance to the attack of the third objective so as to reach their barrage 200 yards beyond the second objective at zero + 2 hours.

Two companies of the 1st Batt. Welsh Guards will be formed up in T.8.a, and will move into X line so as to be ready to occupy the first objective as soon as the 1st Batt. Grenadiers leave that line. In timing their advance to the X line these two companies will seize opportunities offered by any slackening of the hostile barrage.

4. *Consolidation.*—The 4th Batt. Grenadiers and 2nd Batt. Scots Guards will consolidate the second objective. At zero hour + 2 hours the 4th Grenadiers will push a unit forward by the sunken road in N.33.b and d and consolidate a strong point at the northern end, obtaining touch with the 62nd Infantry Brigade. The Battalion will also consolidate a strong point on

CHAPTER XIX.

1st Batt.
Sept.
1916.

the left of the second objective. The O.C. 2nd Batt. Scots Guards will detail one company to push forward at zero hour + 2 hours on his right flank and consolidate a strong point to protect the right rear of the 1st Batt. Grenadiers against attack from the south.

Two companies of the 1st Batt. Welsh Guards will consolidate the first objective, making a strong point on the left flank of that objective and at N.32.d.8.3, and maintaining touch with the 62nd Infantry Brigade.

In the event of the Brigades on our right and left being held up, defensive flanks will be formed. As soon as the situation demands, half a battalion will be advanced to the sunken road in R.34.a and d.

5. *Preliminary Movement.*—Battalions will be moved up to the assembly positions on the night of the 24/25th September. The 1st Batt. Grenadiers will not move before 10 P.M.

Assaulting battalions will cut any wire in front of our trenches on the night of the 24/25th September. Wire-cutters can be drawn at Guillemont station if required. Units will report when they have reached their assembly positions as detailed above on the night of the 24/25th September; special relief of 1st Batt. Welsh Guards will be arranged direct between O.C. 4th Batt. Grenadiers, 2nd Batt. Scots Guards, and 1st Batt. Welsh Guards.

[The remainder of the orders referred to artillery and transport.]

E. C. WARNER, Captain,
Brigade-Major, 3rd Guards Brigade.

The Z line referred to in these orders was a narrow trench about five feet deep, a little way behind the British front line.

The first objective or Green line was the last German trench running north and south, well in front of the villages. The second or Brown line was a sunken road with dug-outs about 800 yards

THE BATTLE OF THE SOMME

in rear of the first, and the third or Blue line was another sunken road some 600 yards farther back still. Zero hour was fixed for 12.35 P.M.

The following officers took part in the attack on September 25:

Lieut.-Colonel M. E. Makgill-Crichton-Maitland	Commanding Officer.
Capt. E. H. J. Duberly	Adjutant.
Lieut. G. F. Pauling	Bombing Officer.
Capt. W. D. Drury-Lowe, D.S.O.	King's Company.
Lieut. P. M. Spence	,, ,,
Capt. E. Sheppard, M.C.	No. 2 Company.
Lieut. R. F. W. Echlin	,, ,,
Lieut. C. H. C. Healy	,, ,,
Lieut. C. T. Swift	No. 3 Company.
Lieut. K. O'G. Harvard	,, ,,
Lieut. R. D. Lawford	No. 4 Company.
Lieut. R. P. le P. Trench, M.C.	,, ,,
Lieut. N. A. C. Flower	Sapping Platoon.

The other officers, and the Sergeant-Major, Drill-Sergeants, Company Sergeant-Majors, and Company Quartermaster-Sergeants remained with the Transport.

Exactly at 12.35 P.M. the assault began, and the 3rd Guards Brigade advanced to the attack with the 2nd Battalion Scots Guards on the right and the 4th Battalion Grenadiers on the left. The first and second objectives were secured with comparatively little loss, considering the strength of the German lines.

With mathematical precision the 1st Battalion started off, and advanced in column of platoons in fours, so as to be close up when the moment arrived for it to pass through the leading battalions at the second objective. The order from right to left was—the King's Company, No. 2, No. 4, and No. 3. The German artillery at once directed a barrage on them with considerable accuracy, causing a number of casualties. Necessarily the advance was slow, but the military precision with which every order was carried out under this shell-fire was truly remarkable. It might have been a Wimbledon field-day, judging by the cool way in which the non-commissioned officers gave their orders, interposed with cautions such as "Steady by the right," etc. And all the while the shells were falling and exploding hideously.

On arrival at the Green line the 1st Battalion had to wait for some time, and spent it in digging itself farther in, pressing into the service some remaining terrified Germans who had been found alive. The men were all eager to get on, and fretted at being left so long in this trench. At last the moment arrived for the Battalion to continue the advance, and again it moved on in a line.

The first two objectives had been taken by the Battalions in front, and the moment had arrived for the 1st Battalion Grenadiers, to which had been entrusted the attack on the third objective and the capture of Lesbœufs, to pass through the front line and continue the advance. It was faced with the usual problem in such attacks— how to guard the flanks of a successful attacking force when the neighbouring division is held up. In this case it was the left flank which remained in the air, and although the 1st Battalion Welsh Guards was forming a protective flank, the 1st

THE BATTLE OF THE SOMME 125

Battalion Grenadiers was subjected to a cruel enfilade fire. Simultaneously on the right the leading battalion of the 1st Guards Brigade was advancing towards the third objective.

CHAPTER XIX.

1st Batt. Sept. 1916.

The order in which the 1st Battalion attacked was now slightly changed: the King's Company under Captain Drury-Lowe was still on the right, but No. 2 came under Captain Sheppard next, with No. 4 under Lieutenant Lawford in support. No. 3 Company under Lieutenant Swift was nearest to the enfilade fire, and found it necessary to swing to the left, in order to face the machine-guns which were causing so many casualties. Both Lieutenant Swift and Lieutenant Harvard, the only two officers with this company, were wounded, in addition to Lieutenant Flower, and the casualties among other ranks were very heavy.

With the forward progress of the Battalion the menace to the left flank increased, and Captain Sheppard threw back his left flank to protect the advance, but this naturally made it difficult for him to keep pace with the King's Company. No. 4 Company under Lieutenant Lawford was therefore ordered to come up between the King's and No. 2 Companies, and the advance continued in perfect lines, never hesitating for a moment in the face of a terrific fire. Lieutenant Healy was wounded, and Sergeant Brooks, who led No. 14 Platoon, behaved with great coolness and gallantry, although all his men but two were killed or wounded. He himself was not touched in the morning, but later in the afternoon had his right hand and wrist blown off by a shell. Sergeant Martin, who was in charge of a Lewis gun, had all his team knocked out, but borrowed some men from No. 2 Company, and kept his gun in action for the rest of the day. He was afterwards awarded the D.C.M.

As the King's Company advanced and took the third objective, its Commander, Captain Drury-Lowe, was killed by a shell, while he was consulting Captain Hargreaves of the Irish Guards. He had already gained the D.S.O. in the artillery battery, in which he had fought all through the first years of the war, and would no doubt have earned further distinction had he lived, for he was a man without fear and a worthy commander of the King's Company. Lieutenant P. M. Spence took command, and directly the Blue line had been secured, ordered the men to dig themselves in, which they did, in a narrow and deep trench.

In order to protect the left flank, General Corkran sent up two companies of the Welsh Guards to watch the left of the Division, and as soon as these arrived No. 3 Company of the 1st Battalion Grenadiers under Lieutenant Pauling, who had been sent up to take charge of this Company, now without officers, was once more free to join the rest of the Battalion. When it reached the front line it was ordered to form a strong point 400 yards in front of the junction of No. 2 and No. 4 Companies. Strong patrols were sent out to deal with any of the enemy's snipers who might still be lurking about in front, and they continued their search well into the night. One patrol under Sergeant Carter did particularly well, and managed to secure a German map showing all their dispositions. Application was

THE BATTLE OF THE SOMME

made that evening to the Guards Division Headquarters for the cavalry to come through, but this was refused on reference to Lord Cavan, on the ground that the situation on the flanks of the Division was still very uncertain.

On the 26th the Germans shelled Lesbœufs with their heavy guns, but the trenches that had been dug were good and little harm was done. No counter-attack was made by the enemy, and that night the 1st Battalion Grenadiers was relieved by the 1st Battalion Scots Guards, and returned to bivouacs at Carnoy.

The total casualties in the 1st Battalion during the consolidation of Ginchy and the two attacks were: officers, killed 4, wounded 12, total 16; other ranks, killed 80, wounded 431, missing 84, total 595.

The 4th Battalion

After a course of training with the other battalions of the 3rd Guards Brigade, the 4th Battalion Grenadiers moved up in omnibuses to the neighbourhood of Carnoy, where it was employed in repairing a road running from Carnoy to Wedge Wood. When this work was finished, it bivouacked in shelters near Talus Boise, about two and a half miles west of Leuze Wood. On September 9 Captain Mitchell left to take up an appointment at the Central Training School at Havre.

On the evening of the 9th the 4th Battalion was sent up to relieve the 47th Brigade, which had just attacked, while the Welsh Guards

CHAPTER XIX.
4th Batt.
Sept.
1916.

took the place of the 48th Brigade. As the attack had succeeded in some places and failed in others, the front line ran in an irregular pattern; in some parts large dents had been knocked in the German line, but in others we had made no progress at all. In the particular section of the line which the 3rd Guards Brigade was to relieve, the 48th Brigade, on the left, had secured all its objectives, but the 47th Brigade, in the centre, had the misfortune to find itself opposite the Quadrilateral. It could not be blamed for failing to advance, for the Quadrilateral was one of the strongest points in the enemy's line, and contained eight machine-guns. Hence its losses were very heavy and it was quite unable to make any headway. On the other hand, the 167th Brigade on its right had been completely successful, and had gone well forward. So at the close of this attack the left of the 167th Brigade and the right of the 48th Brigade were in the air, with a space of 600 yards between the two still in the hands of the enemy.

About midnight the 4th Battalion made its way slowly towards Trônes Wood, and took over the line occupied by what was left of the 47th Brigade between Guillemont and Leuze Wood, with its left on the Wedge Wood Road, 500 yards south of Ginchy. The Battalion advanced across country under a light shell-fire, leaving Guillemont immediately on its left, and heading direct for Ginchy. On reaching its destination No. 1 Company got touch with the supports of the 167th Brigade on the right; No. 2 came next, and No. 3 was on the left, while No. 4

THE BATTLE OF THE SOMME 129

remained in support with the Battalion Headquarters.

The relief was complete by 5 A.M., and patrols were sent out in the thick morning mist to try and locate the enemy. In the trenches that were taken over lay heaps of wounded and dying men, some of whom had been there for five days. There was constant sniping by the enemy in front, and patrols from both sides continually met in No Man's Land (which varied from 80 to 200 yards in width); often neither party knew whether the others were friends or foes. It was difficult for officers commanding companies to send in any clear report of the situation, as whole trenches had been obliterated and the position on both flanks was most obscure. Meanwhile the incessant sniping and shell-fire made any movement almost impossible.

As will have been seen in the account of the 1st Battalion, General Corkran tried to remedy this very unsatisfactory state of things by sending up No. 3 Company from the 1st Battalion Grenadiers to support the Welsh Guards, and No. 2 Company to the 4th Battalion Grenadiers. It was reported at the time that the Quadrilateral was thinly held by a small garrison, which was only waiting for a suitable opportunity to surrender. Nothing further from the truth could well have been imagined, as the 4th Battalion soon discovered. Orders had been sent from Brigade Headquarters for the 4th Battalion to push up north and get touch with the 1st Battalion Welsh Guards, the impression being that these two battalions were in line; but since the Welsh

CHAPTER XIX.

4th Batt. Sept. 1916.

Sept. 10.

Sept. 11.

Guards were 600 yards in front of the Grenadiers' position, it was impossible to carry out these instructions.

Lieut.-Colonel Lord Henry Seymour did his best, and ordered No. 3 Company under Captain Stewart to move off to the left, its place in the line being taken by No. 4 under Captain E. Spencer-Churchill. Captain Stewart eventually got touch with a company of the 2nd Battalion Scots Guards, which had been sent up in support of the Welsh Guards. Noticing this movement of troops, the enemy imagined that an attack was in preparation, and sent up a succession of lights, presumably to call for a barrage. In answer to these signals the German artillery despatched a regular flow of 5·9 shells, and one pitched in the trench occupied by the 4th Battalion Grenadiers; Second Lieutenant R. F. C. Tompson and Sergeant Todd of No. 4 Company were killed, and Captain C. G. Goschen of No. 1 Company was wounded very slightly in the face. All that day the Welsh Guards in their advanced position were very heavily attacked, but managed to retain their trenches with the help of a company from the 1st Battalion Grenadiers.

An attempt was made at 1 o'clock next morning to secure the Quadrilateral, and No. 2 Company from the 1st Battalion carried out a bombing attack; this proved unsuccessful, and Captain Graham, Lieutenant Corry, and a number of other ranks were killed. No. 4 Company from the 4th Battalion went up in support, but as it was found impossible to advance beyond

THE BATTLE OF THE SOMME 131

a certain point, its services were not required. At 3 A.M. the 4th Battalion was relieved by a battalion of the Suffolk Regiment, and No. 2 and No. 4 Companies were placed at the disposal of the officer commanding the 1st Battalion Welsh Guards, while No. 1 and No. 3 Companies retired to Bernafay Wood, which they reached at 5.30 A.M. While No. 2 Company was moving up to support the Welsh Guards, Lieutenant R. Y. T. Kendall was wounded, being shot through the lungs.

CHAPTER XIX.

4th Batt. Sept. 1916.

In the course of the day efforts were made to connect the various parts of the line, and the 1st Battalion Grenadiers and 2nd Battalion Scots Guards were sent up by companies to strengthen the weaker portions. By the evening the line, though not by any means straight, had been joined together in one continuous trench. Even when No. 2 and No. 4 Companies got to Trônes Wood they were still under very heavy shell-fire. Captain Spencer-Churchill reported this by telephone to the Brigade-Major, who inquired whether he wanted any retaliation. "Very much," replied Captain Spencer-Churchill, and instructions were accordingly given. The effect was wonderful, and after a few minutes the German artillery turned their attention to another part of the line. Later on No. 3 Company was sent up and placed at the disposal of the O.C. 1st Battalion Grenadiers. At 10 P.M. the 4th Battalion Grenadiers was relieved by the 1st Battalion Scots Guards and marched back to Happy Valley Camp, remaining there until the 14th.

During the evening of the 14th the Battalion

132 THE GRENADIER GUARDS

CHAPTER XIX.
4th Batt.
Sept. 1916.

moved to Carnoy, and afterwards to a small copse east of Trônes Wood, where it stayed till the following morning.

The officers of the 4th Battalion who took part in the attack of the 15th were :

Major (temp. Lieut.-Colonel) Lord Henry Seymour, D.S.O.	Commanding Officer.
Lieut. (temp. Captain) R. S. Lambert	Adjutant.
2nd Lieut. R. A. Gault	Sapping Platoon.
2nd Lieut. A. F. Newey	No. 1 Company.
2nd Lieut. B. Burman	,, ,,
2nd Lieut. A. C. Flower	,, ,,
Lieut. (temp. Captain) C. R. Britten	No. 2 Company.
2nd Lieut. G. H. T. Paton	,, ,,
2nd Lieut. C. G. Keith	,, ,,
Capt. W. A. L. Stewart	No. 3 Company.
Lieut. R. Farquhar	,, ,,
Lieut. M. H. F. Payne-Gallwey	,, ,,
Capt. E. G. Spencer-Churchill	No. 4 Company.
Lieut. L. Abel-Smith	,, ,,
2nd Lieut. J. W. F. Selby-Lowndes	,, ,,
Capt. N. Grellier, M.C., R.A.M.C.	Medical Officer.

Sept. 15. The attack started at 6.20 A.M., and the 1st and 2nd Guards Brigades advanced with the 3rd Guards Brigade in reserve. After some waiting news was brought down to the 3rd Brigade by the wounded that the first objective had been secured, and about 9 A.M. the Brigade received orders to move up to a position north of Ginchy, and be prepared to support the attack or counter any hostile movement against the right flank of the Division. Originally it had been intended that the 4th Battalion Grenadiers should pass through the rows of massed field-guns, but when the guns began an intense fire this was obviously impossible, and orders were therefore issued for the Battalion

to move by platoons at 100 yards' interval along the old railway. The advance was made with the 4th Battalion Grenadiers on the right and the 2nd Battalion Scots Guards on the left, and they reached trenches near Ginchy in comparative safety, as the German barrage did not extend so far back.

Chapter XIX.
4th Batt.
Sept. 1916.

Second Lieutenant Keith from No. 2 Company and Second Lieutenant Farquhar from No. 3 were sent on to locate and report on a position on the other side of Ginchy, to which the Battalion was to move later. On their return the two battalions moved forward, and passed over what had been the first objective of the two leading brigades, where heaps of dead Germans remained as evidence of the recent fighting. On arrival at their destination 500 yards north of Ginchy, the two battalions dug in in a defensive position, with a support line facing half right. In the line was a stranded tank whose commander claimed to have destroyed two of the enemy's machine-guns. It was hopelessly stuck, and, after the crew had spent most of the day vainly trying to move it, was eventually used to provide excellent cover for a dug-out which was constructed underneath it. At 5 P.M., by order of General Feilding, the 4th Battalion Grenadiers was placed under the command of the G.O.C. 1st Guards Brigade, and the 2nd Battalion Scots Guards under the G.O.C. 2nd Guards Brigade. It was rather disappointing for the 3rd Guards Brigade to be split up in this way instead of going in as a brigade, but of course the situation in front was not known to those who were in reserve.

134 THE GRENADIER GUARDS

CHAPTER XIX.
4th Batt.
Sept. 1916.

At this moment No. 3 Company under Captain Stewart and No. 4 under Captain Spencer-Churchill were sent forward through the German barrage to protect the flanks of the 2nd Battalion Grenadiers in the 1st Brigade. No. 4 Company moved up to an empty trench which it explored as far as it went to the right, and there found a company of the Durham Light Infantry, led by a most gallant officer, a captain, who was killed soon afterwards by a German bomb. In order to expedite matters, Captain Spencer-Churchill sent twenty to thirty men over the top to co-operate with the party working down the trench, and the Germans were soon driven back some distance. Meanwhile No. 3 Company had gone to strengthen the left of the line held by the 2nd Battalion. These two companies remained in their position during the night of the 15th, while No. 1 and No. 2 stayed near Ginchy with the Battalion Headquarters.

Sept. 16.

Next morning Lieut.-Colonel Lord Henry Seymour was ordered to withdraw one company from the line, and sent a message to Lieut.-Colonel de Crespigny, asking him whether he would prefer to keep No. 4 Company on his right or No. 3 on his left. He decided to keep No. 3, and Captain Spencer-Churchill accordingly brought his Company back to Headquarters. While moving back through the barrage with No. 4 Company, Lieutenant Abel-Smith was wounded in the arm, and there were about seventy casualties among other ranks. Second Lieutenant R. Gault, in charge of the sapping platoon, went up to help the 2nd Battalion, and while putting out posts in front of the line was shot through the head. Instructions were given for Corkran's Brigade to pass through the leading brigades and continue the attack on the third objective, but owing to a protest having been referred back to the Corps Commander, the actual attack did not start until 1.15. The 1st Battalion Grenadiers and 1st Battalion Welsh Guards carried it out, with Nos. 2 and 3 Companies from the 4th Battalion Grenadiers in support. But this advance was soon held up by the enemy's machine-guns, and the battalions were told to dig in where they were. No. 3 Company from the 4th Battalion took part in the operation, and Sergeant Higgins particularly distinguished himself by clearing the Germans out of a trench and killing several single-handed.

That night Corkran's Brigade was relieved by the Twentieth Division and returned to Carnoy. There it remained in bivouacs until the 20th, when it returned to the line just north of Ginchy. On the 18th Second Lieutenant H. C. S. Maine joined from the entrenching battalion, and on the 19th Second Lieutenant A. R. Ellice and a draft of thirty men arrived.

Going up to the trenches in front of Lesbœufs at 7 P.M. on the 20th to dig communication and assembly trenches for the attack of the 25th, the 4th Battalion had what seemed an interminable march, owing to the congestion of the traffic and the bad state of the ground. The only available road was one mass of transport, guns, etc., and so deep was the mud in some places that it was difficult to cover more than half-a-mile an hour.

CHAPTER XIX.
4th Batt.
Sept.
1916.

To make matters worse the guides who had been supplied lost their way, and it was not till three o'clock next morning that the relief was complete. The front-line trench was very shallow, and not by any means bullet-proof, while the communication trench called Gas Alley was filled with British and German corpses.

Captain Spencer-Churchill was ordered to go with his company to Gas Alley and dig a trench connecting it with the one on the right, the exact position of which was not known. He was told that the shell-holes round the block in Gas Alley were strongly held by the enemy's snipers, and that he could call for artillery support if he thought it advisable. He decided that it would be useless to send out patrols at night, and determined to find the other trench himself. This he accomplished by going a long way round by the sunken road, and on reaching the block in the other trench he came across a small post with a Lewis gun which had attracted a good deal of attention from the Germans. Having located the other trench he returned to Gas Alley and organised a bombing party, which Lieutenant J. F. J. Joicey-Cecil was to lead.

Sept. 22-24.

Just as the attack was about to start next morning the Germans hurled a succession of bombs at the trench, but they exploded some distance off and no one was hurt. Then the Grenadier party broke down the block and advanced, but discovered that the Germans had retired 100 yards towards their main line, where another block had been made by filling in the trench for 40 yards. Captain Spencer-Churchill followed on and established a bombing post there. On returning to the sunken road, he received orders to take over Gas Alley and the 80 yards of the trench leading into it.

CHAPTER XIX.

4th Batt. Sept. 1916.

Being told by the guide that it was quite safe to go over the top, he did so, with Sergeant Roberts and his runner, Private Woolridge, but hardly had they emerged when they found themselves in full view of the enemy, who fired at them from all directions. One bullet passed through Captain Spencer-Churchill's steel helmet, scratching his face and knocking a piece of the helmet into his eye, while another grazed Sergeant Roberts's ear. It was obvious, therefore, that any attempt to connect the two trenches would have to be made below the surface; as a preliminary, two long sticks with an empty sand-bag on top were put up in the farther trench, and proved to be easily visible from Gas Alley. In the meantime Lieutenant the Hon. E. W. Tennant, who had been left in Gas Alley, had occupied his time shooting at the enemy. Apparently there was some movement by the Germans which led him to shoot with his revolver, and a moment later he fell dead, shot through the head by one of the enemy's snipers. The men of No. 4 Company now set to work to connect the two trenches, and managed to complete the work, though in the gathering dusk they had at first some difficulty in hitting off the exact spot.

That night the 4th Battalion was relieved by the 1st Battalion Welsh Guards and retired to Bernafay Wood. Captain Spencer-Churchill's eyes were now giving him great trouble, and his sight

138 THE GRENADIER GUARDS

CHAPTER XIX.
4th Batt.
Sept. 1916.

became so much affected that he had to be led by his orderly. At Bernafay Wood the surgeon insisted on giving him a tetanus injection and sending him down to hospital. The command of the Company therefore devolved on Second Lieutenant D. O. Constable. During the next two nights the 4th Battalion was again engaged in digging communication and assembly trenches, and had some casualties. On the 24th the orders for next day's attack were issued, and at night the 4th Battalion took up its position in the line.

The officers of the 4th Battalion who took part in the attack of the 25th were:

Major (temp. Lieut.-Colonel) Lord Henry Seymour, D.S.O.	Commanding Officer.
Lieut. (temp. Captain) R. S. Lambert	Adjutant.
Capt. C. G. Goschen	No. 1 Company.
Lieut. A. C. Flower	,, ,,
Lieut. A. R. Ellice	,, ,,
Lieut. (temp. Captain) C. R. Britten	No. 2 Company.
2nd Lieut. C. G. Keith	,, ,,
2nd Lieut. H. C. S. Maine	,, ,,
Capt. W. A. L. Stewart.	No. 3 Company.
Lieut. R. Farquhar	,, ,,
Lieut. J. F. J. Joicey-Cecil	,, ,,
2nd Lieut. M. H. F. Payne-Gallwey	,, ,,
Lieut. D. O. Constable	No. 4 Company.
2nd Lieut. J. W. F. Selby-Lowndes	,, ,,
Capt. N. Grellier, M.C., R.A.M.C.	Medical Officer.

Sept. 25.

The attack on the 25th, with the subsequent capture of Lesbœufs, formed one of the most successful operations in which the Guards Division was engaged in the war. The preparation seems to have been complete, and every possible contingency foreseen. In the first attack on the 15th the 4th Grenadiers had been in reserve, and

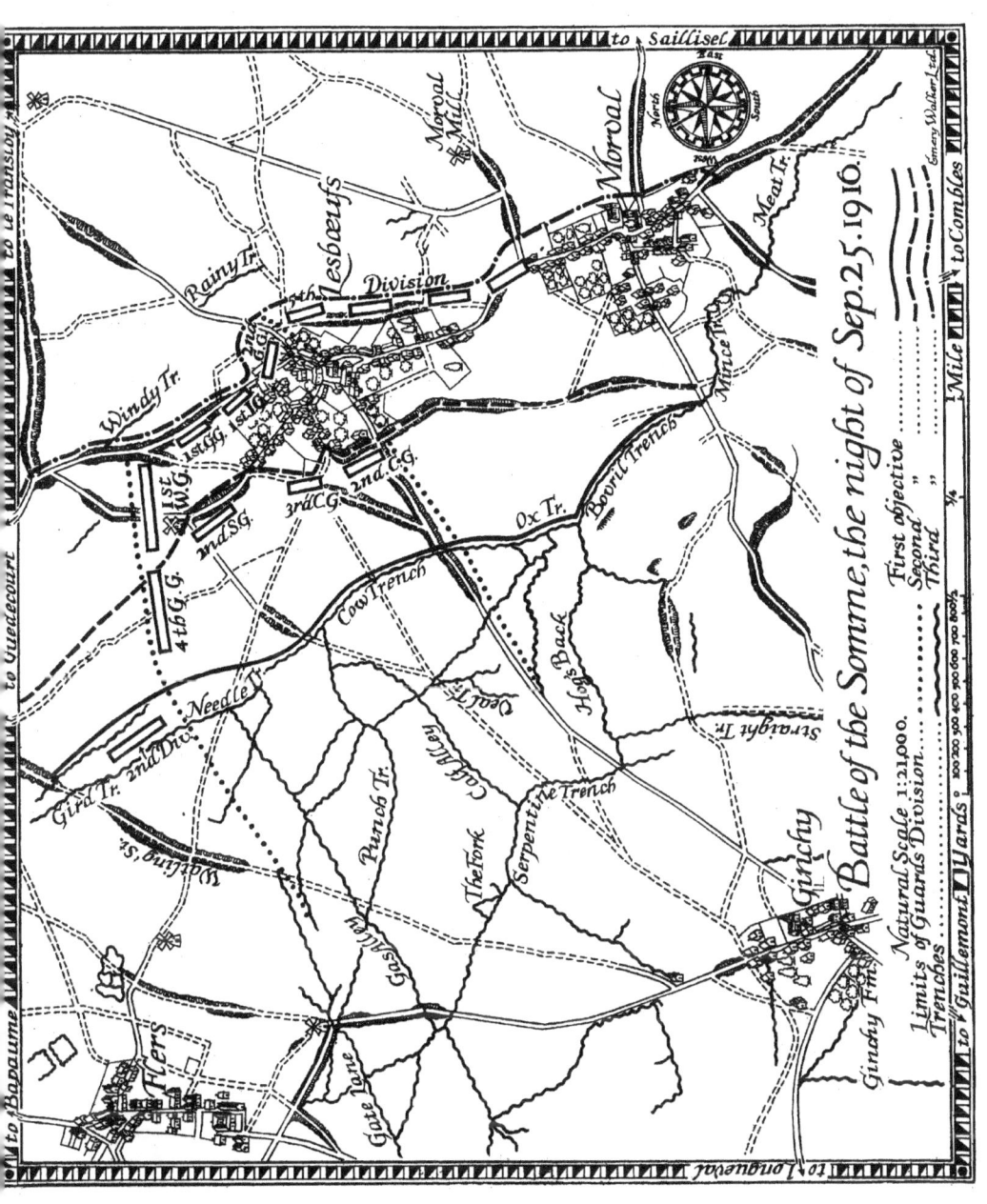

THE BATTLE OF THE SOMME

so had not seen so much of the fighting as the other battalions in the Division, but it was now to take a leading part, and to go through some of the toughest fighting of the whole battle of the Somme. Orders were given for the attack to be carried out by Pereira's Brigade on the right and Corkran's on the left, while Ponsonby's Brigade remained in reserve. In Corkran's Brigade, the 2nd Battalion Scots Guards were to take the right and the 4th Battalion Grenadiers the left.

When the 4th Grenadiers moved up on the night of the 24th, No. 4 Company under Second Lieutenant Constable on the right and No. 2 Company under Captain Britten were sent to the support trenches in front of Ginchy, while No. 1 Company under Captain Goschen and No. 3 under Captain Stewart remained in Trônes Wood. On the left of the Grenadiers was a battalion of the King's Own Yorkshire Light Infantry, but it was to start from a line quite 100 yards in front of the assembly trench occupied by No. 2 Company, which made communication difficult. Captain Britten, realising that it was essential to keep touch with the battalion on the left, made his men deepen a shallow communication trench which ran in that direction. For the last five nights the 4th Grenadiers had been constantly employed in digging, and had been obliged to get what sleep they could during the day—not at all the same thing as a good night's rest.

From 10 to 12 noon the artillery bombardment continued, and was supplemented by the Stokes mortars in the support trenches. During these preliminaries Second Lieutenant Maine was wounded in the foot, and sent down to the dressing station. As zero time approached the men fixed bayonets and remained motionless, waiting for the whistle which was to be the signal to advance. The officers in each company had carefully explained to the platoon and section commanders exactly what was expected of them, and each non-commissioned officer therefore knew as much as the captain.

At 12.35 p.m. the line advanced, preceded by a creeping barrage, which moved 150 yards ahead at the rate of 50 yards per minute. In perfect order, with not a man out of his place, the line swept on until it came to the two intermediate lines, which the officers had been warned to expect somewhere in front of the first objective. These had only recently been discovered, and no one quite knew how strongly they were held. Although the leading companies closed up as near as they could to the creeping barrage, they were met by a terrific machine-gun and rifle fire from the intermediate lines, and terrible gaps were made in the ranks. But the companies pressed on, and made short work of the Germans in these lines. Over 150 were killed there with the bayonet. Re-forming again, the Grenadiers rushed the first objective, which, to their surprise, offered comparatively little resistance. Our guns, however, had dealt effectively with the first objective, and forced the occupants into dug-outs, whereas the intermediate lines had only been passed over by the creeping barrage. On the right the Scots Guards met with little opposition, and easily secured their first objective with no serious loss.

THE BATTLE OF THE SOMME 141

An hour later, at 1.35 P.M., the attack on the second objective started, and the 4th Battalion Grenadiers moved forward, preceded as before by a creeping barrage. Although there was some stiff fighting at the end, the second objective was secured up to time. The brigade on the left had been held up, and the usual difficulty arose of one brigade pressing on while another was kept back. The right of the 4th Battalion under Sergeant Pitt had managed without difficulty to keep touch with the Scots Guards and had reached the second objective, but on the left, which was in the air, Second Lieutenant Keith was unable to advance while he had the Germans on the left in the same trench as his Company. In fact, the situation on the left had resolved itself into a bombing fight, and while the right got forward the left had always to form a defensive flank.

CHAPTER XIX.

4th Batt. Sept. 1916.

At 2.35 P.M. the 1st Battalion Grenadiers passed through the leading battalions and attacked the third objective; but, as the left flank was still exposed, the result was the same—the right got well forward while the left échelonned back and dug in. To fill the gaps the Welsh Guards were sent up, and thus a continuous line, nearly 1400 yards long, was made, protecting the left flank of the Division. That night the position was as follows: the 1st Grenadiers on the right in the third objective, facing east; the 2nd Battalion Scots Guards in the centre, facing east and north-east; the 1st Battalion Welsh Guards and 4th Battalion Grenadiers on the left, facing north. The 1st Battalion Grenadiers were in touch with the 1st Guards Brigade on the northern outskirts of Lesbœufs, and although the enemy made counter-attacks in several places, the situation remained unchanged during the night. In spite of their heavy fighting, the men were in very good spirits and made a hearty meal off the German rations which they found, ending up with German cigars. Water was the difficulty at first, but parties soon came up with this, as well as food and ammunition. The only company officers now left with the Battalion were Lieutenant Farquhar, Second Lieutenant Keith, and Second Lieutenant J. W. F. Selby-Lowndes, and the untiring energy they displayed elicited the highest praise from the Commanding Officer.

A tank made its appearance at 6 A.M., and slowly crawled along on the left of the Division towards the Gird trench, where the brigade on the left had been checked. This trench was very strongly held by the enemy, but when the tank arrived and fired into it 300 Germans surrendered, and the Durham Light Infantry moved up and took possession of it. The Leicester Regiment continued the line to the left towards Gueudecourt. At noon a large number of Germans were seen to leave their trenches between Gueudecourt and Le Transloy and retire across the open in great disorder, dropping their rifles and equipment as they went. Frantic messages were sent back by telephone to our artillery, which opened fire on them and inflicted heavy losses.

A squadron of our cavalry rode up towards Gueudecourt, and a cavalry patrol from the

THE BATTLE OF THE SOMME 143

5th Lancers went towards Lesbœufs, but Lord Cavan decided that the situation did not permit of cavalry going through, and they retired. Between 8 A.M. and noon the enemy ceased shelling, but between 12 noon and 2 P.M. a barrage was sent over by the enemy's artillery on our two front support lines. Subsequently this died down, and the evening was comparatively quiet. Throughout the day the companies in the front line suffered a good deal from small parties of snipers concealed in shell-holes, but the patrols eventually cleared the ground. At 10 P.M. the 4th Battalion was relieved by the 2nd Guards Brigade, and went into bivouacs at Carnoy.

From the 18th to the 26th the casualties in the 4th Battalion were 445, exclusive of officers. Among the officers Captain C. G. Goschen, Captain W. A. L. Stewart, Lieutenant the Hon. E. W. Tennant, Lieutenant J. F. J. Joicey-Cecil, Second Lieutenant D. O. Constable, Second Lieutenant M. H. F. Payne-Gallwey, and Second Lieutenant A. C. Flower were killed, and Captain E. G. Spencer-Churchill, Captain C. R. Britten, Second Lieutenant A. R. Ellice, and Lieutenant H. C. S. Maine were wounded. Second Lieutenant A. R. Ellice died of wounds three days later.

The King, on hearing the result of the attack on the 15th, sent the following telegram:

September 16.

GENERAL SIR DOUGLAS HAIG,
  Commander-in-Chief, British Armies in France.

I congratulate you and my brave troops on the brilliant success just achieved. I have never doubted

144   THE GRENADIER GUARDS

CHAPTER XIX.
4th Batt.
Sept. 1916.

that complete victory will ultimately crown our efforts, and the splendid results of the fighting yesterday confirmed this view.

GEORGE R.I.

To which the Commander-in-Chief sent the following reply:

September 16.

HIS MAJESTY THE KING,
    Windsor Castle.

I have communicated to the troops your Majesty's gracious and inspiring message, for which all ranks respectfully offer grateful thanks.

SIR DOUGLAS HAIG.

General Sir Douglas Haig also congratulated the Fourth Army in the following terms:

O.A.D.151, *September* 17.

GENERAL SIR H. RAWLINSON,
    Commanding Fourth Army.

The great successes won by the Fourth Army on the 15th are most satisfactory, and have brought us another long step forward towards the final victory. The further advance yesterday after such severe fighting was also a fine performance highly creditable to the troops and to Corps, Divisional, and Brigade Staffs. Our new engine of war, the Heavy Section Machine-gun Corps, acquitted itself splendidly on its first trial, and has proved itself a very valuable addition to the Army. My warmest congratulations to you and the Fourth Army on a very fine achievement.

D. HAIG, General,
Commanding-in-Chief, British Armies in France.

The following letters passed between the Commanders-in-Chief of the British and French Armies:

THE BATTLE OF THE SOMME

G.H.Q. OF FRENCH ARMIES,
September 17, 1916.

To GENERAL SIR DOUGLAS HAIG.

MY DEAR GENERAL—I desire to convey to you my most sincere congratulations on the brilliant successes gained by the British troops under your command during the hard-fought battles of the 15th and 16th of September. Following on the continuous progress made by your Armies since the beginning of the Somme offensive, these fresh successes are a sure guarantee of final victory over our common enemy, whose physical and moral forces are already severely shaken.

Permit me, my dear General, to take this opportunity of saying that the combined offensive which we have carried on now for more than two months has, if it were possible, drawn still closer the ties which unite our two Armies—our adversary will find therein proof of our firm determination to combine our efforts until the end, to ensure the complete triumph of our cause.

I bow before those of your soldiers by whose bravery these successes have been achieved, but who have fallen before the completion of our task; and I ask you to convey, in my name and in the name of the whole French Army, to those who stand ready for the fights still to come, a greeting of comradeship and confidence.

(Signed)   J. JOFFRE.

GENERAL HEADQUARTERS,
BRITISH ARMIES IN FRANCE,
September 19, 1916.

To GENERAL JOFFRE.

MY DEAR GENERAL—I thank you most sincerely for the kind message of congratulation and goodwill that you have addressed to me and to the troops under my command on their recent successes. This fresh expression of the good wishes of yourself and of your gallant Army, without whose close co-operation and support those successes could scarcely have been achieved, will be very warmly appreciated by all ranks of the British Armies.

I thank you, too, for your noble tribute to those who have fallen. Our brave dead, whose blood has been shed together on the soil of your great country, will prove a bond to unite our two peoples long after the combined action of our Armies has carried the common cause for which they have fought to its ultimate triumph.

The unremitting efforts of our forces north and south of the Somme, added to the glorious deeds of your Armies unaided at Verdun, have already begun to break down the enemy's powers of resistance; while the energy of our troops and their confidence in each other increases from day to day. Every fresh success that attends our arms brings us nearer to the final victory to which, like you, I look forward with absolute confidence.—Yours very truly,

(Signed)   D. HAIG, General,
Commanding-in-Chief, British Armies in France.

On the 26th Lieut.-General the Earl of Cavan sent the following message to Major-General G. Feilding :

Please convey to the Guards Division my thanks and admiration for the excellent manner in which they carried out their attacks to-day.

A fortnight later General Sir H. Rawlinson conveyed his appreciation of the part taken by the Guards Division in the battle in the following message :

It is only since the reports have come in that it has become clear that the gallantry and perseverance of the Guards Division in the battles of the 15th and 25th September were paramount factors in the success of the operations of the Fourth Army on those days.

On the 15th September especially, the vigorous

THE BATTLE OF THE SOMME 147

attacks of the Guards, in circumstances of great difficulty, with both flanks exposed to the enfilade fire of the enemy, reflects the highest credit on all concerned, and I desire to tender to every officer, N.C.O., and man my congratulations and best thanks for their exemplary valour on that occasion. Their success established the battle front of the Fourteenth Corps well forward on the high ridge leading towards Morval and Lesbœufs, and made the assault of these villages on the 25th a feasible operation.

On the 25th September, the attack of the hostile trenches in front and north of Lesbœufs was conducted with equal gallantry and determination. In this attack the Division gained all the objectives allotted to them, and I offer to all concerned my warmest thanks and gratitude for their fine performance.

H. RAWLINSON,
General Commanding Fourth Army.

CHAPTER XX

OCTOBER, NOVEMBER, DECEMBER 1916

Diary of the War

Chapter XX. 1916.
THE battle of the Somme continued, and further gains by both the British and French armies were announced. On November 13 a successful offensive operation was carried out by the British Army on the Ancre.

The French were still engaged in fighting at Verdun, and eventually succeeded in regaining all the ground they had lost in that part of the line.

The Germans now developed a strong offensive movement against the Roumanians, who, finding themselves outnumbered and out-manœuvred, retired into their own country.

The situation in Greece became very acute, because King Constantine, in direct opposition to the wishes of his people, made persistent overtures to the Germans. The Allies, on the invitation of the Greeks themselves, landed men and blockaded the Greek coast. M. Venizelos was brought back, and acclaimed by the people.

On the 22nd of November the Emperor Francis Joseph of Austria died.

THE 1ST BATTALION

The 1st Battalion remained in bivouacs at Carnoy after the battle of the Somme, and on October 1 proceeded in motor buses, provided by the French, to Fontaine-le-Sec, where it remained till the end of the month. Training was carried out daily with bombing practice and occasional musketry. The following officers joined during the month: on the 5th, Second Lieutenant C. Wilkinson; on the 7th, Second Lieutenant B. L. Lawrence; on the 18th, Lieutenant F. C. St. Aubyn and Second Lieutenant T. P. M. Bevan; on the 19th, Second Lieutenant R. C. Cain.

On November 1 Field-Marshal His Royal Highness the Duke of Connaught, Colonel of the Grenadier Guards, accompanied by Colonel Sir Henry Streatfeild, the Lieut.-Colonel, inspected the Guards Division. His Royal Highness was received with a royal salute, and having ridden down the ranks returned to the saluting base, when the three Brigades marched past.

To relieve the monotony of the training, as well as to be prepared for any eventuality, the Battalions were now trained in open warfare. On the 10th the 1st Battalion moved in French motor buses to the sandpits at Méaulte, where it remained five days. After spending forty-eight hours at D Camp in Trônes Wood, it went into the front trenches east of Gueudecourt, with the Australian Division on the left and the 1st Guards Brigade on the right. The Battalion spent three uneventful days in the trenches, except that

150 THE GRENADIER GUARDS

CHAPTER XX.
1st Batt.
Nov. 1916.

while it was being relieved by the 59th Australian Infantry, Lieutenant V. C. H. Gordon-Lennox was wounded. On the 20th the Battalion proceeded to Montauban, moving on the following day to Méaulte. On the 2nd Captain C. V. Fisher-Rowe joined the Battalion, and on the 13th Lieutenant W. J. Dashwood arrived.

Dec.

After a fortnight at Méaulte the Battalion went into dug-outs in Bouleaux Wood on December 6, and two days later relieved the 4th Battalion in the trenches. On the 11th it retired to Maltzhorn Camp, moving on the following day to Bronfay, and then back to Bouleaux Wood. This routine was followed up to the end of the month, the Battalion spending three days in the trenches followed by a week at Maltzhorn, Bronfay, and Bouleaux, but nothing of importance happened. On the 17th Captain P. J. S. Pearson-Gregory joined, and during the month several drafts arrived to bring the Battalion up to strength.

THE 2ND BATTALION

2nd Batt.
Oct.

After spending the end of September at Morlancourt, the 2nd Battalion proceeded in buses lent by the French Government to Aumont, where it remained for six weeks. The time was spent in training and musketry, with instruction in bombing and Lewis gunnery. The following officers joined during the month: Second Lieutenant W. H. S. Dent on the 2nd; Captain E. O. Stewart on the 5th; Lieutenant the Hon. F. H. Manners and Lieutenant F. A. M. Browning,

INSPECTION OF THE GUARDS DIVISION BY FIELD-MARSHAL H.R.H. THE DUKE OF CONNAUGHT, K.G. NOVEMBER 1, 1916.

Second Lieutenant R. A. W. Bicknell and Second Lieutenant J. H. Jacob on the 6th; Second Lieutenant E. W. Seymour on the 7th; Captain C. F. A. Walker, M.C., and Second Lieutenant J. D. C. Wilton on the 12th; Captain I. St. C. Rose, Captain Lord Frederick Blackwood, D.S.O., Lieutenant A. H. Penn, and Second Lieutenant Lord Basil Blackwood on the 16th. On the 10th Captain the Hon. W. R. Bailey, D.S.O., was granted the temporary rank of Major, and became Second in Command of the Battalion, his place as Adjutant being taken by Lieutenant A. H. Penn.

On November 6 Captain I. Rose was transferred to the 3rd Battalion. On the 10th the 2nd Battalion proceeded in French motor buses *via* Méaulte to the Citadel Camp, where it remained for two days, after which it marched to " H.I." Camp near Montauban. The weather was very bad, and the whole country was a sea of mud, which made marching across country anything but easy. On the 15th the Battalion proceeded to Camps A and B at Trônes Wood, and moved up the following day into the line, relieving the 1st Battalion Irish Guards in the inside right sector between Lesbœufs and Gueudecourt, where the front line consisted of shell-holes joined up, and was held by a succession of small posts. Owing to the frosty condition of the ground, the relief was carried out quickly and without casualties, but a working platoon that had been sent on ahead had two men killed, and Lieutenant J. D. Wilton, the officer in charge, and two men wounded. The line was not good, and as there were no communication trenches considerable difficulty was experienced in bringing up the rations and trench requirements. The second day in the trenches was one of the most trying the Battalion had experienced, as the snow changed to rain, and a thaw began which converted the whole ground to a morass. No one who has not experienced the difficulties of moving about up to the knee in liquid mud can realise the great fatigue it entails: many men were completely exhausted, while some lost their way owing to the tracks having been obliterated. All the time the shelling continued, causing a certain amount of casualties. On the 19th, after a long and difficult relief, the Battalion returned to H.I. Camp, where hot food and warm water for the feet were provided. During the relief Captain C. N. Newton was slightly wounded, but remained at duty. On the 21st the Battalion marched to Méaulte, where it remained until the end of the month. However, it took some days to clean the clothes, rifles, and equipment which were plastered with mud, and training was not commenced until the 23rd. Every day a certain number of men were detailed for work on improving the roads, each company taking it in turns to supply the necessary fatigue parties.

On December 2 the 2nd Battalion marched *via* Bray to Camp 108 at Bronfay, and later moved to Maltzhorn Camp. On the 9th it relieved the 1st Battalion Irish Guards in the trenches at Sailly-Saillisel, where again, owing to the mud, it had a very fatiguing three days, and suffered several casualties. On the 11th it was relieved by the 2nd Battalion Irish Guards, and marched to Maltzhorn Camp. The following day it went to Montauban, and after two days' rest moved up to the front line at Combles, where the trenches were still in a bad state owing to the wet weather. For three days it remained in the line, and the men worked very hard on improving the trenches and making a foundation of timber and rubble. When it was relieved, No. 4 Company was heavily shelled and suffered a number of casualties. On the 18th the Battalion marched to Trônes Wood, where it entrained for Plateau Siding. On the 20th it returned to Combles, where there was little hostile fire, but the sodden condition of the ground made all work very difficult. After three days in the trenches it moved back to Plateau Siding, and subsequently marched to Camp 15. Divine service was held there on Christmas Day, but as the Battalion had to return to the trenches the following day, the Christmas dinners were postponed until later. Three uneventful days were spent in the trenches at Combles, and on the 30th they went back once more to Camp 15. On the 12th Lieutenant J. N. Buchanan joined the Battalion. Brigadier-General C. E. Pereira, C.M.G., D.S.O., was promoted and given command of a Division. He was succeeded by Brigadier-General G. D. Jeffreys, who had fought in every engagement since August 1914, and who had latterly commanded the 2nd Battalion Grenadiers with conspicuous ability.

THE 3RD BATTALION

CHAPTER XX.

3rd Batt. Oct. 1916.

After the battle of the Somme the 3rd Battalion moved from Carnoy to Heucourt by train, and remained there till the end of October. Training was carried out in accordance with the new training schemes, and there were field days in which Advance-guards, Flank-guards, and tactical schemes were practised.

Nov.

On November 1 Field-Marshal His Royal Highness the Duke of Connaught, accompanied by Colonel Sir H. Streatfeild, inspected the Guards Division. On the 6th Captain I. St. C. Rose joined the Battalion. On the 11th, after a journey in French motor lorries, the Battalion arrived at Méaulte, where it remained until the 15th, and then moved to Mansell Camp near Carnoy. There the men were employed in mending the roads until the 27th, when the Battalion marched to the Camp at L'Arbre Fourchée just north of Bray.

From this time onward the Division was divided into two groups, each consisting of six battalions. This necessitated the 2nd Guards Brigade being split up, and two battalions were sent to each group. The right group consisted of the 1st Guards Brigade with the 1st Battalion Coldstream and 2nd Battalion Irish Guards. The left group consisted of the 3rd Guards Brigade with the 3rd Battalion Grenadier Guards and 1st Battalion Scots Guards.

Thus the brigade system was in abeyance, and battalions worked the line in a regular cycle, always going and returning to the same camp or portion

OCTOBER TO DECEMBER 1916

of the line. All blankets and cookers were made camp stores, to reduce the work of the transport.

On December 1 the 3rd Battalion moved to a camp at Maltzhorn Farm, and on the following day marched *via* Trônes Wood, Guillemont, and Combles to Haie Wood, where it was taken by French guides into the front line of trenches north of Sailly-Saillisel and south of Morval. This portion of the line had been only recently captured by the French, who had not had time to organise it properly. The parapets were extremely thin, and there were few if any fire-steps, while communication with the front was entirely overground. There was not a single strand of wire on the frontage, and the enemy was hardly eighty yards away. While the relief was being carried out, forty to fifty Germans attempted to make a raid, and got right up to the parapet, where they shot a French machine-gunner who was sitting on the saddle of his gun. The remainder of the gun-team retreated hastily down a small communication trench, and met No. 4 Company coming up. Rapid fire was at once opened on the raiders, who disappeared carrying off the machine-gun with them, and any further development of the attack was successfully frustrated, although the German barrage on our front line continued for some time. The following day a patrol that went out found the bodies of seven Germans belonging to a storm section of the 23rd Grenadier Regiment of German Infantry, and close by the machine-gun that had been lost. This gun was subsequently returned undamaged to the French.

CHAPTER XX.

3rd Batt. Dec. 1916.

The rest of the time in the trenches passed without incident, but a great deal of work was done in thickening the parapet and making fire-steps. On the 5th the 3rd Battalion was relieved and marched to Maltzhorn Farm. The following days were spent in going by train to Bronfay Farm and then on to Bouleaux Wood. On the 11th the Battalion returned to the trenches, which it found in a deplorable condition, the parapet having fallen in along the greater part of the frontage. Most of the men had to stand with the mud above the knee, and in some places above the waist; some had to be dug out on the way up. Nor did matters improve, as the weather conditions became still worse and rain and snow came down intermittently. So bad were the trenches that it was decided to hold the front line in islands, and to concentrate the work on them. The three days spent in the trenches were some of the most unpleasant the men had ever had, and when they were relieved they were in a most exhausted condition, being encased in mud and quite wet through. After four days' rest, when all the arms and equipment were overhauled, the Battalion returned to the front line for forty-eight hours, but the trenches had already been very much improved. Two days in and two days out of the trenches became the routine till the end of the month, and by degrees the "islands" were made habitable. There had been casualties almost every day in addition to cases of trench feet and chills, but with the trenches in such a state this was inevitable.

THE 4TH BATTALION

The 4th Battalion was sadly depleted after the battle of the Somme, having lost nearly half its number, and a reorganisation and redistribution of the officers and non-commissioned officers was therefore necessary. On the 28th September Major-General Feilding addressed the men on parade, and paid a great tribute to their share in the battle. On the 30th the 4th Battalion moved to the sandpits at Méaulte, and the next day to Morlancourt, where it got into motor buses belonging to the French, and proceeded *via* Amiens to Epaumesnil. There it remained for five weeks ; the billets were good, the weather on the whole was fine, and the Battalion was able gradually to recover its spirits and normal proportions. Company training was carried out in addition to musketry practice on the rifle-range and Lewis-gun instruction. On the 4th Brigadier-General C. E. Corkran, commanding the 3rd Guards Brigade, addressed the Battalion on parade, and said that their splendid behaviour during the recent fighting could not have been surpassed. He thought that the part played by the Battalion in the battle of the Somme equalled in brilliance what it had achieved in any of the battles whose names were embroidered on the Regimental Colours.

The following officers joined the Battalion during the month : on the 2nd, Captain the Hon. F. E. Needham ; on the 4th, Captain E. G. Spencer-Churchill ; on the 5th, Captain E. O. Stewart and Lieutenant R. Farquhar ; on the 6th,

158   THE GRENADIER GUARDS

CHAPTER XX.
4th Batt.
Oct. 1916.

Second Lieutenant A. C. Adams; on the 14th, Lieutenant H. J. Boyton and Second Lieutenant the Hon. A. H. L. Hardinge; on the 17th, Captain M. Williams and Second Lieutenant E. H. Tuckwell.

Nov.

On November 1 Field-Marshal His Royal Highness the Duke of Connaught, accompanied by Colonel Sir Henry Streatfeild, inspected the Guards Division. On the 10th the Battalion left Epaumesnil, and was transported in French motor buses *via* Amiens to the sandpits at Méaulte. Two days later it moved to Carnoy, and on the 13th went up into the trenches in front of Lesbœufs and Gueudecourt, with two companies in the front line, one in support and one in reserve. The front line was much battered, and was also 3 feet deep in mud, which made the relief a matter of some difficulty. In addition to the continual sniping there was considerable activity on the part of the enemy's artillery, which resulted in a considerable number of casualties. The weather had now turned very cold, and it was freezing, with snow and rain at intervals. On the 17th the 4th Battalion retired to H Camp at Carnoy, where it remained until the end of the month. On the 19th Lieut.-Colonel Lord Henry Seymour left to take temporary command of the 2nd Brigade.

Dec.

On December 5 the 4th Battalion took over a line of trenches near Sailly-Saillisel, and two companies of the 2nd Battalion Scots Guards were attached. The front line was a long one, and there were no communication trenches, which made the relief more dangerous than usual.

THE GRENADIER GUARDS MARCHING IN FOURS PAST THEIR COLONEL, FIELD-MARSHAL H.R.H. THE DUKE OF CONNAUGHT, K.G. NOVEMBER 1, 1916.

OCTOBER TO DECEMBER 1916

After four days, during which there was little shelling, the Battalion retired to Bouleaux Wood, and the next day proceeded to Bronfay Farm. On the 9th Lieut.-Colonel G. C. Hamilton arrived and took over command, and on the 14th the Battalion returned to the front line. During this relief the Germans put down a barrage, and Lieutenant H. J. Boyton was killed by a shell and a few men wounded. After the first day the shelling diminished considerably, and there were no more casualties, but the mud was as bad as ever. Private James behaved with the greatest gallantry the first night, and went over to bring in three men who were wounded within fifty yards of the enemy. There were again a certain number of casualties, and Lieutenant J. W. F. Selby-Lowndes was wounded. Returning to the line again on the 27th, the Battalion had a quiet time, and suffered no casualties.

CHAPTER XX.
4th Batt.
Dec. 1916.

CHAPTER XXI

JANUARY, FEBRUARY, MARCH 1917

Diary of the War

CHAPTER XXI.
1917.

AT the beginning of 1917 events of the highest importance succeeded each other with startling rapidity. On the British front a series of operations was commenced on the Ancre, beginning at Sailly-Saillisel Ridge; and so successful was the British offensive that village after village was captured. The Germans adroitly retired to what was known as the Hindenburg line, and after Bapaume and Peronne had been captured Sir Douglas Haig pressed forward towards Cambrai on a 100-miles front. The French had some very stiff fighting between the Aisne and the Argonne, and also between Tahure and Massiges where the Germans broke through. There was still fighting round Verdun, and the Germans claimed some successes there; but, on the other hand, in conjunction with the British, the French made an advance between La Fère and St. Quentin.

In Russia some progress had been made in the Bukovina and also near Riga, when a revolution broke out in Petrograd. The Czar was forced to abdicate, and Kerensky proclaimed a Russian Republic. Under the delusion that this change

JANUARY TO MARCH 1917

would assist either Russia or the Allied cause, the British Government sent messages of congratulation. In Roumania the situation was hopeless, and the Germans were masters of Wallachia. The Greek Government accepted all the Allies' demands, and even sent apologies; and when the junction of the French and the Italians in South Albania isolated Greece from the Central Powers, the activities of King Constantine in the German cause were much lessened.

On January 31 the policy of unrestricted naval warfare was adopted by the Germans, who announced their intention of sinking every ship neutral or otherwise. With Russia in a state of revolution, the Germans calculated that they would be able to dispose of the other Allies before the United States Army was ready. This was a plausible theory, since with the tightening up of the submarine blockade there was some prospect of Great Britain being starved into submission before America could move. On February 3 the United States broke off diplomatic relations with the Central Powers and declared war.

In Mesopotamia General Sir Stanley Maude commenced a series of brilliant operations which resulted in the fall of Kut-el-Amara on February 24, and the capture of Baghdad on March 11. In Palestine General Sir A. Murray succeeded in inflicting a blow on the Turks at Gaza, and took 900 prisoners, but these operations were only partially successful.

On March 13 China broke off diplomatic relations with Germany.

THE 1ST BATTALION

Chapter XXI.
1st Batt. Jan. 1917.

The officers of the 1st Battalion on January 1, 1917, were :

Lieut.-Colonel M. E. Makgill-Crichton-Maitland	Commanding Officer.
Major E. N. E. M. Vaughan, D.S.O.	Second in Command.
Capt. E. H. J. Duberly	Adjutant.
Capt. P. J. S. Pearson-Gregory	Bombing and L.-G. Officer.
Lieut. D. H. S. Riddiford	Transport Officer.
Lieut. and Quartermaster J. Teece	Quartermaster.
Capt. L. G. Fisher-Rowe	King's Company.
Lieut. F. C. St. Aubyn	,, ,,
Lieut. C. Wilkinson	,, ,,
Lieut. B. L. Lawrence	No. 2 Company.
Lieut. T. P. M. Bevan	,, ,,
2nd Lieut. H. Bird	,, ,,
Capt. P. M. Spence	No. 3 Company.
Lieut. G. F. Pauling, M.C.	,, ,,
Lieut. W. J. Dashwood	,, ,,
2nd Lieut. J. F. Eastwood	,, ,,
Capt. R. D. Lawford	No. 4 Company.
Lieut. R. P. le P. Trench, M.C.	,, ,,
2nd Lieut. W. H. Lovell	,, ,,
Capt. J. C. B. Grant, R.A.M.C.	Medical Officer.

At the beginning of 1917 the 1st Battalion was in camp at Maltzhorn, where it had retired after the usual tour of duty in the trenches. On the 2nd it moved to Méaulte, and on the 10th to Billon Wood Camp, where it remained for twelve days' training by companies. On the 22nd it proceeded to Priez Farm, and on the 25th to Maurepas. Lieutenant C. S. de Cerjat joined on the 14th, and Lieutenant C. D. Baker on the 24th.

On the 30th the 1st Battalion moved into

JANUARY TO MARCH 1917

the line about fifteen miles north of St. Quentin, and during the first three days spent in the trenches nothing occurred worth recording. Just before it was relieved, however, the Germans attempted a raid on the advanced posts. An intense bombardment lasting for thirty-five minutes warned the 1st Battalion of the impending attack, and the King's Company, which was holding the part of the line selected by the Germans, was easily able to repulse the raiders by rifle-fire. The casualties were 1 man killed, 1 missing, and 2 wounded. In the evening the 1st Battalion was relieved by the 4th Battalion, and proceeded to camp at Maurepas.

After four days' rest it returned to the trenches, placing two companies in the front line and two companies in reserve, and carrying out inter-company relief. On the 10th of February, about 5 A.M., the enemy launched a bombing attack, and tried to raid the two right posts of the right companies, but it was a half-hearted affair, and the enemy succeeded in reaching the wire in front of our trenches; the Lewis-gun and rifle fire was too strong for them, and none of the bombs they threw reached our men. The remainder of the month was spent at Mericourt, where training was carried on by companies. Second Lieutenant S. Y. P. Gardner and Second Lieutenant O. F. Stein arrived on the 13th, and on the 21st Lieutenant M. Thrupp joined the Battalion. On the 17th a Guard of Honour consisting of Captain L. G. Fisher-Rowe, Lieutenant W. J. Dashwood, and Lieutenant C. Wilkinson, with 100 rank and file from the King's Company, proceeded to the 4th Army Headquarters for the reception of General Nivelle, the Commander-in-Chief of the French Armies.

On March 3 the 1st Battalion moved to Bronfay Farm, and on the following day to the trenches at Fregicourt and Haie Wood, where it was employed in improving the dug-outs. On the 5th a shell most unluckily fell among the King's Company. Company Sergeant-Major Bradbury had both his legs blown off, and three other Sergeants were wounded. Captain Fisher-Rowe was knocked down but not hurt, and Brigadier-General Lord Henry Seymour and Lieut.-Colonel Maitland, who were only a few yards off, were untouched. Sergeant-Major Bradbury was carried back on a stretcher, but it was plain to every one, including himself, that he could not live. As he was being borne away he asked to speak to the Adjutant, Captain Pearson-Gregory, who at once came up thinking it was some personal request or last wish the dying man wanted to communicate. " You won't forget, sir," said Bradbury, " the Battalion has to find a fatigue party of a hundred men to-morrow early." Unselfish to the last, no thought of himself in his terrible condition crossed his mind. His sole idea, to the very last, was to do his duty to the Battalion.

Another four days in the trenches caused further casualties, and Lieutenant H. B. Vernon was wounded. On the 11th the 1st Battalion retired to Bronfay Farm, where it remained resting for a week, after which it returned to the front line. The Germans were now retiring along the whole front, and a close and unremitting pursuit had to be maintained. The 1st Battalion was employed on outpost duty with orders to accelerate the retirement as much as possible. This necessitated constant advances, but each line, as it was reached, had to be consolidated in case of counter-attack. After four days of this the Battalion retired to Maurepas, and subsequently to Camp 15 at Billon. Second Lieutenant R. B. St. Q. Wall joined on the 8th of March, Lieutenant P. G. Simmons on the 14th, Lieutenant R. H. Rolfe and Second Lieutenant R. F. W. Echlin on the 30th.

THE 2ND BATTALION

The officers of the 2nd Battalion on January 1, 1917, were :

Lieut.-Colonel C. R. Champion de Crespigny, D.S.O.	Commanding Officer.
Major Hon. W. R. Bailey, D.S.O.	Second in Command.
Lieut. A. H. Penn	Adjutant.
Lieut. G. G. M. Vereker	Transport Officer.
Hon. Lieut. and Quartermaster W. E. Acraman, D.C.M.	Quartermaster.
Lieut. J. N. Buchanan	No. 1 Company.
Lieut. F. A. M. Browning	,, ,,
Lieut. E. W. Seymour	,, ,,
Lieut. A. McW. Lawson-Johnston, M.C.	,, ,,
Lieut. J. C. Cornforth	,, ,,
Captain E. O. Stewart	No. 2 Company.
Lieut. Hon. F. H. Manners	,, ,,
Lieut. F. H. G. Layland-Barratt, M.C.	,, ,,
Lieut. T. A. Combe	,, ,,
Captain C. F. A. Walker, M.C.	No. 3 Company.

166   THE GRENADIER GUARDS

CHAPTER XXI.
2nd Batt.
Jan. 1917.

Lieut. K. O'G. Harvard	No. 3 Company.
2nd Lieut. Lord I. B. G. T. Blackwood	,, ,,
2nd Lieut. H. M. Wilson	,, ,,
Capt. Lord F. T. H. T. Blackwood, D.S.O.	No. 4 Company.
Lieut. R. Terrell	,, ,,
Lieut. R. A. W. Bicknell	,, ,,
Lieut. A. T. A. Ritchie	,, ,,
Lieut. J. Tabor	,, ,,
Capt. J. A. Andrews, R.A.M.C.	Medical Officer.

From January 2 to 25 the 2nd Battalion remained at Méaulte, training by companies, providing fatigue parties, and receiving instruction in bombing, Lewis gunnery, and precautions against gas attacks. Each company went through a course of musketry, and constantly had route marches. On the 25th orders were received to move to **Priez Farm** in motor buses and lorries, but owing to some unexplained mistake only seven buses and nine lorries arrived, so that a large part of the Battalion had to march. Priez Farm, which is between Combles and Rancourt, consisted of dug-outs which were constantly subjected to the enemy's shells. The men were employed in filling sand-bags, but owing to a sharp frost the ground was hard as iron, and it was by no means easy to obtain the requisite soil. One shell pitched among the cookers, killing 2 men and wounding 4, while another fell on the water-cart, wounding 2 men. On the 29th the Battalion was relieved by the 3rd Battalion Coldstream and marched to Billon Camp near Maricourt. The weather was bitterly cold, and the men suffered a good deal in spite of the warm clothing provided for them.

JANUARY TO MARCH 1917

The following officers joined during the month: on the 2nd, Lieutenant J. C. Cornforth; on the 14th, Lieutenant K. O'G. Harvard; on the 24th, Captain G. C. FitzH. Harcourt-Vernon, D.S.O.

For the first ten days in February the 2nd Battalion remained at Billon Camp, where the companies trained. A sporting event somewhat out of the ordinary was held on the 6th, 7th, and 8th, when Lord Cavan started a ratting competition, and promised an extra ration of rum to the Battalion that succeeded in killing the largest number of rats. The 2nd Battalion, accustomed to excel in all forms of sport, succeeded in securing this coveted prize by capturing as many as 386 rats. On the 10th the Battalion marched to Maurepas Ravine, and two days later took over from the 1st Battalion the trenches between Peronne and St. Pierre Vaast Wood. This part of the line consisted of a series of isolated posts, which were dry and well revetted, on the forward slope of the hill. The Battalion remained in the trenches five days, and although there was a good deal of shelling there were fortunately no casualties. On the 15th it was relieved by the 1st Battalion Irish Guards, and returned to camp at Maurepas. The weather was now warmer, and a thaw which had set in made the whole camp very muddy. After four days' rest the Battalion returned to the trenches and again carried out inter-Company reliefs. On the 21st Lieutenant A. McW. Lawson-Johnston and Lieutenant R. Terrell were wounded by the same shell: the latter recovered, but Lieutenant Lawson-Johnston, who was hit in

Chapter XXI.

2nd Batt. Jan. 1917.

Feb.

168   THE GRENADIER GUARDS

CHAPTER XXI.
2nd Batt.
Feb. 1917.

twenty places, died from his wounds the following day. There were no casualties among other ranks. The mornings were very foggy, and Lieut.-Colonel de Crespigny took advantage of this fact to reconnoitre the ground to his immediate front. On the 23rd the Battalion, after being relieved by the 21st Battalion of the Middlesex Regiment, returned to Maurepas, and on the 26th proceeded to Camp 107 at Billon, remaining there until March 14.

March.

The German retirement necessitated by the battle of the Somme had now begun, but it was impossible to tell at first what exactly the enemy's intentions were. After four days at Maurepas the Battalion moved up into the line at Sailly-Saillisel, where no German could be seen and no gun heard. The outpost line had been advanced to within 1000 yards of Le Mesnil, and cavalry patrols were being pushed forward to establish touch with the enemy. The difficulty presented itself of how to make the guns and supplies keep pace with the advance, and all available battalions were employed in road-making.

One curious incident happened during this advance. Two Russian soldiers who had remained hidden after the German retirement were found in Etricourt. Originally taken prisoner on the Russian frontier, they had been transferred to the Western front, and employed in digging. Hearing the orders given by the German officers to retire, they managed to conceal themselves, and waited until the British troops arrived. They were overjoyed at finding themselves once more free, and delighted at their cordial reception.

JANUARY TO MARCH 1917

The interesting duty of following up the Germans did not fall to the 2nd Battalion, which was employed till the end of the month in making roads and filling up shell-holes.

CHAPTER XXI.

2nd Batt. March 1917.

THE 3RD BATTALION

The officers of the 3rd Battalion on January 1, 1917, were:

3rd Batt. Jan.

Lieut.-Colonel A. F. A. N. Thorne, D.S.O.	Commanding Officer.
Major G. E. C. Rasch, D.S.O.	Second in Command.
Capt. O. Lyttelton, D.S.O.	Adjutant.
Lieut. the Hon. F. O. H. Eaton	Bombing Officer.
Lieut. the Hon. A. G. Agar-Robartes	Lewis Gun Officer.
Lieut. M. Duquenoy	Transport Officer.
Lieut. G. H. Wall	Quartermaster.
Capt. J. C. Craigie, M.C.	No. 1 Company.
Capt. I. St. C. Rose	No. 2 Company.
Lieut. G. F. R. Hirst	,, ,,
Lieut. F. Anson	,, ,,
Lieut. C. A. Hall	,, ,,
Lieut. P. M. Walker, M.C.	No. 3 Company.
Lieut. W. W. S. C. Neville	,, ,,
2nd Lieut. L. Holbech	,, ,,
Capt. R. W. Parker	No. 4 Company.
Lieut. W. G. Orriss	,, ,,
Lieut. C. H. Bedford	,, ,,
Capt. J. N. L. Thoseby, R.A.M.C.	Medical Officer.

The 3rd Battalion came out of the trenches on January 2, and spent the next ten days training at Corbie, Billon Farm, and Priez Farm. This was followed by three uneventful days in the trenches from the 12th to the 15th, and again from the 21st to the 24th, after which it returned to Mericourt. On the 28th it marched to La Briqueterie, where the men were employed in making the foundation for the Decauville railway, a tiring fatigue owing to the frozen nature of the ground and the long distances to be covered.

During the greater part of February the 3rd Battalion remained at Mericourt training. On the 7th it was chosen from the 2nd Guards Brigade to drill at Ville before General MacMahon, who expressed himself much pleased with the smart appearance of the Battalion. The parade was rendered more impressive by the presence of the band of the regiment under Lieutenant Williams. On the 9th an unfortunate bombing accident occurred: a defective bomb of the Mills Adapter type burst at the muzzle, and wounded Lieutenant W. G. Orriss, Lance-Sergeant Dugmore, and two men. Brigadier-General Lord Henry Seymour and Major Rasch, who was temporarily in command of the Battalion, were looking on at the time, and fortunately were not hit. On the 26th the 3rd Battalion marched to Maurepas, and on the following day went into the front line, where it remained for five days, carrying out inter-Company reliefs. On the last day the Fifteenth Corps carried out an attack east of Bouchavesnes, and the Battalion was to have assisted with a discharge of smoke-bombs, but owing to an unfavourable wind the orders were cancelled. Several patrols were, however, sent out to ascertain how strongly the enemy's posts were held, and the nature and strength of his wire.

Early on the 5th the Battalion was relieved,

and retired for three days' rest to Maurepas. Three more uneventful days were spent in the trenches from the 8th to the 11th, but the retirement of the Germans had begun, and their lines were therefore only thinly held. On the 15th two companies were ordered to move up into the reserve trenches, while the rest of the Battalion remained at Priez ready to move at a moment's notice. On the following day Lieut.-Colonel A. Thorne took charge of the centre of the whole line, while Major Rasch commanded the Battalion, and Captain R. W. Parker took command of the vanguard composed of two companies. The advance began on the 16th, and met with little resistance, the patrols pushing forward through St. Pierre Vaast Wood to Vaux Wood. On the 18th the Battalion was relieved, and spent the rest of the month on fatigues and work on the railway.

THE 4TH BATTALION

The officers of the 4th Battalion on January 1, 1917, were:

Lieut.-Colonel G. C. Hamilton, D.S.O.	Commanding Officer.
Major W. S. Pilcher	Second in Command.
Capt. R. S. Lambert, M.C.	Adjutant.
Lieut. I. H. Ingleby	Act.-Quartermaster.
2nd Lieut. C. E. Benson	Transport Officer.
Lieut. C. G. Keith, M.C.	No. 1 Company.
Lieut. B. Burman	,, ,,
Lieut. J. N. F. Pixley	,, ,,
2nd Lieut. E. H. Tuckwell	,, ,,
Capt. the Hon. F. E. Needham	No. 2 Company.
Lieut. G. E. Shelley	,, ,,

172 THE GRENADIER GUARDS

CHAPTER XXI.
4th Batt.
Jan. 1917.

Lieut. the Hon. A. H. L. Hardinge	No. 2 Company.
2nd Lieut. G. H. T. Paton	,, ,,
Capt. C. H. Greville	No. 3 Company.
Lieut. R. Farquhar, M.C.	,, ,,
Lieut. G. C. Sloane-Stanley	,, ,,
Lieut. J. B. M. Burke	,, ,,
Lieut. C. S. Nash	,, ,,
Capt. E. G. Spencer-Churchill	No. 4 Company.
Lieut. R. H. G. Leveson-Gower	,, ,,
Lieut. C. E. Irby	,, ,,
2nd Lieut. B. J. Hubbard	,, ,,
Capt. N. Grellier, M.C., R.A.M.C.	Medical Officer.

The first week in January was spent by the 4th Battalion at Mericourt, and on the 9th Major-General Feilding presented medal ribbons to the N.C.O.'s and men of the Battalion who had been awarded the Military Medal. On the 10th the Battalion proceeded to Billon Camp, where it was employed in road-making and improving the camp, and on the 14th it moved to Priez Farm. The weather was now very cold, and there was continual snow. Occasional shells reminded the men forcibly of the presence of the enemy, but there were no casualties. On the 18th the Battalion retired to Billon Camp, remaining there until the 25th, when it moved to Maurepas. The following day it took over the trenches immediately east of Rancourt on the edge of St. Pierre Vaast Wood. This part of the line was held by a series of posts or islands, which were duckboarded; it was a quiet spot, and there was practically no shelling.

Feb. After four days' rest the Battalion returned to the line, and during the relief came in for a heavy barrage, but after it had settled down, the

JANUARY TO MARCH 1917

shelling died away. On February 7 it was relieved, and retired to Maurepas. Two days later it went by train to Méaulte, and marched from there to Ville-sur-Ancre, where it remained till the end of the month going through the usual routine of training. The French War Minister, General Lyautey, inspected the 3rd Guards Brigade, and was reported to have been much impressed by all he saw.

CHAPTER XXI.

4th Batt. Feb. 1917.

On March 1 the Battalion moved to Bronfay, and on the following day to Combles with two companies at Haie Wood. There it went into the trenches until the 6th. During this tour it came in for a good deal of shelling, and Lieutenant B. Burman and seventeen other ranks were wounded. After four days' rest at Fregicourt, the Battalion returned to the same line of trenches, but this time found everything far quieter. On the 13th it moved to Billon Camp, and on the 19th to Priez Farm, whence it moved up to the trenches for four uneventful days. On the 24th it retired to Bronfay Farm, and on the 27th marched to Clery, where it was employed on railway work.

March.

CHAPTER XXII

APRIL, MAY, JUNE, JULY 1917

Diary of the War

CHAPTER XXII.
1917.

THE British offensive operations still continued with great success, and considerable progress was made on the famous Vimy Ridge. An advance on a 50-miles front was undertaken in the direction of Cambrai, and 19,343 prisoners were taken, in addition to 257 guns and 227 trench mortars. The Germans made fierce counter-attacks, but were not sufficiently strong to check the advance, and even the Hindenburg switch line was broken through. A further offensive from Ypres to Armentières was commenced, and there was some very stiff fighting on the Messines-Wytschaete ridge. The French were equally successful, and having gained positions between Soissons and Craonne they pushed forward on a 100-miles front, taking 20,000 prisoners. In May they succeeded in capturing Craonne, and the important position on the Chemin des Dames. During the Allied offensive 52,000 Germans were taken prisoner, and 446 guns and 1000 machine-guns fell into our hands.

The Italians made good progress on the slopes

of Monte Santo and on the heights of Gorizia, and there was some fierce fighting on Monte Vodia. Later San Giovanni was taken and the Timavo crossed, when there was more fighting on the Corso Plateau. In Russia the war was at a standstill, although a certain amount of fighting still continued in isolated places. In Greece the situation was still so unsatisfactory that the Allies agreed to let France undertake the whole Greek question. M. Jonnart was accordingly sent to Athens, where he at once demanded the abdication of King Constantine. Two days later King Constantine abdicated in favour of his second son Alexander, who was proclaimed King.

In Mesopotamia General Sir Stanley Maude gained two victories over the retreating Turks near Deltawa and Istabulat.

The following nations severed relations with Germany and joined the Allies: Cuba, Brazil, Bolivia, Liberia, and Honduras.

THE 1ST BATTALION

The officers of the 1st Battalion on April 1, 1917, were:

Lieut.-Colonel M. E. Makgill-Crichton-Maitland, D.S.O.	Commanding Officer.
Major E. N. E. M. Vaughan, D.S.O.	Second in Command.
Capt. P. J. S. Pearson-Gregory	Adjutant.
Lieut. W. J. Dashwood	Signalling Officer.
Lieut. R. P. le P. Trench, M.C.	Bombing Officer.
Lieut. T. P. M. Bevan	Lewis Gun Officer.
Lieut. D. H. S. Riddiford	Transport Officer.
Lieut. and Quartermaster J. Teece	Quartermaster.

176   THE GRENADIER GUARDS

Chapter XXII.
1st Batt.
April 1917.

Capt. L. G. Fisher-Rowe	King's Company.
Lieut. C. Wilkinson	,, ,,
Lieut. R. F. W. Echlin	,, ,,
2nd Lieut. F. T. Maurice	,, ,,
2nd Lieut. R. H. Rolfe	,, ,,
Capt. C. D. Baker	No. 2 Company.
2nd Lieut. S. Y. P. Gardner	,, ,,
Capt. P. M. Spence	No. 3 Company.
Lieut. P. G. Simmons	,, ,,
2nd Lieut. J. F. Eastwood	,, ,,
2nd Lieut. H. Bird	,, ,,
2nd Lieut. O. F. Stein	,, ,,
Capt. R. D. Lawford	No. 4 Company.
Lieut. N. G. Chamberlain	,, ,,
2nd Lieut. W. H. Lovell	,, ,,
Capt. J. C. B. Grant, R.A.M.C.	Medical Officer.

The whole of April was spent by the 1st Battalion in working on the railway and in training. Second Lieutenant A. S. Chambers joined on the 11th; Lieutenant E. G. L. King, Second Lieutenant H. G. Johnson, and Second Lieutenant J. W. Chapple on the 30th. On the 26th Captain C. V. Fisher-Rowe arrived to take up the duties of Second in Command, but did not remain long, as he was appointed a week later Brigade-Major to the 51st Infantry Brigade.

May.   May was spent in very much the same way, with three companies on railway fatigue and one company training. The Commanding Officer, Lieut.-Colonel Maitland, started competitions in all the various arts of war, and there seems no doubt that these competitions made the men keen and fostered a spirit of friendly rivalry between the various teams. There were also tactical schemes in open warfare, so that if by any chance the German line should break, the men would

APRIL TO JULY 1917

know how to act. The latter part of the month was devoted solely to training, and the Commanding Officer was able to assemble the whole Battalion. Captain Viscount Lascelles arrived on the 2nd, and a few days later was promoted to the rank of temporary Major, and appointed Second in Command. Lieutenant G. F. Pauling, M.C., joined on the 2nd. On the 31st the Battalion went by train to St. Omer, and subsequently to Campagne.

For the first fortnight in June it remained training at Campagne, and then proceeded to Zudausques. On the 18th it moved to Herzeele, where it remained until July 13.

The officers of the 1st Battalion on July 1, 1917, were:

Lieut.-Colonel M. E. Makgill-Crichton-Maitland, D.S.O.	Commanding Officer.
Major H. G. C. Viscount Lascelles	Second in Command.
Capt. P. J. S. Pearson-Gregory	Adjutant.
2nd Lieut. O. F. Stein	Bombing Officer.
Lieut. W. H. Lovell	Lewis Gun Officer.
Lieut. D. H. S. Riddiford	Transport Officer.
Lieut. and Quartermaster J. Teece, M.C.	Quartermaster.
Capt. L. G. Fisher-Rowe, M.C.	King's Company.
Lieut. G. F. Pauling, M.C.	,, ,,
Lieut. T. P. M. Bevan	,, ,,
Lieut. M. Thrupp	,, ,,
Capt. C. D. Baker	No. 2 Company.
Lieut. B. L. Lawrence	,, ,,
Lieut. E. G. L. King	,, ,,
2nd Lieut. S. Y. P. Gardner	,, ,,
Capt. P. M. Spence	No. 3 Company.
Lieut. W. J. Dashwood	,, ,,
Lieut. P. G. Simmons	,, ,,
Capt. R. D. Lawford	No. 4 Company.

178 THE GRENADIER GUARDS

CHAPTER XXII.
1st Batt.
July 1917.

Lieut. N. G. Chamberlain	. .	No. 4 Company.
Lieut. R. P. le P. Trench, M.C.	. .	,, ,,
Lieut. R. F. W. Echlin .	. .	,, ,,
2nd Lieut. F. W. Chapple	. .	,, ,,
2nd Lieut. A. S. Chambers	. .	,, ,,
Capt. J. C. B. Grant, R.A.M.C.	.	Medical Officer.

The 3rd Guards Brigade now moved up into the line in order to take part in the attack by the Guards Division on the 31st. The Battalion Headquarters were at Boesinghe Château, and all four companies had two platoons in the front line. The two days spent in the trenches were uncomfortable and noisy, but there were no casualties. The Germans raided the 1st Battalion Irish Guards which was on the right, and the platoon on the right of the Grenadiers' line was involved, but Second Lieutenant Johnson, who was in command, succeeded in preventing the enemy reaching our lines.

On the 15th the 1st Battalion came out of the line, and retired to de Wippe Cabaret, where for ten days it was employed in carrying up ammunition and war material to the front line. This necessitated constant visits to the front trenches always under shell-fire, and there were in consequence many casualties. On the 22nd Lieutenant E. G. L. King was killed by a shell close up to the front trench while in command of a fatigue party. The loss of so promising and keen an officer just before the attack was most unfortunate for the Battalion. On the 24th Second Lieutenant R. H. Rolfe, who had only just rejoined from hospital, was wounded in the same way. Second Lieutenant

APRIL TO JULY 1917

L. de J. Harvard joined the Battalion on the 15th, and on the 28th the Battalion moved up to Forest Camp so as to be ready to take its place in the line for the attack on the 31st.

THE 2ND BATTALION

The officers of the 2nd Battalion on April 1, 1917, were :

Lieut.-Colonel C. R. C. de Crespigny, D.S.O.	Commanding Officer.
Major the Hon. W. R. Bailey, D.S.O.	Second in Command.
Lieut. A. H. Penn	Adjutant.
Lieut. G. G. M. Vereker	Transport Officer.
Quartermaster and Hon. Lieut. W. E. Acraman, D.C.M.	Quartermaster.
Capt. J. N. Buchanan	No. 1 Company.
Lieut. F. A. M. Browning	,, ,,
Lieut. J. C. Cornforth	,, ,,
2nd Lieut. R. G. Briscoe	,, ,,
2nd Lieut. T. Smith	,, ,,
Lieut. A. T. A. Ritchie, M.C.	No. 2 Company.
Lieut. the Hon. F. H. Manners	,, ,,
Lieut. F. H. G. Layland-Barratt, M.C.	,, ,,
Lieut. T. A. Combe	,, ,,
Lieut. R. G. C. Napier	,, ,,
Capt. C. F. A. Walker, M.C.	No. 3 Company.
Lieut. A. W. Acland	,, ,,
Lieut. K. O'G. Harvard	,, ,,
2nd Lieut. Lord I. B. G. T. Blackwood	,, ,,
2nd Lieut. H. M. Wilson	,, ,,
2nd Lieut. I. FitzG. S. Gunnis	,, ,,
Capt. G. C. FitzH. Harcourt-Vernon, D.S.O.	No. 4 Company.
Lieut. R. A. W. Bicknell	,, ,,
Lieut. J. H. Jacob	,, ,,
Lieut. J. Tabor	,, ,,
Lieut. R. E. H. Oliver	,, ,,
Capt. J. A. Andrews, M.C., R.A.M.C.	Medical Officer.

Hon. Captain A. Williams, with Regimental Band.

CHAPTER XXII.
2nd Batt.
April 1917.

During the first week in April the 2nd Battalion remained in camp at Ginchy, and was employed in road-making. Later it moved to Rocquigny for a week, and then on to Bronfay to train. The monotony of company training was relieved by brigade competitions, and No. 11 Platoon under Lieutenant Gunnis succeeded not only in winning the prize, but also in being first in every event—a very remarkable performance.

May.

On May 9 the Battalion marched *via* Maricourt, Guillemont, and Ginchy to a camp near Lesbœufs, and three days later moved to Le Mesnil, where it worked on the railway. On the 20th it returned to Bronfay, and on the way halted for half-an-hour to enable the men to view the memorial to officers and men of the Regiment who had been killed there in September 1916. It consisted of an oak cross about ten feet high, made out of wood collected from the ruins of Lesbœufs. On May 22 the Battalion went to Sailly-le-Sec, where it remained till the end of the month, when it went by train *via* Cassel and Bavinchove to Renescure.

June.

During the first fortnight in June the 2nd Battalion remained at Renescure training and going through a course of musketry, and on the 16th marched to Winnezeele. The weather was fine, and though the heat was great the men stood the marching well. On the 18th the Battalion marched into Belgium, and went into bivouacs at Proven, where it remained for two days and then moved to Herzeele. On the 20th it attended a parade at which General Antoine, commanding the First French Army, presented

APRIL TO JULY 1917

crosses of the Legion of Honour and medals to officers of the Fifth British Army. At the conclusion of the parade the Battalion marched past followed by the 2nd Battalion Coldstream Guards, and then returned to billets. On the 24th it marched to de Wippe Cross-roads, where it remained a week. The enemy's big guns carried out some long-distance shelling, chiefly on the roads at night, but fortunately the 2nd Battalion suffered no casualties. On the 28th it marched to Cardoen Farm.

The officers of the 2nd Battalion on July 1, 1917, were :

Lieut.-Colonel C. R. C. de Crespigny, D.S.O.	Commanding Officer.
Major the Hon. W. R. Bailey, D.S.O.	Second in Command.
Lieut. A. H. Penn	Adjutant.
Lieut. G. G. M. Vereker	Transport Officer.
Hon. Lieut. W. E. Acraman, M.C., D.C.M.	Quartermaster.
Capt. J. N. Buchanan	No. 1 Company.
Lieut. F. A. M. Browning	,, ,,
Lieut. J. C. Cornforth	,, ,,
2nd Lieut. P. A. A. Harbord	,, ,,
2nd Lieut. R. G. Briscoe	,, ,,
Capt. A. T. A. Ritchie, M.C.	No. 2 Company.
Lieut. A. S. L. St. J. Mildmay	,, ,,
Lieut. the Hon. F. H. Manners	,, ,,
Lieut. F. H. G. Layland-Barratt, M.C.	,, ,,
Lieut. R. G. C. Napier	,, ,,
Capt. C. F. A. Walker, M.C.	No. 3 Company.
Capt. Sir A. L. M. Napier, Bart.	,, ,,
Lieut. K. O'G. Harvard	,, ,,
Lieut. A. W. Acland	,, ,,
2nd Lieut. H. M. Wilson	,, ,,
2nd Lieut. Lord I. B. G. T. Blackwood	,, ,,
2nd Lieut. I. FitzG. S. Gunnis	,, ,,
Capt. G. C. FitzH. Harcourt-Vernon, D.S.O.	No. 4 Company.

182 THE GRENADIER GUARDS

CHAPTER XXII.
2nd Batt.
July 1917.

Lieut. J. H. Jacob . . . No. 4 Company.
Lieut. R. E. H. Oliver . . . ,, ,,
Lieut. J. Tabor . . . . ,, ,,
2nd Lieut. F. H. J. Drummond . ,, ,,
Capt. J. A. Andrews, M.C., R.A.M.C. Medical Officer.
Capt. C. F. Lyttelton . . . Chaplain of the Forces.

On July 2 the 2nd Battalion relieved the 3rd Battalion Coldstream Guards in the Boesinghe Sector, which was soon to become the site selected for an offensive. The Belgians at the time were on the right, and were subsequently relieved by the French. The trenches occupied by the Battalion were extended for about 1500 yards along the western bank of the Yser Canal. The first day was spent in improving the position, and as soon as it became dark the men were mostly employed in carrying up material of all kinds to the front area. At 11.30 P.M. orders were received from the Brigadier to make two raids into the enemy's lines, with a view to obtaining identification of the German regiments employed there, as well as information as to the whereabouts of the German trench. Lieut.-Colonel de Crespigny decided to send out two parties: the first consisting of No. 11 Platoon, under Second Lieutenant I. FitzG. S. Gunnis, whose task it was to capture, if possible, a prisoner; and the second under Second Lieutenant Lord Basil Blackwood with a party of five men from No. 10 Platoon, who received orders to reconnoitre in a certain direction. It was a very dark night, and this was all in favour of the enterprise, but on the other hand the difficulties of crossing the canal and advancing into " No Man's Land," where the exact disposition of the German defences were unknown, in absolute darkness, were only too obvious. The first obstacle to be overcome was the passage of the Yser Canal, and this was accomplished by means of 5-feet mats made of canvas and wire netting, nailed to wooden slats. Two of these were used, being placed in position by two specially detailed parties, and proved most effective in providing a foothold over the muddy bed of the canal. Thus the two parties succeeded in crossing without detection by the enemy.

On arrival on the east side of the canal, Lord Basil Blackwood led his party on into the darkness, but instead of the trench which they had expected to find from a previous study of the aeroplane map, there was nothing but a mass of shell-holes with heavy wire entanglement, which made it difficult for the party to keep together. After going a considerable distance over rough and broken ground, rifle-fire was suddenly opened on them from a dug-out. Lord Basil Blackwood's orderly was wounded, while a sapper from the Royal Engineers, who formed one of the party, was killed. The remainder at once lay down in shell-holes, and as they waited bombs were thrown at them from the same direction. Owing to the two men who originally followed him having become casualties, the party now became scattered. Beyond this point little is known. A corporal of the Royal Engineers who accompanied the party, and who was wounded, said that he saw Lord Basil Blackwood crawl forward after the shots were fired, but subsequently lost sight of him. The two remaining men of the Grenadiers assert that they saw him fall, but that owing to the darkness they completely lost touch with him, and after crawling about for some time they returned to the canal bank. Unfortunately they omitted to report all this to their Company Commander, Captain Walker, who with Colonel de Crespigny and Major Bailey was waiting on the canal bank for any news of the raiding party. It did not at first occur to Captain Walker that anything was amiss, but when time wore on, and Lord Basil Blackwood failed to return, he became uneasy. The difficulty was, however, that no one could be found to give any information which would enable a patrol to go out with any hope of tracing the missing party.

The movements of the other party under Second Lieutenant Gunnis are even more obscure. After crossing the canal, one portion of the party went on to form a block on the north side, whilst the remainder worked south in search of a prisoner. Eventually they found a German trench and walked down it, until an obstruction of barbed wire made farther progress impossible. As the sides were too steep to admit of egress, Second Lieutenant Gunnis gave the order to turn about, with the intention of retracing his steps and getting out farther back. The order was apparently misunderstood, and some of the men became detached. Second Lieutenant Gunnis then entered another trench. He went along it until he was suddenly fired at, at very close range. Undeterred by this, he retired a short distance and returned again outside the trench. Having passed the point from which he was fired at, he appears to have lost direction, for he went on until he came upon the dead body of a British soldier, most probably that of the Engineer, who had accompanied Lord Basil Blackwood's party. He told the two men next to him to carry the body back. He intended the remainder of the party to follow him, but, owing to the darkness, combined with the broken state of the ground, the orders were misunderstood. At that moment several bombs were thrown. The men took what cover they could in shell-holes. When the bombing ceased Second Lieutenant Gunnis was no longer with the party. Whether he walked on under the impression that the others were following him, or whether he was killed by a bomb it is impossible to say. The enemy about this time sent up S.O.S. signals which brought down a heavy barrage on the British lines, and this no doubt prevented the survivors of the party returning in time to enable a patrol to go out before daylight.

During the following day the shelling continued intermittently, but it was not until the 5th that the Germans began to search the ground in earnest. Two heavy Minenwerfers were firing from the left front, and the bombs were falling near the support line. The range was gradually lengthened until the Battalion Headquarters were reached. Then came a gas alarm, but the discipline was so good, and gas helmets were put on so promptly, that although a large number of gas shells pitched on our front line, there were no casualties. On the 6th the shelling continued, and one shell pitched in the support line, wounding

CHAPTER XXII.

2nd Batt. July 1917.

Chapter XXII.
2nd Batt.
July 1917.

Lieutenant Hermon-Hodge and three sergeants, one of whom subsequently died.

On the 7th the Battalion was relieved, and retired into billets at Roussel Farm, where it remained until the 11th, ostensibly for a rest, though the men were constantly employed in carrying material to the front line. On the 11th they went up into the support system, where they were employed in repairing the trenches which were being constantly blown in by shell-fire. All available officers and N.C.O.'s were taken over the ground which had been selected as the forming-up area of the Battalion in the coming offensive, and were shown objectives and landmarks. On the 13th the Battalion was relieved and marched to Elverdinghe, where it entrained for Proven. On the following day it marched to Honflond, where it remained for a fortnight, carefully practising every stage of the attack over ground exactly representing the German lines, until even the men knew by heart the lie of the land and the position of the strong points and farmhouses. On the 15th Lieutenant F. A. Magnay arrived, and on the 16th Lieutenant G. R. Westmacott and Second Lieutenant S. H. Pearson joined the Battalion. On the 28th the Battalion moved up to Roussel Farm, and then to the Forest Area, preparatory to taking part in the offensive on the 31st.

The 3rd Battalion

3rd Batt.
April.

The officers of the 3rd Battalion on April 1, 1917, were :

APRIL TO JULY 1917

Lieut.-Colonel A. F. A. N. Thorne, D.S.O.	.	Commanding Officer.
Major G. E. C. Rasch, D.S.O.	.	Second in Command.
Lieut. the Hon. F. O. H. Eaton	.	Adjutant.
Lieut. K. Henderson	.	Intelligence Officer.
Lieut. M. Duquenoy	.	Transport Officer.
Lieut. G. H. Wall	.	Quartermaster.
Capt. J. C. Craigie, M.C.	.	No. 1 Company.
Lieut. the Hon. A. G. Agar-Robartes		,, ,,
Lieut. F. J. Siltzer	.	,, ,,
2nd Lieut. A. G. Elliott	.	,, ,,
Lieut. G. F. R. Hirst	.	No. 2 Company.
Lieut. E. R. M. Fryer	.	,, ,,
Lieut. F. W. R. Greenhill	.	,, ,,
Lieut. C. A. Hall	.	,, ,,
2nd Lieut. A. H. S. Adair	.	,, ,,
2nd Lieut. L. Holbech	.	,, ,,
Capt. W. W. S. C. Neville	.	No. 3 Company.
Lieut. N. Thornhill	.	,, ,,
Lieut. J. C. D. Tetley	.	,, ,,
2nd Lieut. the Hon. A. M. Borthwick		,, ,,
2nd Lieut. G. A. I. Dury	.	,, ,,
Capt. R. W. Parker	.	No. 4 Company.
Lieut. F. J. Heasman	.	,, ,,
Lieut. J. F. Worsley	.	,, ,,
2nd Lieut. C. W. Carrington	.	,, ,,
Capt. J. N. L. Thoseby, R.A.M.C.	.	Medical Officer.

CHAPTER XXII.

3rd Batt.
April 1917.

April was spent by the 3rd Battalion in road-mending, loading trucks, and other fatigues. As a rule half the Battalion was engaged on these works, while the other half, with the exception of those men required for the ordinary duties, was occupied in training.

During May the Battalion continued training at Clery, Billon, Ville, and Wardrecques.

May.

On June 5 Lieut.-Colonel A. F. A. N. Thorne was obliged to go to hospital with a strained leg, and Captain Craigie temporarily commanded

June.

188   THE GRENADIER GUARDS

CHAPTER XXII.
3rd Batt.
June 1917.

the Battalion until the 10th, when Major Rasch returned. On the 17th the Battalion relieved the 1st Battalion Scots Guards in the support line with their headquarters at Bluet Farm, and although at first there was not much firing the shelling increased in intensity each day, with the result that there were quite a number of casualties. On the 22nd the Battalion was relieved, and returned to Roussel Farm, where it remained until the end of the month. There were a great number of hostile aeroplanes over this part of the line, and the men had constantly to be warned to keep under cover. The Battalion spent another two days in the trenches on the 26th, and came in for a great deal of shelling. Second Lieutenant B. J. Dunlop had a lucky escape; he had just been called away from the bomb-store, where he had been all day, when a high-explosive shell pitched on it, killing the men to whom he had been speaking.

July.

The officers of the 3rd Battalion on July 1, 1917, were :

Lieut.-Colonel G. E. C. Rasch, D.S.O.	Commanding Officer.
Capt. E. D. Ridley, M.C.	Second in Command.
Lieut. the Hon. A. G. Agar-Robartes	Adjutant.
Lieut. M. Duquenoy	Transport Officer.
Lieut. G. H. Wall	Quartermaster.
Lieut. K. Henderson	Bombing Officer.
Capt. J. C. Craigie, M.C.	No. 1 Company.
Lieut. E. R. M. Fryer	,, ,,
Lieut. F. J. Siltzer	,, ,,
2nd Lieut. A. G. Elliott	,, ,,
2nd Lieut. E. G. A. Fitzgerald	,, ,,
Capt. the Hon. F. O. H. Eaton	No. 2 Company.

APRIL TO JULY 1917

Lieut. G. F. R. Hirst	. . .	No. 2 Company.
Lieut. C. A. Hall .	. . .	,, ,,
2nd Lieut. L. Holbech .	. . .	,, ,,
2nd Lieut. F. W. R. Greenhill .	.	,, ,,
Capt. W. W. S. C. Neville, M.C.	.	No. 3 Company.
Lieut. J. C. D. Tetley	. . .	,, ,,
Lieut. N. Thornhill	. . .	,, ,,
2nd Lieut. the Hon. A. M. Borthwick		,, ,,
2nd Lieut. B. J. Dunlop	. .	,, ,,
Capt. R. W. Parker	. . .	No. 4 Company.
Lieut. F. J. Worsley	. . .	,, ,,
2nd Lieut. C. W. Carrington .	.	,, ,,
2nd Lieut. L. E. Dunlop	. .	,, ,,
2nd Lieut. H. R. Ogle .	. .	,, ,,
2nd Lieut. G. V. G. A. Webster	.	,, ,,
Lieut. H. Dearden, R.A.M.C. .	.	Medical Officer.

CHAPTER XXII.

3rd Batt. July 1917.

On July 1 the 3rd Battalion went to Wylders, and the following day moved on to Herzeele. Every detail of the projected attack on the 31st was carefully rehearsed over specially prepared trenches, and every officer and N.C.O. was made familiar with the plan of the German lines and the prominent landmarks. On the 12th Lieut.-Colonel Thorne resumed command of the Battalion, and Major Rasch went to hospital, his place as Second in Command being taken by Captain Ridley. On the 13th the Battalion moved up to the Forest Area and was bivouacked in two fields. The enemy's aeroplanes were so busy overhead that the greatest attention had to be paid to " camouflage," and everything had to be hidden as far as possible. The men were constantly employed in carrying up ammunition and war material to the front trenches, an arduous and dangerous task since they were continually under shell-fire. Private Bignell of

190 THE GRENADIER GUARDS

CHAPTER XXII.
3rd Batt.
July 1917.

No. 4 Company behaved with great coolness and gallantry in carrying from a dug-out a box of Véry lights which had been set on fire by a pine-apple bomb. For this he received the Military Medal.

On the 18th Second Lieutenant W. H. S. Roper joined, and on the 21st the Battalion took over the right Brigade Sector near Boesinghe, with Nos. 1 and 2 Companies in the front trench. For five days the Battalion remained in the trenches, during which time it suffered much from shellfire. Second Lieutenant H. R. Ogle was wounded but remained at duty, and the casualties among other ranks were 27 killed, 11 died of wounds, 45 wounded, 10 gassed, 7 to hospital from concussion. Second Lieutenant G. Webster made an excellent reconnaissance of the Canal, and discovered four places where it could be crossed without the men getting very wet. No. 4 Company was to have carried out a raid to ascertain the strength of the enemy, but at the last moment the order was cancelled. On the night of the 26th the Battalion was relieved by the 3rd Battalion Coldstream Guards, and retired again to the Forest Area to rest before the attack by the Division on the 31st.

THE 4TH BATTALION

4th Batt.
April.

The officers of the 4th Battalion on April 1, 1917, were:

Lieut.-Colonel G. C. Hamilton, D.S.O.	Commanding Officer.
Major W. S. Pilcher	Second in Command.
Capt. R. S. Lambert, M.C.	Adjutant.

Lieut. I. H. Ingleby	Act.-Quartermaster.	CHAPTER XXII.
Lieut. J. B. M. Burke	Intelligence Officer.	
2nd Lieut. C. E. Benson	Transport Officer.	4th Batt.
Capt. C. G. Keith, M.C.	No. 1 Company.	April 1917.
Lieut. J. N. F. Pixley	,, ,,	
2nd Lieut. E. H. Tuckwell	,, ,,	
2nd Lieut. G. R. Green	,, ,,	
Capt. the Hon. F. E. Needham	No. 2 Company.	
Lieut. G. H. T. Paton	,, ,,	
Lieut. the Hon. A. H. L. Hardinge	,, ,,	
2nd Lieut. M. P. B. Wrixon	,, ,,	
Capt. C. H. Greville	No. 3 Company.	
Lieut. R. Farquhar, M.C.	,, ,,	
Lieut. G. C. Sloane-Stanley	,, ,,	
Lieut. C. S. Nash	,, ,,	
2nd Lieut. T. T. Pryce, M.C.	,, ,,	
Capt. E. G. Spencer-Churchill	No. 4 Company.	
Lieut. E. R. D. Hoare	,, ,,	
Lieut. R. H. G. Leveson-Gower	,, ,,	
Lieut. C. E. Irby	,, ,,	
2nd Lieut. B. J. Hubbard	,, ,,	
2nd Lieut. N. A. Pearce	,, ,,	
Capt. N. Grellier, M.C., R.A.M.C.	Medical Officer.	

Lieut.-Colonel G. Hamilton, having been given a command in England, left to take up his duties and was succeeded by Captain (Brevet Major) the Viscount Gort, D.S.O., M.V.O., M.C. After a fortnight at Clery the 4th Battalion moved to Cartigny, where it remained for six weeks. On arrival it had to pitch camp on sodden ground. Though it was snowing hard and almost dark, the men managed in an incredibly short time to collect timber from the ruined houses, bring up braziers and pitch tents, so that a tolerably habitable camp soon sprang up. On the 14th Captain M. Williams assumed temporary command of the 58th Prisoners of War Company.

192   THE GRENADIER GUARDS

CHAPTER XXII.

4th Batt. April 1917.

The greater portion of the Battalion worked on the railway, but each company in turn remained behind to do steady drill.

By degrees the Battalion made itself very comfortable, and a canteen with a recreation room was built, two football grounds were made, and a cricket-ground begun. The pioneers of the Battalion collected the debris from the neighbouring ruins and erected stables and various other buildings. On the 23rd the work on the railway ceased, and all the companies were left at the disposal of the Commanding Officer.

May.

The 4th Battalion remained at Cartigny until May 18, practising all the latest developments of the attack, but the work on the railway again claimed three companies, and it was only occasionally that the Commanding Officer had the whole Battalion at his disposal for training purposes. Second Lieutenant R. G. West joined the Battalion on the 1st of May, Second Lieutenant R. C. Denman on the 2nd, Second Lieutenant H. W. Windeler on the 16th, and on the 12th Second Lieutenant N. A. Pearce was appointed Transport Officer. On the 18th the Battalion marched to Bronfay, and on the way was inspected by Major-General Feilding commanding the Guards Division. The following day it proceeded to Corbie, where it remained training until the end of the month.

June.

At the beginning of June it moved on by train to Le Rons. Second Lieutenant J. M. Chitty joined the Battalion on the 4th, and Second Lieutenant F. R. Oliver and Second Lieutenant J. J. M. Veitch on the 7th. Company training

APRIL TO JULY 1917

and musketry were carried out during the fortnight spent at Le Rons, and on the 17th the Battalion moved to Herzeele, where the whole Brigade manœuvred together. On the 21st Captain E. O. Stewart joined the Battalion, and on the 29th Second Lieutenant D. J. Knight arrived.

CHAPTER XXII.

4th Batt.
June 1917.

July.

The officers of the 4th Battalion on July 1, 1917, were:

Lieut.-Colonel the Viscount Gort, D.S.O., M.V.O., M.C.	Commanding Officer.
Major W. S. Pilcher, D.S.O.	Second in Command.
Capt. C. R. Gerard	Adjutant.
Lieut. I. H. Ingleby	Act.-Quartermaster.
Lieut. Lord E. D. J. Hay	Intelligence Officer.
2nd Lieut. N. A. Pearce	Transport Officer.
Capt. C. G. Keith, M.C.	No. 1 Company.
Lieut. J. N. F. Pixley	,, ,,
2nd Lieut. E. H. Tuckwell	,, ,,
2nd Lieut. G. R. Green	,, ,,
2nd Lieut. G. C. Burt	,, ,,
2nd Lieut. J. M. Chitty	,, ,,
Capt. the Hon. F. E. Needham	No. 2 Company.
Capt. E. O. Stewart	,, ,,
Lieut. R. G. West	,, ,,
2nd Lieut. T. T. Pryce, M.C.	,, ,,
2nd Lieut. R. C. Denman	,, ,,
2nd Lieut. W. H. Windeler	,, ,,
Capt. C. H. Greville, D.S.O.	No. 3 Company.
Lieut. R. Farquhar, M.C.	,, ,,
Lieut. J. B. M. Burke	,, ,,
Lieut. G. C. Sloane-Stanley	,, ,,
Lieut. C. S. Nash	,, ,,
2nd Lieut. D. J. Knight	,, ,,
Capt. G. H. T. Paton	No. 4 Company.
Lieut. R. H. G. Leveson-Gower	,, ,,
Lieut. C. E. Irby	,, ,,
Lieut. B. J. Hubbard	,, ,,
2nd Lieut. J. J. M. Veitch	,, ,,

194 THE GRENADIER GUARDS

CHAPTER XXII.
4th Batt.
July 1917.

2nd Lieut. F. R. Oliver . . . No. 4 Company.
2nd Lieut. C. E. Benson . . ,, ,,
Capt. N. Grellier, M.C., R.A.M.C. . Medical Officer.

The 4th Battalion now made its way to the area opposite the portion of the German line which had been selected for an attack on July 31. The camp consisted of a few bivouac sheets in a wood, and was well within the range of the German shells; almost as soon as the Battalion arrived some shells fell in the Transport lines, but fortunately did no damage. Lieut.-Colonel Lord Gort went up to the line to make himself acquainted with the trenches from which the Battalion would attack, and took with him Captain Paton, Lieutenant Pixley, and Lieutenant Burke. During the first week in July the Battalion had to find between 500 and 600 men for fatigues in the forward area. On the 5th the camp was again shelled, but luckily there were no casualties. Lord Gort made a second visit to the front line, and took with him this time Captain the Hon. F. E. Needham, Captain Greville, Captain Keith, and Lieutenant Lord E. Hay. During these days there were constant gas alarms, and on one occasion the men were ordered to sleep with their helmets in the " alert " position.

July 14 was a red-letter day for the 4th Battalion, as it was the second anniversary of its formation, but owing to the large number of men required for fatigue work Lord Gort decided to keep this anniversary on the 15th. The celebrations consisted of a football match, a tug-of-war, and a sergeants' dinner, followed by a Battalion concert, and last, but not least, a free issue of beer to all the men. The Corps Commander, Lord Cavan, attended the sergeants' dinner, and made a speech which aroused the greatest enthusiasm. Major-General G. Feilding also attended.

The fatigue parties worked day and night, and as the work necessitated going up into the front trenches there were almost daily a number of men wounded. On the 16th the Battalion moved up nearer to the front line and received orders to raid the German trenches on the whole Divisional front in eight different places. The men selected for this were trained separately, and for three days the raid was rehearsed so that every man knew exactly what to do.

On the 18th the Battalion moved up into the front line of the Boesinghe Sector, and was unlucky enough to come in for considerable artillery fire while the relief was being carried out, as the enemy put up the S.O.S. signal, when he was being raided by the neighbouring Brigade. As soon as the relief was completed, gas was discharged from our Stokes mortars, while the enemy's artillery put down a heavy barrage on our front line. No. 1 Company was placed in the front line; No. 2 Company placed two platoons in S line and two platoons in Y line; and X line was occupied by No. 4 Company. The raiding parties from No. 3 Company were posted at Paradou Farm.

At 1 A.M. on the 20th the raids took place, and in accordance with the orders received the German front line was penetrated in four places. No. 1 party started off, and had nearly reached the German line when it found that the mat which had been provided to help it over the mud was too short. There was nothing to be done but to plunge into the Canal, and in spite of being up to their knees in mud the men succeeded in entering the German trench at the right place. After moving down the trench for 100 yards, they came upon a German double sentry post which was engaged in sending up Véry lights. They determined to work round this post, but one of the raiders lost his head, and fired point-blank at the Germans. This would in any case have raised the alarm, but in addition to this another of the raiders dropped a bomb, killing his neighbour and wounding himself, so that all attempt at surprise was at an end. The German sentries rushed off yelling, but had not gone far when one of them dropped dead. Showers of Véry lights were soon sent up by the Germans in rear, and men were seen advancing with bombs and hand grenades in all directions. This raiding party therefore withdrew, bringing with it the body of the man who had been killed by the bomb. They were able to see a good deal of the German trench, and reported it to be badly knocked about.

No. 2 party under Second Lieutenant T. T. Pryce was more successful. The mat in this case was the right length, and enabled the men to cross over the mud quickly. They saw five Germans, who immediately ran over the Yperlee into Crapouillot Wood. They visited two German dug-outs, but found them unoccupied and empty, and reported that they had some difficulty in moving along the trench, which was badly damaged. No. 3 party arrived at its destination without difficulty, but the Germans who had bolted across the Yperlee opened fire on it from the opposite bank. The raiders afterwards claimed that they had silenced this fire with bombs, but there was no evidence to prove that they succeeded in killing any of the enemy. However, they were able to make a tolerably accurate report on the state of the trench.

No. 4 party was heavily handicapped, as the part of the parapet over which it had to start was on the sky-line, and therefore clearly visible to the enemy. No sooner had the men started than the alarm was given, and they found the Germans waiting for them. Again the mat proved too short, and the men were obliged to advance knee-deep in mud. Bombs were thrown at them from the start, and one bomb reached the covering party, wounding all three men. Sergeant Waterfall was hit as he topped the parapet, but continued to advance, and succeeded in effecting an entry into the German line. Then a regular bombing fight took place, during which Sergeant Waterfall was again wounded and knocked down into a shell-hole. The Germans determined to catch this raiding party, and commenced an outflanking manœuvre on each flank, but this attempt was stopped by the covering party and mat men. There was no object in pursuing the enterprise any further, and the raiders therefore returned bringing back with them the eight wounded men.

On the whole the result of these raids was very

satisfactory, and a great deal of valuable information was obtained, but none of the parties succeeded in bringing back a live prisoner. It had been proved that the enemy only held his front line in posts, all of which had been located, and that the concrete dug-outs or pill-boxes were what the Germans mostly relied on for protection. The wire on the whole length of the trench, although not continuous, was passably good, and formed an obstacle difficult to pass.

On the 23rd the Battalion was relieved by the 2nd Battalion Scots Guards, and retired to Battle Area Camp, having lost 3 men killed, 1 died of wounds, and 10 wounded during the three days it had been in the front line. In this camp it remained until the 31st.

Brigadier-General G. F. Trotter, C.B., C.M.G., D.S.O.

CHAPTER XXIII

BOESINGHE, JULY 1917

Diary of the War

During this month the Germans made a determined attack on Nieuport in the Dune country near the coast, and succeeded in penetrating 600 yards into the British line, in spite of the stout resistance of the British troops; but a counter-attack was successfully launched, and restored the line to its original position. At the end of July a combined attack by the British and French troops in Flanders commenced in the neighbourhood of Ypres.

On the French front the Germans made strong attacks on the Chemin des Dames and gained some ground after severe fighting, but a week later the French were able to regain all the lost ground.

The Russians, under General Korniloff, advanced in Galicia, and even gained some victories over the Austrians, but disaffection was beginning to show itself among the men, and the Germans found no difficulty in driving them back over the frontier. This retirement on the part of the

Russians ended in an ignominious retreat and open mutiny.

London was raided by a large number of German aeroplanes, and many people were killed and wounded by the bombs which were dropped.

The Guards Division

When the attack on the Boesinghe Sector was decided upon, the great difficulty of crossing the Canal under the enemy's artillery fire at once presented itself to the Corps and Divisional Commanders. It would be necessary to construct bridges, and under an accurate barrage the loss of life entailed in crossing the Canal would certainly be very heavy. Lord Cavan thoroughly appreciated the drawbacks, but thought a well-organised attack would succeed. He ordered every detail of the attack to be carefully rehearsed over dummy representations of the Canal and the German trenches, and by the end of July every officer, N.C.O., and even every man knew exactly what he had to do. During this time the enemy seem to have been completely ignorant of the preparations that were being made, and imagined that so long as their positions farther south remained intact there was small probability of an attack on this sector of the line.

The date of the attack, or zero day, was originally fixed for the 28th, but on the 24th it was postponed until the 31st. About a week before zero day British aeroplanes reported that, although the German trenches were fully manned

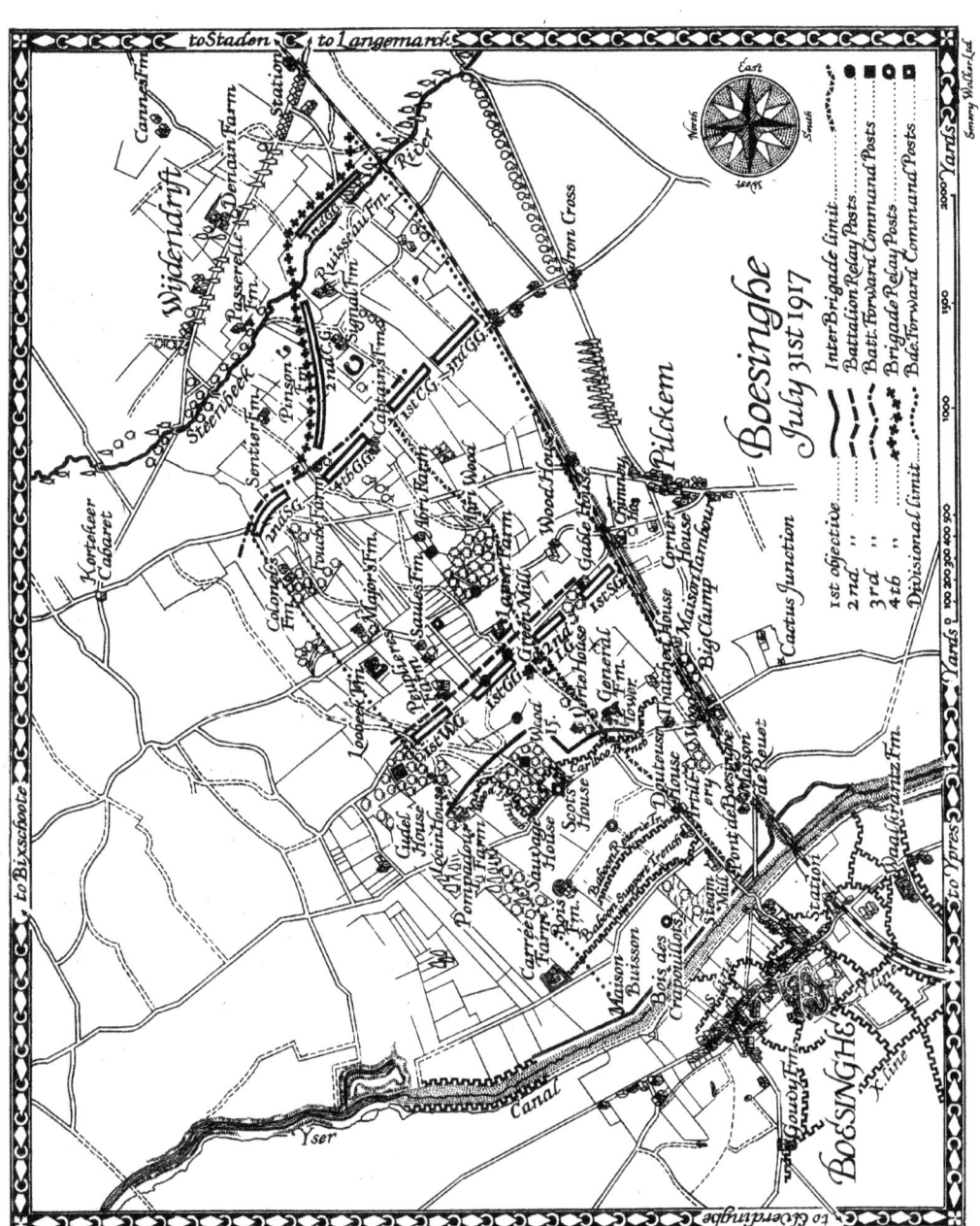

at dawn, the greater part of the garrison was withdrawn during the day to avoid the shells. A small incident occurred which left no doubt in General Feilding's mind on this point. Two wounded British soldiers who had been left behind during a night raid were observed on the far side of the Canal, and Lieutenant C. J. Hambro and Private Smith of the 3rd Battalion Coldstream Guards volunteered to go across the Canal and bring them in. This they succeeded in doing, and Lieutenant Hambro reported that not only had he not been fired on during his successful venture, but that he had seen no signs of the enemy at all.

General Feilding thereupon conceived the audacious plan of seizing the Canal in broad daylight without the aid of an artillery barrage. If the information which he had gained was correct, the enterprise would certainly succeed, but if on the other hand the absence of the Germans was only momentary, as had so often happened, it might prove a costly failure. He decided not to wait but to strike at once, and accordingly sent for Lieut.-Colonel Crawfurd commanding the 3rd Battalion Coldstream Guards, and told him to send out strong patrols properly supported at 5 P.M. as far as Baboon Support Trench, Artillery Wood, and Cactus Junction. As the matter was urgent, these orders were given verbally, and were later confirmed in writing, but it was not found possible to start before 5.20. The whole scheme, although planned at a moment's notice, was well thought out. The patrols pushed forward closely followed by supporting platoons

CHAPTER XXIII.
The Guards Division.
July 1917.

and moppers-up, and succeeded without difficulty in reaching their objectives, where they surprised the Germans who had been left in charge of the trenches. Many prisoners were made, but so quickly and unobtrusively was the raid carried out that the Germans in rear were totally ignorant of what was happening in front. The Division on the right attempted a similar raid somewhat later, but owing to no moppers-up having been ordered to accompany the raiders, the patrols were captured or killed by Germans who emerged from dug-outs in rear of them. The following day, however, it succeeded in gaining a foothold on the farther bank of the Canal.

For the best part of two days the 3rd Battalion Coldstream Guards remained in its advanced positions unmolested. When the men of a German patrol advanced on their usual rounds, they were allowed to enter the trench, and were then quietly made prisoners. On the 29th an officers' patrol sauntered along down a communication trench quite unconscious of the danger it was approaching; the officer himself and the leading men were made prisoners, but the N.C.O. in rear escaped, although he was fired upon. Presumably he dashed off, and telephoned that the front German trenches were in our hands. It was not long before enemy aeroplanes came soaring over at a comparatively low height to investigate the situation, and then the enemy's artillery deluged these trenches unmercifully with shells.

However, the Canal had been gained, and the enormous advantage of this could not well be over-estimated. The attack was started on the far bank, and thus hundreds of men were saved from being killed in the initial stages.

On the night of the 29th the 3rd Battalion Coldstream Guards and 1st Battalion Irish Guards were relieved by battalions from the 2nd and 3rd Guards Brigades. On the left the 1st Battalion Grenadiers and 1st Battalion Welsh Guards from the 3rd Guards Brigade, and on the right the 1st Scots Guards and 2nd Irish Guards from the 2nd Guards Brigade, moved up to take over their attack frontages.

CHAPTER XXIII.

The Guards Division. July 1917.

The order of battle of the Guards Division was as follows:

3RD GUARDS BRIGADE (SEYMOUR)		2ND GUARDS BRIGADE (PONSONBY)	
1st Welsh Gds. (Gordon)	1st Gren. Gds. (Maitland)	2nd Irish Gds. (Greer)	1st Scots Gds. (Ross)
2nd Scots Gds. (Orr-Ewing)	4th Gren. Gds. (Gort)	1st Cold. Gds. (Brand)	3rd Gren. Gds. (Thorne)

1ST GUARDS BRIGADE (JEFFREYS)	
2nd Cold. Gds. (Follett)	2nd Gren. Gds. (De Crespigny)
3rd Cold. Gds. (Crawfurd)	1st Irish Gds. (Pollock)

The first objective, or Blue line, consisted of Cariboo Trench, Wood 15 Trench, and Wood 15.

The second objective, or Black line, some 600 yards farther on, ran parallel to the Pilckem road.

The third objective, or Green line, was not a line of trenches, but an imaginary line 100 yards beyond the Iron Cross—Kortekeer Cabaret road.

The fourth objective, or Dotted Green line, was not parallel to the others, and while it crossed

Chapter XXIII.
The Guards Division.
July 1917.

the Steenbeek on the right joined up with the Green line on the left. The total depth was about $1\frac{3}{4}$ miles from the Canal.

The French First Division was on the left, and the Thirty-eighth Welsh Division on the right of the Guards Division.

The 2nd and 3rd Guards Brigades were to take the first three objectives, and the 1st Guards Brigade was then to pass through and secure the fourth. In the 2nd and 3rd Brigades the leading Battalions were responsible for the first and second objectives, and the Battalions in support for the third.

So carefully had the whole attack been rehearsed that from the first there was never a moment's hesitation: each Company knew exactly what was expected of it. If General Feilding with his staff had thought out every eventuality, he could not have asked for more prompt execution of his orders. Each successive objective was captured exactly according to the time stated in the orders. The creeping barrage was perfect. The Field Companies of the Royal Engineers did admirable work, and nothing could have been better than the arrangements for bringing up ammunition, water, and rations. There appears to have been no hitch throughout the attack.

Ponsonby's Brigade on the right occupied the frontage from the railway to Boesinghe Bridge, while Seymour's Brigade continued the line to the left for 600 yards. The frontage of Ponsonby's Brigade, although much smaller than that of Seymour's, included more enclosed and difficult country with many strong points. Whether it was wise to have the railway as a boundary between the Guards and the Thirty-eighth Division is open to doubt. There was a number of concrete block-houses on the railway which gave a great deal of trouble, and required the united efforts of the troops on the flanks of both Divisions. Now the junction of two Divisions is admittedly the weakest part in the line, and therefore it would have been better had the difficult task of capturing these block-houses been entrusted wholly to one Division.

These concrete block-houses or "pill-boxes" were built in the ruins of the numerous farms scattered about the country. They were cunningly concealed under old roofs and screened from frontal view by bricks and rubble, and the tops were often covered with old tiles, grass, or earth. They were generally built to accommodate eight or twelve men, and were strong enough to resist a direct hit from a field-gun or light howitzer, but their weakness seems to have been the restricted field of fire from the loopholes. This enabled troops to work round them and often close up to them without difficulty.

The morning was excessively dark and cloudy, although it was not raining. Zero hour was at 3.50, but it was not until 4.10 A.M. that the 2nd Battalion Irish Guards and 1st Battalion Scots Guards advanced in four waves, with an interval of 100 yards between each wave, moving at the rate of 100 yards in four minutes behind the creeping barrage. The first objective was captured at 4.30. During the barrage

Chapter XXIII.
*The Guards Division.
July 1917.*

which the enemy's artillery put down on the Canal, the Scots Guards had the misfortune to lose the services of their Commanding Officer, Lieut.-Colonel Romilly, who was wounded by a shell, and soon after the attack started Lieut.-Colonel E. B. Greer commanding the 2nd Battalion Irish Guards was killed. This was a serious loss to the Guards Division, as he had proved himself a most able officer.

Punctually the attack on the second objective started, and although the pill-boxes proved hard nuts to crack, the Black line was successfully taken. The Scots Guards had their right flank constantly exposed to enfilade fire from the railway, and were consequently obliged to throw back a defensive flank, so that when they reached the Black line they had hardly sufficient men for the front allotted to them. The 3rd Battalion Grenadiers and 1st Battalion Coldstream in support, however, made good the deficiency when they advanced to the third objective. The 3rd Battalion Grenadiers which passed through the Scots Guards had to contend with precisely the same difficulty, and as it advanced was continually obliged to leave men to guard its right flank. In spite of all this, the Green line fell into our hands, and was at once consolidated.

Meanwhile the 1st Battalion Grenadiers and 1st Battalion Welsh Guards in Seymour's Brigade had the advantage of starting the attack from Baboon Reserve Trench some 500 yards on the far side of the Canal, and had to wait some time to enable Ponsonby's Brigade to come up on their right. They advanced behind the creeping barrage and had no difficulty in reaching the first objective. Nor did the Black line present any great stumbling-block, although the casualties here were heavier. As soon as this line was consolidated, the 4th Battalion Grenadiers and 2nd Battalion Scots Guards passed through and attacked the Green line. Here there was a slight delay, as the French Division on the left was held up near Colonel's Farm. It was only a momentary check, and as the 2nd Battalion Scots Guards passed this farm the French were able to capture it. So the Green line was reached.

The moment had now arrived for Jeffreys' Brigade to pass through, and the 2nd Battalion Grenadiers on the right, and the 2nd Battalion Coldstream on the left, taking up the whole Divisional frontage, swept over the ground in perfect formation. The task of the Grenadiers involved the more severe fighting, since they were confronted with a large number of "pill-boxes." They also had the same difficulty as their predecessors with the railway, but after severe fighting succeeded in one place in gaining a foothold on the farther side of the Steenbeek River. No. 2 Company of the 2nd Grenadiers, on the extreme right, reached the river, but found it impossible to cross it. Although the Coldstream did not encounter so much opposition, they had to wheel to the left in the course of the advance—by no means an easy manœuvre when the shells were falling thick; but they carried out their task most successfully, and joined up with the Grenadiers. By 11 A.M. Brigadier-General

208   THE GRENADIER GUARDS

CHAPTER XXIII.
The Guards Division.
July 1917.

Jeffreys was able to report that, except by the extreme right Company, all the objectives had been secured. No counter-attack was attempted against the front held by the Guards Division, no doubt because the Germans were thoroughly disorganised.

At the end of the attack our barrage became thin and uncertain, making it impossible for the companies in front to send out patrols; but when it became dark the barrage ceased, and the 2nd Battalion Coldstream Guards succeeded in establishing advanced posts at Pinson and Sentier Farms.

During the advance the dash and gallantry displayed by the 201st French Regiment on the left, often in circumstances of exceptional difficulty, gained the admiration of the whole Guards Division. The ground over which it passed was covered with block-houses; there were several strong posts which had to be reckoned with; but in spite of all this it managed to keep pace with the Division.

The total casualties in the Guards Division during these operations were 59 officers and 1876 men, while 750 Germans were taken prisoner, and 30 machine-guns and 1 howitzer were captured.

THE 3RD BATTALION

3rd Batt. On the evening of the 30th of July the 3rd Battalion left Forest Area, and moved up with the remainder of the 2nd Brigade to the assembly area on the western side of the Canal. On the

BOESINGHE, JULY 1917

way it halted in a field just east of Elverdinghe, and the men were provided with hot tea and rum. This halt had a very good effect, for not only did it give the men rest on a long and tiring march, but it saved them from the nervous tension of a long period of waiting in the line for the battle to begin.

The east side of the Canal had fallen into our hands a few days previously, and it was therefore possible to hold that side lightly. On the right of the Guards Division the Thirty-eighth Division had been equally successful, and had established itself on the east bank; but it had not been able to push its line any farther forward.

The 1st Battalion Scots Guards and the 2nd Battalion Irish Guards were to be in the front line, and their leading companies were to start from the farther side of the Canal, which had fallen into our hands a few days previously. The 3rd Battalion Grenadiers and 1st Battalion Coldstream were in reserve some 400 yards from the Canal. The two leading Battalions were to take the first and second objectives, and the two Battalions in reserve were then to pass through and secure the third objective. The final objective was left to the 1st Guards Brigade, which formed the Divisional Reserve.

The following officers took part in the attack:

Lieut.-Colonel A. F. A. N. Thorne, D.S.O.	Commanding Officer.
Lieut. K. Henderson	Acting Adjutant.
2nd Lieut. L. Holbech	Intelligence Officer.
Lieut. E. R. M. Fryer	No. 1 Company.
Lieut. F. J. Siltzer	,, ,,
2nd Lieut. A. G. Elliott	,, ,,

210   THE GRENADIER GUARDS

CHAPTER XXIII.
3rd Batt.
July 1917.

Capt. the Hon. F. O. H. Eaton . No. 2 Company.
Lieut. F. W. R. Greenhill . . ,, ,,
Lieut. J. F. Worsley . . . ,, ,,
Capt. W. W. S. C. Neville, M.C. . No. 3 Company.
2nd Lieut. the Hon. A. M. Borthwick ,, ,,
2nd Lieut. B. J. Dunlop . . ,, ,,
Lieut. F. J. Heasman . . . No. 4 Company.
2nd Lieut. C. W. Carrington . . ,, ,,

Attached—Capt. G. W. East, R.A.M.C.

The whole Brigade took up its battle positions without any difficulty: the two leading Battalions each placed two companies less two platoons on the farther bank, and left two platoons as moppers-up on the western bank. The shelling of the Canal by the German artillery never ceased for a moment, and caused a good many casualties. The attack was timed to start at 3.50 A.M., but in order to conform with the creeping barrage the actual advance of the Brigade did not take place till twenty minutes later. The leading Battalions advanced behind the creeping barrage in four waves, with an interval of over 100 yards between each wave. The attack was assisted by a machine-gun barrage: eight guns from the Divisional Machine-Gun Company were detailed for this work, as well as the 4th Guards and the 29th Machine-Gun Companies. Both by the attacking troops, and by prisoners who were subsequently taken in the advance, this barrage was reported to have been most effective.

The attack was completely successful, and the first objective or Blue line was secured at 4.30 A.M., but there was naturally a considerable

BOESINGHE, JULY 1917

number of casualties, especially on the right, where the Scots Guards were exposed to enfilade fire. The 3rd Battalion Grenadier Guards waited in its trenches until 5 A.M., by which time it was light; and although the enemy continued with all the German thoroughness to shell the Canal itself, it never seems to have occurred to him to put barrages down farther back. This was undoubtedly a bad mistake on his part.

At 5 A.M., according to orders, the 3rd Battalion started off with No. 1 Company under Lieutenant E. R. Fryer on the right, and No. 2 Company under Captain the Hon. F. Eaton on the left. In support came No. 3 Company, commanded by Captain W. Neville, while No. 4 Company under Lieutenant F. Heasman was employed in carrying up material to the various objectives, and was directly under the orders of the Brigade. The passage across the Canal was successfully accomplished, though owing to the broken bridges there was a certain amount of delay. In some places, indeed, these bridges, consisting of petrol tins, had been so much damaged that there was practically nothing to walk upon. However, the barrage thrown on the Canal was by no means continuous, and as a certain amount of latitude was allowed in the choice of a crossing, officers were able to select comparatively safe courses, with the result that there were no casualties. Having crossed the Canal, the Battalion advanced in artillery formation towards Artillery Wood over the most difficult ground, while the German artillery sent high-explosive shells over, directing them to any strong points that might be made use of by the attacking force. So the 3rd Battalion arrived at the Blue line.

Meanwhile the battalions in front had been pushing on to the second objective or Black line. This phase of the attack was more complicated, for the enemy's machine-guns were scattered about in "pill-boxes," which were difficult to capture, and a great many casualties occurred not only from the machine-guns, but also from the German infantry, which was holding positions in the shell-holes in front of its trenches.

When the 3rd Battalion Grenadier Guards approached the Black line it found that there were hardly any British troops in front of it, as the Scots Guards, having suffered heavy casualties, were mostly employed in dealing with the "pill-boxes" on their right. Captain Eaton at once disengaged No. 2 Company, and brought it up on the left of No. 1. The enemy's machine-guns at Maison Tambour had been very troublesome, and had caused twenty casualties in No. 1 Company on the way up. Leaving Captain Neville to deal with this difficulty, Captain Eaton and Lieutenant Fryer extended their companies in two waves, and with the help of the Scots Guards, who were now freed from guarding the right flank, rushed on, and seized the second objective or Black line. At the same time Captain Neville brought up Lewis guns and rifle grenades, and with the help of hand grenades succeeded in silencing the obstructive enemy post. The Adjutant, Lieutenant Henderson, finding that the Division on the right was not keeping pace, went out to find the Royal Welsh

Fusiliers, but before he was able to accomplish his mission he was shot through the body, and eventually carried back into safety.

Although the Black line had been captured, the situation on the right was still unsatisfactory, and part of No. 1 Company had to face to that flank. The duty of reporting the position of the Battalion to the contact aeroplanes was then accomplished by waving large flappers above sheets laid on the ground.

The advance to the third objective or Green line was now timed to begin, and this was entrusted to the 3rd Battalion Grenadiers and 1st Battalion Coldstream. As the advance progressed considerable opposition was met with from the block-houses on the railway. These block-houses were also holding up the Thirty-eighth Division. Nor was No. 2 Company on the left of the Grenadiers free to advance, as there were several "pill-boxes" in front of it to be disposed of. Captain Eaton began to deal with these methodically, and with the aid of Lewis guns and bombs demolished each in turn. As No. 1 Company approached a house which it had surrounded, a large white flag was seen to be waved frantically from one of the apertures, and eventually three German officers and fifty men emerged and surrendered.

Captain Neville was occupied in dealing with the situation on the right, while Nos. 1 and 2 Companies continued their advance. Just beyond Wood House he brought up two machine-guns and got them into action under cover of the low railway embankment. Lieutenant Dunlop was told to advance with No. 9 Platoon, and started off most gallantly in the face of a withering fire when he was shot dead. Captain Neville at once brought up No. 12 Platoon, while Lieutenant Borthwick, with No. 11 Platoon, guarded the right flank. This enabled Nos. 1 and 2 Companies to push on and secure the Green line. During the last advance Captain Eaton had been unable to keep touch with the 1st Battalion Coldstream Guards, who had had to bear to the left to retain touch with the 3rd Guards Brigade, but on reaching the Green line every unit was at its allotted post. While Captain Eaton and Lieutenant Fryer were ordering their Companies to consolidate the position, Captain Neville noticed that the Thirty-eighth Division was still being held up by three "pill-boxes" which were situated in rear of his Company on the other side of the railway line. Rifle-fire was quite useless against 2 feet of ferro-concrete, and he therefore determined to make a bombing attack. Though there was, of course, considerable danger of the attackers being shot by the Thirty-eighth Division, it seemed the only way of dealing with this obstruction. The attack was led by Sergeant Browning and Private Baker, both of whom were wounded, and was wonderfully successful, the enemy being completely dislodged from their position, and losing 20 killed and 42 captured. Lieut.-Colonel Thorne came up soon after, and expressed his approval of all the dispositions that had been made. In order to adhere strictly to the orders, he told Captain Neville to take his men from the front line into support, and Lieut.

Fryer to occupy the whole of the front-line trench. At this moment, however, the 2nd Battalion Grenadier Guards, of the 1st Brigade, was seen advancing to pass through, and in order to prevent any confusion Captain Neville decided to wait until it had passed before sorting out his men. Having carried out his orders he was just looking round to see if there were no more men of his Company in the front line when he was hit by a bullet.

During the whole attack No. 4 Company, under Lieutenant Heasman, acted as a carrying party for the whole Brigade, and was split up into five small parties of about twenty men, each under a Sergeant. Yukon packs which the men wore were of great service for carrying shells and water-bottles. Each man carried four Stokes-gun shells and a coil of French wire during the initial stages of the attack, but later in the day two or three tins of water were carried instead. One party made no less than five journeys to the Blue line, a distance of 1000 yards, and the average number of journeys was three. After the third objective had been taken Lieutenant Heasman received orders to go himself to Battalion Headquarters, and to send Second Lieutenant Carrington with the whole of No. 4 Company up to the second objective to relieve the Scots Guards.

The total casualties in the 3rd Battalion were 2 officers killed (Second Lieutenant B. J. Dunlop and Captain G. W. East, R.A.M.C.), 4 officers wounded (Lieutenant K. Henderson, Lieutenant J. F. Worsley, Second Lieutenant A. G. Elliott, and Captain W. Neville, M.C.), whilst among other ranks there were 26 killed, 113 wounded, and 12 missing.

THE 1ST BATTALION

Although the attack at Boesinghe was, comparatively speaking, a simple operation, since the Germans had brought in the " crater zone " theory of defence, and the ground therefore was not strongly defended, it was most successful, and the manner in which the distances between the various waves were maintained during the attack, and the promptitude with which the fire positions were taken up and consolidated, won the warmest praise from the Brigadier, Lord Henry Seymour. The morning of the 31st was very misty, and the enemy's aeroplanes were unable to locate the attacking troops and incapable of directing the barrage. The comparatively light casualties may therefore be attributed to this fortunate state of the atmosphere.

The dispositions of the 3rd Guards Brigade were as follows: The 1st Battalion Grenadier Guards on the right, and the 1st Battalion Welsh Guards on the left, were to take the first two objectives, the Blue and Black lines, while the 4th Battalion Grenadier Guards and 2nd Battalion Scots Guards were to capture the third objective. The 1st Guards Brigade was then to pass through and take the fourth objective or Dotted Green line.

On July 29 the King's Company under Lieutenant Pauling and No. 2 Company under Captain Baker left Forest Camp to take over from the Irish Guards their battle front, while the officers and men who were not to take part in the battle returned to Herzeele under Captain L. Fisher-Rowe. Owing to a most fortunate reconnaissance by the 1st Guards Brigade, some days before, advanced positions on the eastern side of the Canal had been seized by the 3rd Battalion Coldstream Guards, and had since been maintained. This proved of the greatest value to the 1st Battalion, since it enabled the leading companies to start the attack on the farther bank, instead of having to cross the Canal under fire.

As soon as it was dark the King's and No. 2 Companies crossed the Canal by means of petrol tin bridges, which swayed so much that several men fell into the water, until orders were given that not more than four men at a time were to cross. Each company pushed forward two platoons as far as Baboon Reserve Trench, leaving one platoon in Baboon Support Trench and the remaining platoon on the Canal bank. This movement was naturally not carried out without a certain number of casualties. Captain Baker and his servant were killed by a direct hit from a shell, and Acting Company Sergeant-Major Wheatley of No. 2 Company was wounded in addition to a number of other ranks. The Battalion Headquarters, which was on the west side of the Canal at the end of Bridge Street, was also constantly shelled, but as Nos. 3 and 4 Companies remained in Forest Area till the 30th, the greater part of the German shells were wasted.

CHAPTER XXIII.
1st Batt.
July 1917.

On the 30th, subsections of the 3rd Guards Brigade Machine-Gun Company and the Trench Mortar Battery moved up to their assembly positions. No. 3 Company under Lieutenant Dashwood and No. 4 under Captain Lawford moved up into the trenches known as X line, just short of the Canal. Brigadier-General Lord Henry Seymour came round as soon as these positions were taken up to see that everything was ready. All through the day the two leading companies in their advanced position came in for a great deal of shelling, although mercifully the German artillery did not seem to know their precise position. Lieutenant Pauling, in command of the King's Company, and Lieutenant Lawrence, who had been sent up to command No. 2 after Captain Baker had been killed, were both wounded, and the two Company Sergeant-Majors, who had replaced those wounded the day before, were both killed. These losses were particularly unfortunate just as the attack was about to start. It rained intermittently all day, and the trenches were consequently in a marshy condition. On the night of the 30th the Battalion was formed up ready to attack the following morning.

The officers who took part in this attack were as follows :

Lieut.-Colonel M. E. Makgill-Crichton-Maitland, D.S.O.	Commanding Officer.
Capt. P. J. S. Pearson-Gregory	Adjutant.
Lieut. W. H. Lovell	Lewis Gun Officer.
Capt. P. M. Spence	Attached to Batt. Headquarters.
Lieut. M. Thrupp	King's Company.

BOESINGHE, JULY 1917

2nd Lieut. O. F. Stein	. . .	King's Company.
Lieut. T. P. M. Bevan	. . .	No. 2 Company.
2nd Lieut. S. Y. P. Gardner	. .	,, ,,
Lieut. W. J. Dashwood	. .	No. 3 Company.
Lieut. P. G. Simmons	. . .	,, ,,
2nd Lieut. H. G. Johnson	. .	,, ,,
Capt. R. D. Lawford	. .	No. 4 Company.
2nd Lieut. A. S. Chambers	. .	,, ,,
2nd Lieut. J. W. Chapple	. .	,, ,,
Capt. J. C. B. Grant, R.A.M.C.	.	Medical Officer.

CHAPTER XXIII.

1st Batt. July 1917.

During the night of the 30th our artillery bombarded the German artillery with gas shells. The result was very satisfactory, for, although the British front line received a good proportion of shells, the assembly was carried out without a hitch, and almost without a casualty. Zero hour was at 3.50 A.M., but, as the 3rd Guards Brigade was so far in advance of the rest of the line, the 1st Battalion Grenadiers had to wait till 4.28 A.M. before advancing behind the barrage. The enemy put down a heavy barrage on the Canal, but seeing no attack start on our front evidently assumed that none was intended, and lifted the barrage to another sector. During this preliminary bombardment Lieutenant Thrupp had his wrist smashed by a splinter of a shell, but after he had had it bound up by his runner he joined the advance, when a bullet through his leg stopped him a second time. Although he was carried down to the dressing-station, he never recovered, and died that evening.

The order of the advance was as follows:

First Wave.   2 Platoons of the King's Company.
              2 Platoons of No. 2 Company.

CHAPTER XXIII.
1st Batt.
July
1917.

Moppers-up.	2 Platoons of No. 4 Company.	
	2 Sections of the King's Company.	
	2 Sections of No. 2 Company.	
Second Wave.	No. 3 Company in support.	
Third Wave.	2 Platoons of the King's Company (less 2 sections).	
	2 Platoons of No. 2 Company (less 2 sections).	
	Remainder of No. 4 Company.	

There were ten paces between the lines and seventy-five paces between the waves.

At 4.36 a protective barrage was put down on the southern half of the Blue line, and a quarter of an hour later it was continued on the northern half. The King's and No. 2 Companies advanced in perfect order, but so eager were they to get at the enemy that the officers and N.C.O.'s found it difficult to prevent the men going too fast, and getting dangerously near the creeping barrage. Owing to the mist the 1st Battalion went a little too much to the right, but this tendency was easily corrected later on. At first the moppers-up did not make many prisoners, but as the advance continued they found dug-outs full of Germans, and captured about fifty. The first objective or Blue line was taken with comparative ease, but just as the Battalion reached it Captain Lawford and Lieutenant Dashwood were wounded. The former recovered, but Lieutenant Dashwood died two days afterwards in hospital. Within twenty minutes of the capture of this line the consolidation was complete. French wire was run out and strong points were dug. While this was being done the attack on the second objective or Black line was started by the third wave followed by the second wave. Everything went like clockwork, and there was no hitch of any kind. At zero + 3 hours and 24 minutes the 4th Battalion passed through to assault the Green line. No. 3 Company was placed under the direct orders of the officer commanding the 4th Battalion, and was ordered to make a strong point just north of Abri Farm. The 101st French Regiment on the left was held up for a time, but the 4th Battalion Grenadiers by its advance lessened the pressure on the French front and enabled them to seize the enemy's strong point at Colonel's Farm. While No. 4 Company was consolidating the Black line Second Lieutenant Chapple was seriously wounded, and died a few days later in hospital. As the advance to the third objective started, the two platoons of the King's Company, which had reached the Black line, returned to the Battalion in the Blue line, and at 9.50 A.M. Lieut.-Colonel Maitland received orders to withdraw his Battalion.

During the attack the 1st Battalion captured four machine-guns and two Minenwerfers. The casualties in the Battalion were 2 officers and 24 other ranks killed, 2 officers and 3 other ranks died of wounds, and 3 officers and 85 other ranks wounded. The medical arrangements were perfect, and the whole battlefield was cleared by 10 A.M.

THE 4TH BATTALION

At 9 o'clock on the night of the 30th the 4th Battalion left Forest Bivouac Area, and marched *via* Artillery Track 12, Bridge Street, and Clarges

CHAPTER XXIII.
4th Batt.
July
1917.

Street through Boesinghe to its forming-up areas, which it reached without suffering any casualties. By 1.20 A.M. all companies were reported to be in their places. No. 1 under Lieut. Pixley and No. 4 under Captain Paton, with two mopping-up platoons from No. 2 Company, were in the front trench, with the rest of the Battalion some distance in rear. The 4th Battalion was to follow the 1st Battalion until the first two objectives, the Blue and Black lines, had been secured. It was then to pass through that Battalion, and attack the Green line. After this had been taken the 1st Guards Brigade would pass through and go on to the Dotted line over the Steenbeck River.

The following officers took part in the attack :

Lieut.-Colonel Viscount Gort, D.S.O., M.V.O., M.C.	Commanding Officer.
Capt. C. R. Gerard	Adjutant.
Lieut. J. B. M. Burke	Intelligence Officer.
Lieut. I. H. Ingleby	Act.-Quartermaster.
2nd Lieut. N. A. Pearce	Transport Officer.
Lieut. J. N. F. Pixley	No. 1 Company.
2nd Lieut. G. R. Green	,, ,,
2nd Lieut. E. H. Tuckwell	,, ,,
2nd Lieut. J. M. Chitty	,, ,,
Capt. the Hon. F. E. Needham	No. 2 Company.
Lieut. R. G. West	,, ,,
2nd Lieut. H. W. Windeler	,, ,,
2nd Lieut. F. R. Oliver	,, ,,
Capt. C. H. Greville	No. 3 Company.
Lieut. R. Farquhar, M.C.	,, ,,
Lieut. C. S. Nash	,, ,,
Capt. G. H. T. Paton, M.C.	No. 4 Company.
2nd Lieut. B. J. Hubbard	,, ,,
Lieut. C. E. Irby	,, ,,
2nd Lieut. J. J. M. Veitch	,, ,,
Capt. N. Grellier, M.C., R.A.M.C.	Medical Officer.

At 3.50 A.M. the barrage began, and the noise was terrific. The whole sky blazed, and it seemed as if every gun that had ever been made was firing. Nos. 1 and 4 Companies, followed by the Battalion Forward Command Party and the moppers-up, crossed the Canal, moving in artillery formation. The left of No. 4 Company was heavily shelled as it crossed, and two platoons became rather scattered and lost direction. Second Lieutenant Hubbard with great coolness succeeded in rallying them and bringing them back to their correct position. There was at the time a considerable amount of machine-gun fire from Crapouillot Wood, and in the terrific noise and semi-darkness it was not easy to keep the platoons together. During the first stages of the advance both companies found it difficult to recognise landmarks, and compass bearings had to be used. There was a marked tendency to mistake Artillery Wood for Wood 15, which in the circumstances was hardly to be wondered at. Some loss of direction was inevitable, and at one time Grenadier, Irish, and Scots Guards seemed inextricably mixed south of Artillery Wood. But the private soldier of to-day is extremely intelligent, and if he can only see his officer he will disentangle himself, and get into his right place. Captain Pixley soon managed to re-form his Company, and take it on in the right direction, while the companies and platoons from the other Battalions sorted themselves out in an incredibly short time. No. 4 Company had also lost direction, and had come in for very heavy shelling, but Captain Paton was able by the aid of his compass to bring it back to the correct line of advance. A 5·9 shell fell right among the Battalion Forward Command Party, wounding many men and throwing it into great confusion. Lieutenant J. B. Burke quickly reorganised the party with the few remaining men, and was able to maintain the chain of communications.

When the Black line was reached, the 4th Battalion deployed into line. The hostile shelling had completely died down, and except for some machine-gun fire from the direction of Abri Wood the deployment was not interfered with. A smoke barrage proved most effective, and completely covered the Battalion as it deployed. The 1st Battalion had succeeded in capturing the Blue and Black lines in accordance with the scheduled time, and the advance on the Green line now commenced. On the right of the 4th Battalion was the 1st Battalion Coldstream, and on the left the 2nd Battalion Scots Guards. No. 1 Company was delayed for a short time by the water surrounding Lapin Farm, but managed to catch up the barrage again before entering Abri Wood. The creeping barrage was perfect, and gave the men great confidence. On the left of the 3rd Guards Brigade the 101st French Regiment had been held up by machine-guns, with the result that the left flank of the Brigade was in the air. The 2nd Battalion Scots Guards had to throw back a defensive flank, so as to keep touch with its neighbours.

There was a considerable amount of machine-gun fire from " pill-boxes " in Abri Wood, and also enfilade fire from the right, but the advance was not delayed on this account. The " pill-boxes " were rapidly surrounded, and the occupants of dug-outs immediately emerged and surrendered; only in a few cases was it necessary to bomb them. Three trench mortars were captured in a position near Abri Farm, and the whole attack was most successful.

As soon as the Green line was secured, consolidation was begun. The front occupied by the Battalion extended from Captain's Farm to Fourche Farm, with strong points at both these places, and a support line consisting of fortified shell-holes fifty yards in rear. Machine-guns, Stokes mortars, and Lewis guns were brought up and posted at different points in the front line. No. 3 Company of the 1st Battalion, which had been placed under Lord Gort's orders, dug a large cruciform post in rear of the support trench, and by 2 P.M. the whole of the defences were complete and efficiently wired.

Meanwhile the 2nd Battalion Coldstream Guards had passed through, and had succeeded in reaching the Green Dotted line, with its left on Fourche Farm and its right on Signal Farm. For the first two hours after the Green line had been captured the shelling was negligible, but when three German contact aeroplanes flew very low over the line, and located the Battalion, every one feared the worst. It was not long before a heavy bombardment took place, and the shells fell with alarming rapidity. Captain Pixley had a somewhat lucky escape: he had selected a

CHAPTER XXIII.
4th Batt.
July 1917.

concrete dug-out in Captain's Farm for his headquarters when he was requested by the 1st Battalion Coldstream Guards to hand it over to be used as its Battalion Headquarters. He had hardly left it when it was blown to pieces by a shell. He then changed his quarters to a hut, but had to move farther to the left when the Battalion took over the whole line, and soon after he vacated it the hut was demolished by a shell.

Orders were now received for the 4th Battalion to take over the whole frontage, from Captain's Farm to Colonel's Farm, so that the 2nd Scots Guards might be withdrawn. This operation was carried out in pouring rain, and the Battalion spent a miserable night, being soaked to the skin and continually shelled. The next morning, August 1, the trenches were in a shocking condition owing to the rain, and the shell-holes were full of water. A heavy bombardment took place in the morning, and died down later. At 7 that evening the 4th Battalion was relieved by the 3rd Battalion Coldstream, and returned to Forest Area Bivouac Camp. Both officers and men were dead-beat, having had no sleep for three days: they were so wet that everything they had with them was ruined by the rain, and any paper or book was like pulp.

There were 2 officers wounded (Lieut.-Colonel Lord Gort and Captain C. H. Greville), while the casualties amongst the other ranks were: killed 15, wounded 94, gassed 1, shell-shock 3, died of wounds 4, missing 5. On Lord Gort being sent to hospital, Captain the Hon. F. E. Needham took over the command of the Battalion.

BOESINGHE, JULY 1917

THE 2ND BATTALION

The assembly march on the night of the 30th of July was carried out by the 1st Guards Brigade without any difficulty, and all units were in position by 1 A.M. The 2nd Battalion Grenadier Guards moved from bivouacs in the Forest Area, $2\frac{1}{2}$ miles west of Elverdinghe, to a field near Roussel Farm, where cookers, sent on with the platoon guides, provided tea and rum for the men before they bivouacked in the open.

The following officers of the 2nd Battalion took part in the attack on the 31st:

Lieut.-Colonel C. R. C. de Crespigny, D.S.O.	Commanding Officer.
Capt. C. F. A. Walker, M.C.	Acting Second in Command.
Lieut. A. H. Penn	Adjutant.
Capt. J. N. Buchanan	No. 1 Company.
2nd Lieut. R. G. Briscoe	,, ,,
2nd Lieut. P. A. A. Harbord	,, ,,
Capt. A. T. A. Ritchie, M.C.	No. 2 Company.
Lieut. A. S. L. St. J. Mildmay	,, ,,
Lieut. F. H. G. Layland-Barratt, M.C.	,, ,,
Lieut. R. G. C. Napier	,, ,,
Capt. Sir A. L. M. Napier, Bart.	No. 3 Company.
Lieut. K. O'G. Harvard	,, ,,
2nd Lieut. H. Minto-Wilson	,, ,,
Lieut. J. H. Jacob	No. 4 Company.
Lieut. R. M. Oliver	,, ,,
2nd Lieut. F. H. J. Drummond	,, ,,
Capt. J. A. Andrews, M.C., R.A.M.C.	Medical Officer.

The task assigned to the 1st Guards Brigade was the capture of the farthest objective, after the first three objectives had been secured by the

CHAPTER XXIII.
2nd Batt.
July 1917.

1st and 2nd Guards Brigades. During the first phases of the attack the 1st Guards Brigade was therefore in reserve, advancing in rear so as to be prepared to pass through the leading Brigades when the moment arrived.

Zero hour was fixed for 3.50 A.M., and at 4 A.M. the 1st Guards Brigade advanced with the 2nd Battalion Coldstream on the left and the 2nd Battalion Grenadiers on the right, moving in artillery formation. The 3rd Battalion Coldstream Guards and 1st Battalion Irish Guards were under the direct orders of the G.O.C. Guards Division. On the right of the Guards Division, the battalion which had to undertake the attack on the last objective was the 17th Battalion Royal Welsh Fusiliers in the Thirty-eighth Division.

During the early stages of the advance the shelling was very slight, and it was not until the Canal was reached that the 2nd Battalion began to suffer casualties. A considerable amount of shelling was met with on both sides of the Canal, but the crossing was effected without serious difficulty, although in places the bridges were broken, and some of the men fell into the mud. The Battalion advanced in very good order, the intervals and distances being kept with great precision. Lieut.-Colonel de Crespigny, finding that he was gaining on the time allotted to him, and noticing that the German barrage was irregular, gave orders that commanders of platoons might use their discretion, and halt occasionally in shell-holes, in order to avoid any zones which appeared to be receiving particular attention from the German artillery. The enemy was continually shortening his range, and there is no doubt that, by avoiding the shelling as necessity demanded, many casualties were avoided.

After going on in this way for about 2000 yards the leading companies, No. 1 under Captain Buchanan, and No. 2 under Captain Ritchie, M.C., having come under machine-gun fire, deployed into line, their example being followed by the companies in rear. The German barrage seemed to follow the Battalion as it advanced, but without ever reaching it. One howitzer shell, however, fell among the men of the Battalion Headquarters, knocking over no less than five. When the Battalion reached a point 500 yards southwest of the Green line, some 3000 yards from our old front line, it halted in accordance with orders, and Lieut.-Colonel de Crespigny went forward to confer with Lieut.-Colonel Thorne, commanding the 3rd Battalion. In the meantime the 2nd and 3rd Guards Brigades had captured the Green line, which was not a line of trenches but a line on the map, 100 yards beyond the Iron Cross—Korteker Cabaret road, and therefore easily recognisable as a landmark. At 8.20 A.M. the 1st Guards Brigade advanced through the leading Brigades, which were to dig in and consolidate the Green line.

When the leading companies of the 2nd Battalion reached the Green line, Captain Ritchie with No. 2 Company found, as he expected, the 3rd Battalion Grenadier Guards digging itself in, and consolidating the line; but Captain Buchanan with No. 1 Company could find no

Chapter XXIII.
2nd Batt.
July 1917.

trace of the 1st Battalion Coldstream Guards, which should have been on the left of the 3rd Battalion Grenadiers. As he had arrived somewhat ahead of his time he commenced to dig in, as the position was on the crest of a hill and exposed to a considerable amount of machine-gun fire. The Company soon began to suffer heavy casualties. Captain Ritchie on the right sent word to say that he was being held up by machine-gun fire from the right, and was being subjected to enfilade fire from a partially destroyed house on the east of the Boesinghe-Staden Railway. He added that he could see no trace of the Royal Welsh Fusiliers on his right. The whole line was under machine-gun and rifle fire, and not long afterwards Captain Ritchie and Lieutenant Napier were hit by machine-gun bullets, so that the command of No. 2 Company now devolved on Lieutenant A. St. J. Mildmay.

Captain Buchanan considered that while it was possible to push on he should do so, even if the Company on his right was unable to advance. He therefore decided to move forward, and sent back to Captain Sir A. L. Napier, commanding No. 3 Company, asking him to garrison the Green line. As the 1st Battalion Coldstream Guards, which, it was afterwards discovered, had gone too far to the right, did not appear, and as the Royal Welsh Fusiliers were unable to reach their objective, the advance was delayed and not continued until fifteen minutes after the creeping barrage was timed to move on. However, our barrage had now become uncertain, shells falling sometimes far ahead and sometimes alarmingly close, so that the two leading companies could not well have advanced any sooner. Captain Buchanan, regardless of the situation on his flanks, continued to advance with No. 1 Company in the most gallant manner, and succeeded in reaching Signal and Ruisseau Farms, where thirty of the enemy were captured, including a battalion commander and a number of officers. A platoon of No. 3 Company, under the command of Lieutenant Harvard, who showed considerable ability in handling his men in exceptionally difficult circumstances, was now sent up as reinforcements. No. 1 Company dashed on, and managed to cross the Steenbeek River, on the farther side of which it dug itself in.

Meanwhile the position on the right was full of difficulties. The 17th Battalion Royal Welsh Fusiliers had been held up, and the usual problem demanded solution: how to keep pace with the advance, and at the same time to guard the exposed flank? A platoon of No. 4 Company, under Lieutenant Oliver, at once formed a defensive flank to the right; but this was an insufficient safeguard, and as No. 2 Company continued to advance, Lieutenant Mildmay, now in command, was forced to waste half his strength in protecting the right flank. Lieutenant Jacob, who commanded No. 4 Company, sent forward one platoon to assist No. 2 in their advance, and after consultation with Captain Buchanan despatched a third platoon under Second Lieutenant Drummond to prolong the left of No. 3 Company, which was now advancing in support of No. 1. This platoon had not gone far before

CHAPTER XXIII.
2nd Batt.
July 1917.

Lieutenant Drummond was wounded by a shell, but in spite of this, and even another wound in the neck from a bullet, he insisted on remaining with his Company until the Battalion was relieved, dealing coolly with every situation which arose. During the advance Sergeant Sharpe and two men captured a block-house 150 yards west of the railway, securing no less than twenty-one prisoners.

By now the Royal Welsh Fusiliers had succeeded in demolishing the block-houses which impeded their advance, and had gained ground on the right. This enabled Lieutenant Mildmay to push on with No. 2 Company to within 80 yards of the Steenbeek, but there he was held up by machine-gun fire from Langemarck village. Any endeavour to cross the river in the circumstances would be doomed to failure, nor was there any advantage to be gained by the attempt, since the men now occupied a position with a good field of fire dominating the approaches to the river.

The section of the Machine-Gun Company which followed the 2nd Battalion during this advance suffered very much from shell-fire. Lieutenant Cottle, the officer in command, was killed whilst going forward to reconnoitre, and shortly afterwards one of the guns of this section with its entire team was knocked out by a shell. The remaining guns, however, were brought up into good positions in the front line.

Three German aeroplanes made a complete and leisurely reconnaissance of our position, although they were freely engaged with Lewis guns and rifle-fire. Meanwhile, the 2nd Battalion Coldstream on the left, which had not experienced much opposition, but had had a very difficult wheel to perform, had succeeded in reaching its objective, and was established with its left on the Green line and its right in touch with the 2nd Battalion Grenadiers on the Steenbeek. As soon as it was dark, the line was straightened and strengthened, and touch was established between all units. A steady downpour of rain commenced that night and continued unceasingly until the Battalion was relieved two days later. The ground became one large morass, and the trenches were mere ditches, in which the men had to stand up to their knees in water. The hardships which the men had to endure cannot be over-estimated. Not only were they soaked through and covered with mud, but they were under continual shell-fire. Being for the most part on the forward slope of a hill, they were unable to move about in daylight to keep warm, and no hot food of any description could be brought up to them. The only way to ensure warmth was to dig a new trench at dusk and dawn every day. The advanced position of the trenches made it a precarious line to hold, more especially as it was impossible to dig down very deep on account of the water. There were consequently many casualties, amongst whom was Lieutenant K. Harvard, who was so badly wounded that he never recovered. He died the same evening at the dressing-station. The situation was not made easier by the Thirty-eighth Division on the right, which continually sent up S.O.S. signals without any apparent reason.

CHAPTER XXIII.
2nd Batt.
July 1917.
Aug.

This not only brought down our barrage, some shells of which fell in the Battalion's own advanced trenches, but it also caused retaliation from the enemy's artillery.

On the night of August 2 the 2nd Battalion was relieved, and marched to Bluet, where hot tea was provided. It was a very trying march; every one was knee-deep in mud, and the weight of the mud and soaked equipment was almost intolerable. Later the Battalion moved on to Elverdinghe in order to entrain for Proven, but a shell had blown up a part of the line, and no train was therefore available. A move was made instead into bivouacs near Cardoen Farm, where the Battalion remained until lorries arrived to convey it to Proven.

The casualties amongst the officers were: Lieutenant K. O'G. Harvard, killed; Lieutenant R. G. C. Napier, died of wounds; Captain A. T. A. Ritchie, M.C., Lieutenant J. H. Jacob, Lieutenant A. S. L. St. J. Mildmay, and Second Lieutenant F. H. J. Drummond, wounded. Amongst other ranks: 44 killed, 191 wounded, 15 missing, 11 slightly wounded.

CHAPTER XXIV

AUGUST AND SEPTEMBER 1917

Diary of the War

THERE was much fighting on the British front during these two months. Early in August the Germans counter-attacked near Ypres, and succeeded in regaining St. Julien, but only for a short time, for it was retaken by the British a week later. On the Ypres—Menin road there was fierce fighting; the British gained some ground north-west of Lens, and also reached the Bois Hugo. In co-operation with the French they made good progress in the direction of Langemarck, and crossed the Steenbeek River. A general offensive east of Ypres was undertaken in September, and the line was advanced considerably.

The French launched a determined attack at Verdun on an 11-mile front, and captured several villages.

The Italians advanced in strong force on a 30-mile front from the Isonzo to the sea, and captured the Austrian front-line trenches beyond the Piave. They also had successes at Monte Gabriele and Val Sagana.

236 THE GRENADIER GUARDS

CHAPTER XXIV.
1917.

The Russian *débâcle* continued, and the Germans captured Czernowitz and Riga. General Korniloff, finding that the Army was in a state of mutiny, marched on Petrograd, apparently with the intention of taking over the Government of Russia, but his insurrection ended in failure, and he was forced to submit to the Provisional Government under Kerensky.

In Mesopotamia Sir Stanley Maude defeated the Turks at Ramadie, and there was some further fighting in East Africa. China declared war on the Central Powers.

During these months several air raids were carried out against England, and not only London but many other towns were severely bombed.

THE 1ST BATTALION

1st Batt.
Aug.

After the operations at Boesinghe the 1st Battalion retired for a few days' rest to Forest Area, but returned to the front trenches on August 5. While it was being relieved by the 3rd Battalion Royal Fusiliers, Second Lieutenant H. G. Johnson was killed. On the 8th it proceeded to Putney Camp near Proven, where it remained for four days, and then moved on to Reinforcement Camp at Herzeele. On the 12th Captain J. C. B. Grant, R.A.M.C., who had been attached to the Battalion for over a year, left, and Captain P. H. Wells arrived to take up the duties of Medical Officer. On the 26th Second Lieutenant W. A. Fleet joined from the base, and on the 22nd Captain A. T. G. Rhodes arrived. At

AUGUST AND SEPTEMBER 1917

the end of the month the Battalion moved to Rugby Camp in the Bluet Farm Area.

On September 1 it went into the line for four days, and came in for a certain amount of shelling. Second Lieutenant R. H. Carson received a bad wound in the side from a shell, and although he was carried down to the dressing-station, where it was at first thought that his wound was not serious, he died the next day. Second Lieutenant S. Y. P. Gardner was wounded, and Second Lieutenant W. A. Fleet was gassed. On September 5 the Battalion entrained at Lunéville Siding for Ondank, whence it marched to Cariboo Camp. On the 13th it moved to Harrow Camp, and on the 21st to Purbrook Camp. The following officers joined during the month: Lieutenant A. A. Moller, Lieutenant J. F. Tindal-Atkinson, Second Lieutenant F. H. Ennor, Second Lieutenant C. C. Mays, Second Lieutenant R. Hall-Watt, Lieutenant J. P. Bibby, Second Lieutenant W. U. Timmis, Lieutenant C. Wilkinson, Second Lieutenant F. T. Maurice, Lieutenant the Hon. P. P. Cary, Second Lieutenant J. A. Lloyd.

The first few days in October were spent by the Battalion at Putney Camp, and on the 3rd it moved to the Elverdinghe Area, where the following officers rejoined: Captain Spence, Captain Chamberlain, Lieutenant Bevan, and Second Lieutenant Timmis.

LIST OF OFFICERS OF THE 1ST BATTALION AT THE BEGINNING OF OCTOBER

Lieut.-Colonel M. E. Makgill-Crichton-Maitland, D.S.O. . Commanding Battalion.
Major H. G. C. Viscount Lascelles Second in Command.

238 THE GRENADIER GUARDS

CHAPTER XXIV.
1st Batt.
Oct. 1917.

Capt. P. J. S. Pearson-Gregory	Adjutant.
Lieut. D. H. S. Riddiford	Transport Officer.
Capt. and Quartermaster J. Teece, M.C.	Quartermaster.
Capt. L. G. Fisher-Rowe, M.C.	King's Company.
Lieut. T. P. M. Bevan, M.C.	,, ,,
Lieut. L. de J. Harvard	,, ,,
2nd Lieut. R. B. St. Q. Wall	,, ,,
2nd Lieut. R. C. Bruce	,, ,,
Capt. A. T. G. Rhodes	No. 2 Company.
2nd Lieut. L. G. Byng	,, ,,
2nd Lieut. W. U. Timmis	,, ,,
2nd Lieut. R. Hall-Watt	,, ,,
Capt. P. M. Spence	No. 3 Company.
Lieut. P. G. Simmons	,, ,,
Lieut. J. P. Bibby	,, ,,
2nd Lieut. F. H. Ennor	,, ,,
Lieut. A. A. Moller	No. 4 Company.
Lieut. the Hon. P. P. Cary	,, ,,
Lieut. R. P. le P. Trench, M.C.	,, ,,
Lieut. J. F. Tindal-Atkinson	,, ,,
2nd Lieut. A. S. Chambers	,, ,,
2nd Lieut. C. C. Mays	,, ,,
Capt. P. H. Wells, R.A.M.C.	Medical Officer.

THE 2ND BATTALION

2nd Batt.
Aug.

The 2nd Battalion reached Plumstead Camp between Herzeele and Proven on August 3, and remained there training until the 21st, when it moved into bivouacs at Bluet Farm. On the 28th it went to Harrow Camp, and was employed in carrying up material to the front line. There was a great deal of promiscuous shelling by the enemy's artillery, and one shell pitched on the cookers of the 3rd Battalion Coldstream Guards, killing 3 men and wounding 14, while later two of its travelling cookers were blown to pieces, but the 2nd Battalion only had one man wounded. On the 31st it moved back out of the shelled area. During the month the following officers joined: Lieutenant H. White, Captain C. N. Newton, M.C., Second Lieutenant R. H. R. Palmer, and Second Lieutenant H. B. G. Morgan.

On September 8 the Battalion took over the front trenches immediately to the left of the Staden Railway, where the line was held by a series of posts running across the Broembeek. This was a very unpleasant line to occupy, as it was wet and marshy, and the enemy was able practically to overlook the trenches. Captain Walker, M.C., commanded the Battalion, while Major Rasch temporarily took command of the Brigade. During the three days in the line, 6 men were killed and 32 wounded. Second Lieutenant H. B. G. Morgan and three other ranks were slightly wounded, but remained at duty. On the 10th the Battalion spent four very disagreeable days at Rugby Camp, where it was continually bombed, shelled, and gassed. The men were employed in carrying up material to the front line, but considering they were constantly subjected to shell-fire they suffered very little: 3 men were killed, 3 wounded, and 11 gassed. Just as the Battalion was leaving camp, six 8-inch shells fell close by, but fortunately without causing any casualties. After a fortnight at De Wippe Camp, where it was employed on fatigues, the Battalion moved on the 23rd to Plumstead Camp, where it remained until October 6. On September 22 Brigadier-General

G. D. Jeffreys, C.M.G., having been given command of the Nineteenth Division, left the 1st Guards Brigade to take up his new appointment, and was succeeded by Lieut.-Colonel C. R. C. de Crespigny. Lieutenant R. Y. T. Kendall and Second Lieutenant H. D. Stratford joined the Battalion on the 14th, and Second Lieutenant G. H. Hanning on the 21st.

LIST OF OFFICERS OF THE 2ND BATTALION AT THE BEGINNING OF OCTOBER

Major G. E. C. Rasch, D.S.O.	Commanding Battalion.
Major the Hon. W. R. Bailey, D.S.O.	Second in Command.
Capt. A. H. Penn	Adjutant.
Hon. Capt. W. E. Acraman, M.C.	Quartermaster.
Lieut. G. G. M. Vereker, M.C.	Transport Officer.
2nd Lieut. H. M. Wilson	Intelligence Officer.
Capt. J. N. Buchanan, M.C.	No. 1 Company.
Lieut. J. C. Cornforth (Battalion Bombing Officer)	,, ,,
2nd Lieut. P. A. A. Harbord, M.C.	,, ,,
2nd Lieut. S. H. Pearson	,, ,,
2nd Lieut. H. D. Stratford	,, ,,
Capt. Sir A. L. M. Napier, Bart.	No. 2 Company.
Lieut. F. A. M. Browning (Asst. Adjutant)	,, ,,
Lieut. the Hon. F. H. Manners	,, ,,
Lieut. F. H. G. Layland-Barratt, M.C.	,, ,,
Lieut. W. H. S. Dent	,, ,,
2nd Lieut. R. H. R. Palmer	,, ,,
2nd Lieut. H. B. G. Morgan	,, ,,
Capt. C. N. Newton, M.C.	No. 3 Company.
Lieut. R. Y. T. Kendall	,, ,,
Lieut. F. A. Magnay	,, ,,
Lieut. A. W. Acland	,, ,,
2nd Lieut. H. White	,, ,,

AUGUST AND SEPTEMBER 1917 241

Capt. G. C. FitzH. Harcourt-Vernon, D.S.O.	. . . No. 4 Company.	
Lieut. G. R. Westmacott .	. ,, ,,	
Lieut. R. A. W. Bicknell (Battalion L.G. Officer) .	. . . ,, ,,	
Lieut. J. Tabor	. . . ,, ,,	
2nd Lieut. G. H. Hanning .	. ,, ,,	
Capt. J. A. Andrews, M.C., R.A.M.C.	. . . . Medical Officer.	
Capt. the Rev. Hon. C. F. Lyttelton	Chaplain.	

CHAPTER XXIV.

2nd Batt. Oct. 1917.

THE 3RD BATTALION

After three days' rest in Forest Area the 3rd Battalion went by train to Elverdinghe, and marched up from there to the front line. While the relief was being carried out there was a good deal of shelling, and Second Lieutenant G. V. G. A. Webster, a keen young officer of great promise, was killed by a shell. After a week's rest at Herzeele, the 3rd Battalion moved into Corps Reserve, while the Twentieth and Twenty-ninth Divisions attacked on the 16th. It returned to Herzeele on the 19th, and on the 22nd went to De Wippe Camp.

3rd Batt. Aug.

On September 4 the Battalion moved to Eton Camp, which was close to the railway, and therefore exposed to attacks by the enemy's aircraft. There were no less than forty casualties from bombs dropped from aeroplanes. On the 12th the Battalion moved to Rugby Camp, which was regularly shelled at night, and then took over the trenches in the Broembeek sector. For four days it was subjected to considerable shelling, and on the 20th it prolonged the line to the left, where the 10th King's Royal Rifle Corps

Sept.

VOL. II   R

242 THE GRENADIER GUARDS

CHAPTER XXIV.
3rd Batt.
Sept. 1917.
Oct.

attacked, and took their objective. The casualties during the four days were 6 killed and 28 wounded, including Lieut. the Hon. A. M. Borthwick, Lieut. E. D. Tate, and Lieut. R. W. Eliot Cornell.

The first week in October was spent in training at Herzeele and Proven.

LIST OF OFFICERS OF THE 3RD BATTALION AT THE BEGINNING OF OCTOBER

Lieut.-Colonel A. F. A. N. Thorne, D.S.O.	Commanding Battalion.
Capt. E. D. Ridley, M.C.	Second in Command.
Capt. the Hon. A. G. Agar-Robartes, M.C.	Adjutant.
2nd Lieut. L. Holbech	Assistant Adjutant.
Lieut. C. C. Carstairs	Intelligence Officer.
Lieut. M. Duquenoy	Transport Officer.
Lieut. G. H. Wall	Quartermaster.
2nd Lieut. F. W. R. Greenhill	,,
Capt. J. C. Craigie, M.C.	No. 1 Company.
Lieut. E. R. M. Fryer, M.C.	,, ,,
2nd Lieut. E. G. A. Fitzgerald	,, ,,
Lieut. E. W. Seymour	,, ,,
Lieut. W. H. Beaumont-Nesbitt, M.C.	No. 2 Company.
2nd Lieut. W. H. S. Roper	,, ,,
2nd Lieut. C. B. Hollins	,, ,,
2nd Lieut. J. Chapman	,, ,,
Lieut. J. C. D. Tetley	No. 3 Company.
Lieut. G. P. Bowes-Lyon	,, ,,
Lieut. N. Thornhill	,, ,,
Lieut. the Hon. H. E. Eaton	,, ,,
2nd Lieut. A. C. Knollys	,, ,,
Capt. G. F. R. Hirst	No. 4 Company.
Lieut. F. J. Heasman	,, ,,
2nd Lieut. C. W. Carrington	,, ,,
2nd Lieut. C. L. F. Boughey	,, ,,
2nd Lieut. F. S. V. Donnison	,, ,,

Attached—Lieut. H. Dearden, R.A.M.C.

THE 4TH BATTALION

The first few days in August were spent by the 4th Battalion in Forest Area; its strength was made up to 32 officers and 882 men. From the 5th to the 7th the Battalion went up into the trenches, where it came in for a good deal of shelling. The casualties were 15 killed, 35 wounded, 3 missing, 1 case of shell-shock, total 54. Lieutenant J. B. Burke was slightly wounded, but remained at duty. A patrol under Second Lieutenant D. J. Knight was sent out to reconnoitre the ground on the far side of the Steenbeek, and returned without having encountered any Germans. On the 8th the Battalion marched to Zonnerbloom Cabaret, where it entrained for Proven, whence it marched to Penton Camp. On the 27th it proceeded to Herzeele, where Lieutenant M. Chapman joined, and on the following day moved up into the line, where it remained for four days. At first all was quiet, but later shells began to fall very heavily. Second Lieutenant Benson took out his platoon from No. 4 Company, and advanced the bridgehead positions a distance of 100 yards, thus gaining a fresh field of observation over three-quarters of a mile. He also went out with a daylight patrol to locate the enemy, and succeeded in going as far as 200 yards before two machine-guns opened fire on his party. One man was killed by a low-flying aeroplane, which flew along the front line firing a machine-gun, and the total casualties during the four days in the trenches were 4 killed and 7 wounded.

On the evening of September 1 the Battalion

244 THE GRENADIER GUARDS

CHAPTER XXIV.
4th Batt.
Sept. 1917.

retired to Rugby Camp near Bluet Farm, where it remained for a week. On the 5th a German aeroplane flew over the camp, and dropped bombs, which wounded Lieutenant R. G. West and Lance-Sergeant S. G. Bull. After a week at Dublin Camp a move was made to Charterhouse Camp, where Lieutenant R. Farquhar, M.C., was killed by a shell. He was a fearless officer who had seen much fighting, and already distinguished himself; his death was a great loss to the Battalion. On the 21st the Battalion moved to Herzeele, and on the 24th to Penton Camp, where it remained training until the operations of October 5.

Oct.

LIST OF OFFICERS OF THE 4TH BATTALION AT THE BEGINNING OF OCTOBER

Lieut.-Colonel Viscount Gort, D.S.O., M.V.O., M.C. . . . . Commanding Battalion.
Major W. S. Pilcher, D.S.O. . Second in Command.
Capt. C. R. Gerard . . . Adjutant.
Capt. G. C. Sloane-Stanley . Assistant Adjutant.
Lieut. M. Chapman . . . Intelligence Officer.
Lieut. I. J. Ingleby . . . Act.-Quartermaster.
2nd Lieut. N. A. Pearce . . Transport Officer.
Capt. J. N. F. Pixley . . . No. 1 Company.
Lieut. C. E. Irby . . . ,, ,,
2nd Lieut. E. H. Tuckwell (Battalion L.G. Officer) . . ,, ,,
2nd Lieut. G. R. Green . . ,, ,,
2nd Lieut. J. M. Chitty . . ,, ,,
Capt. the Hon. F. E. Needham . No. 2 Company.
2nd Lieut. C. E. Benson, D.S.O. ,, ,,
2nd Lieut. T. T. Pryce, M.C. . ,, ,,
2nd Lieut. R. C. Denman . . ,, ,,
2nd Lieut. H. W. Windeler . ,, ,,
Capt. J. B. M. Burke, M.C. . No. 3 Company.

AUGUST AND SEPTEMBER 1917

Lieut. C. S. Nash (Battalion Bombing Officer)	No. 3 Company.
2nd Lieut. D. J. Knight . .	,, ,,
2nd Lieut. R. L. Murray Lawes .	,, ,,
Capt. G. H. T. Paton, M.C. .	No. 4 Company.
Lieut. H. H. Sloane-Stanley .	,, ,,
Lieut. E. R. D. Hoare . .	,, ,,
2nd Lieut. B. J. Hubbard, M.C. .	,, ,,
2nd Lieut. F. R. Oliver . .	,, ,,
2nd Lieut. N. R. Abbey . .	,, ,,
Capt. N. Grellier, M.C., R.A.M.C.	Medical Officer.

CHAPTER XXIV.

4th Batt.
Oct.
1917.

CHAPTER XXV

THE CROSSING OF THE BROEMBEEK (THE GUARDS DIVISION)

Chapter XXV.
The Guards Division.
Oct. 9-12. 1917.

THE crossing of the Broembeek and the occupation of the southern edge of Houthulst Forest by the Guards Division was one of those brilliantly executed attacks which are apt to be counted among minor operations simply because of their success. There had been plenty of time to make the arrangements, and General Feilding was determined to ensure the success of the whole operation. The weather was an important factor, as the ground was low, and there had been much rain. If the Broembeek should become swollen by the rain, it would develop into a serious obstacle, and the ground, already very deep in places, might become a morass over which the troops would pass with difficulty. Two patrols, which had gone out the week before the attack, reported that mats would be necessary for crossing the stream, but the weather fortunately improved, and on the day of the attack the passage of the Broembeek presented few difficulties.

General Feilding decided to hold the line with Seymour's Brigade until the 9th, and to carry out

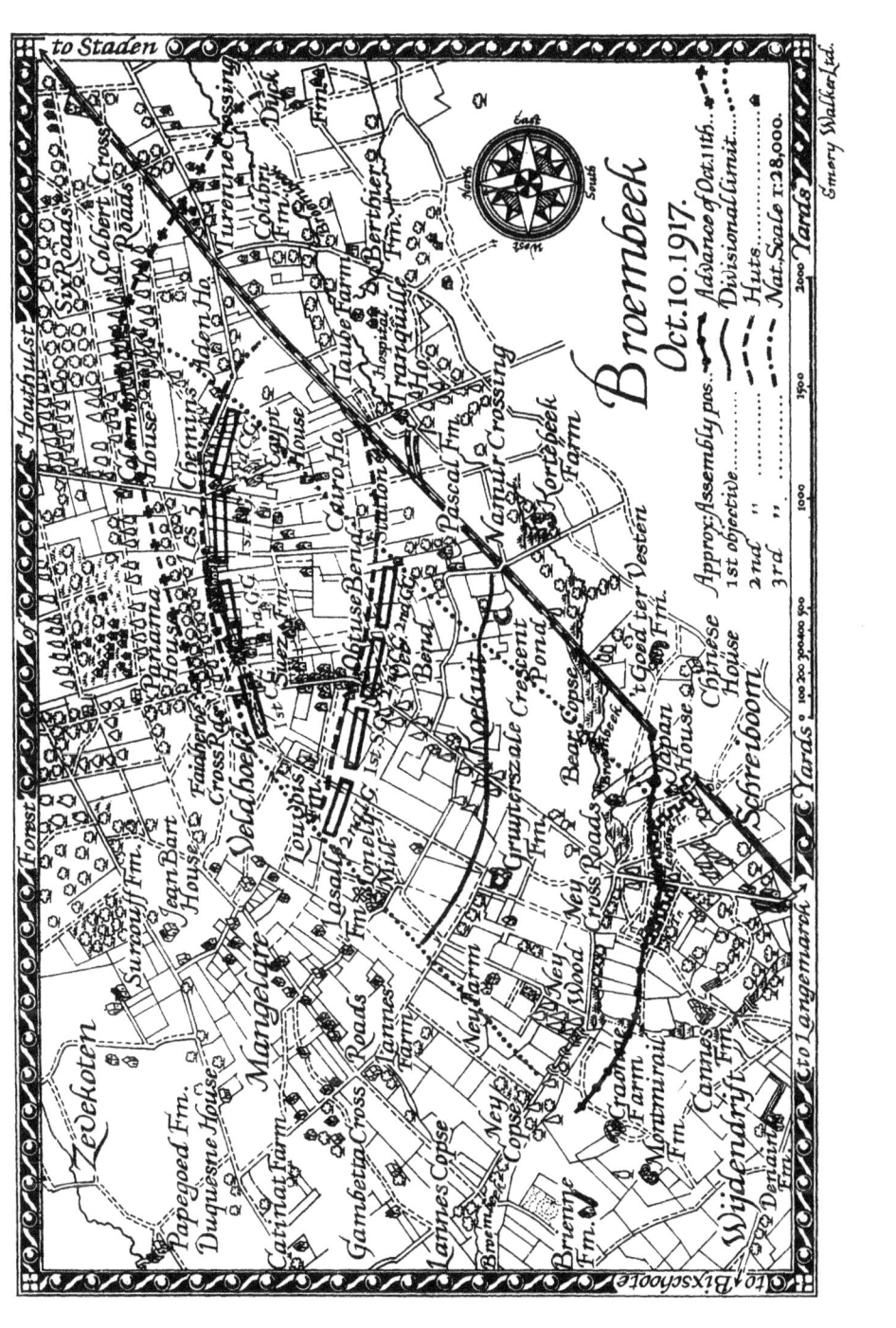

the attack with De Crespigny's Brigade on the right and Sergison-Brooke's Brigade on the left. De Crespigny's Brigade was to cross the Broembeek from Panther and Leopard trenches, and continue on either side of the Koekuit Road through Vee Bend to its final objective, on the edge of the forest, from Egypt House to about 800 yards east of Les Cinq Chemins. Sergison-Brooke's Brigade, starting from Craonne Farm and Panther trench, was to advance across the stream through Ney Wood and Gruyterszaale Farm to Louvois Farm, and a strong point beyond on its left, while on the right the group of houses from Obtuse Bend to Suez Farm was to be taken, so that the line up to the road to Les Cinq Chemins on the edge of the wood would be secured.

Brigadier-General Lord Henry Seymour, who had to hold the original line for the two days before the attack, placed the 4th Battalion Grenadiers and 2nd Battalion Scots Guards in the front trenches, and these two Battalions had a strenuous time preparing accommodation for the other two Brigades, and placing mats in readiness for the crossing of the stream. The 1st Battalion Grenadiers and 1st Battalion Welsh Guards had also to work hard forming forward dumps, and dragging guns into their new position.

On the evening of the 7th the relief was successfully accomplished, and De Crespigny's and Sergison-Brooke's Brigades moved up into their assembly positions.

At 5.20 A.M. on the 9th the attack began. In De Crespigny's Brigade, the 2nd Battalion Grenadiers and 2nd Battalion Coldstream advanced after an intense bombardment, which lasted four minutes, and having crossed the stream with comparatively little difficulty secured the first objective. In Sergison-Brooke's Brigade, the 1st Battalion Scots Guards and the 2nd Battalion Irish Guards succeeded in crossing the stream, and reaching the first objective by the appointed time. They, however, experienced some difficulty at Ney Wood, where the enemy had posted a strong machine-gun nest.

At 7 A.M. the advance to the second objective commenced, and was equally successful, although in De Crespigny's Brigade the 2nd Battalion Coldstream met with some resistance from a group of block-houses at Vee Bend.

As soon as the second objective had been secured, the remaining Battalions in each Brigade moved up, and passing through the leading Battalions attacked the third objective. In De Crespigny's Brigade the 3rd Battalion Coldstream and 1st Battalion Irish Guards advanced, but found that their task was not so easy as that of their predecessors. Concrete block-houses had to be disposed of, and in some places a very determined resistance was encountered. The Newfoundland Battalion of the 88th Brigade had been unable to keep pace with the advance of the Guards Division, whose right flank was consequently exposed. But the third objective was reached according to the scheduled time.

In Sergison-Brooke's Brigade the 3rd Battalion Grenadiers and 1st Battalion Coldstream encountered little opposition, and seized Suez Farm, where they captured two field-guns. The 3rd

Battalion Grenadiers reached the third objective so quickly that it was able to open fire on the Germans retreating into Houthulst Forest and inflict on them heavy casualties. The 1st Battalion Coldstream had some difficulty with a strong point at Louvois Farm, but after working round it succeeded in effecting its capture, together with the forty Germans who formed the garrison.

When the third objective was secured the two Brigades dug themselves in, and prepared for the expected counter-attack, but, although the enemy showed some signs of activity, no actual attack took place. The position was maintained until the night of the 10th, when Seymour's Brigade took over the line. The 1st Battalion Grenadiers was placed on the right, the 4th Battalion in the centre, and the 1st Battalion Welsh Guards on the left. In order to improve the front line, and at the same time slightly to alter its direction, General Feilding decided on a farther advance. The Welsh Guards had to remain where they were; the 4th Battalion in the centre had to advance a short distance, and the 1st Battalion on the right had to go somewhat farther. All this was successfully carried out under a protective barrage, though the 1st Battalion found it difficult to maintain contact with the 51st Brigade on the right flank.

The new line was held until the evening of the 13th, when De Crespigny's Brigade took over the line. On the 17th the Guards Division was relieved, and retired for a period of rest. The casualties in the Division amounted to 67 officers and 1899 other ranks. The total number of prisoners captured was 28 officers and 1152 other ranks, in addition to 3 field-guns, 1 howitzer, 36 machine-guns, and 9 trench mortars.

THE 2ND BATTALION

On October 7 the 2nd Battalion with the remainder of the 1st Guards Brigade reached Charterhouse Camp between the Yser Canal and Elverdinghe. The afternoon was spent in distributing fighting stores to the companies who were to undertake the attack.

The following officers took part in these operations :

Lieut.-Colonel G. E. C. Rasch, D.S.O.	Commanding Officer.
Capt. G. C. FitzH. Harcourt-Vernon, D.S.O.	Second in Command.
Lieut. F. A. M. Browning	Acting Adjutant.
Lieut. J. C. Cornforth	No. 1 Company.
2nd Lieut. S. H. Pearson	,, ,,
2nd Lieut. H. D. Stratford	,, ,,
Capt. Sir A. L. M. Napier, Bart.[1]	No. 2 Company.
Lieut. the Hon. F. H. Manners	,, ,,
2nd Lieut. H. B. G. Morgan	,, ,,
Capt. C. N. Newton, M.C.	No. 3 Company.
Lieut. A. W. Acland	,, ,,
2nd Lieut. H. White	,, ,,
Lieut. G. R. Westmacott	No. 4 Company.
Lieut. R. A. W. Bicknell	,, ,,
Lieut. J. Tabor	,, ,,
Capt. J. A. Andrews, M.C., R.A.M.C.	Medical Officer.

Nos. 1 and 2 Companies took up their battle positions on the night of the 7th, but the relief

[1] Captain Sir A. Napier, Bart., was the only officer who had taken part with the 2nd Battalion in the operations on July 31.

CROSSING OF THE BROEMBEEK 251

was long and troublesome owing to the sodden and shattered state of the ground, and the night was cold and windy. On the following day Nos. 3 and 4 Companies came up into their places behind Nos. 1 and 2. The day was fine until 4 P.M., when a steady rain commenced, which increased to a downpour, and continued until early the next morning. It was a miserable night for the men who were going to attack the next morning, and well calculated to depress the spirits of the boldest. Rum and rations were sent up in addition to hot tea, and everything possible was done to make the position bearable.

Chapter XXV.
2nd Batt.
Oct. 1917.

The condition of the Broembeek, which ran parallel to our front line, was a matter for great anxiety. During the past week patrols had reported it to be impassable at various places, and it was feared that the recent rains had converted it into a serious obstacle. Both companies sent out patrols to reconnoitre it during the night without very reassuring results, although Lieutenant the Hon. F. Manners found one or two points at which he was able to wade across. Mats and light bridges were carried to the front companies to be used by the leading waves of the attack.

The 2nd Battalion was on the right of the Guards Division, with the 2nd Battalion Coldstream on its left, and the 4th Battalion Worcestershire Regiment on its right. Nos. 1 and 2 Companies were to capture the first objective, and Nos. 3 and 4 were then to pass through and secure the second objective. The capture of the third objective was allotted to the 1st Battalion

CHAPTER XXV.
2nd Batt.
Oct. 1917.

Irish Guards, which was to pass through the Battalion after the second objective had been taken. The line of advance of the 1st Guards Brigade was parallel to and 300 yards from the Staden—Langemarck railway.

There was no preliminary bombardment, but at zero hour, 5.20 A.M., an intense barrage from 18-pounder guns and Stokes mortars dropped on and beyond the Broembeek. It was considered of the first importance that the effects of the barrage should not be lost by delay in crossing the stream, but in the half light its exact line was not easy to determine, and some casualties were caused by men pressing too close to it. The stream proved far easier to cross than was anticipated, and fallen trees, planks, and duckboards were of great assistance. The German Division who held this part of the line appears to have been taken by surprise, for it made a very poor resistance, and in places where the crossing was difficult, the curious sight of Germans holding out their hands to help our men out of the mud could be seen. Its line was held by a series of posts, mostly converted shell-holes. In spite of the line of advance being oblique to the trench from which they started, No. 1 Company under Lieutenant Cornforth, and No. 2 Company under Captain Sir A. Napier, managed to keep the direction, and the advance continued unchecked. Minor adjustments were necessary from time to time with the Battalion on the right, which at one time lost direction, and swerved too far to the left, but the first objective was gained and consolidated without any great opposition or serious loss. No. 3 Company under

CROSSING OF THE BROEMBEEK 253

Captain Newton and No. 4 under Lieutenant Westmacott passed through, and advanced on the second objective. This attack was equally successful, and this objective also was secured and consolidated up to time. Both advances had been carried out with the greatest steadiness and precision, and the skilful way in which the N.C.O.'s handled their sections was remarkable. Although the task allotted to the Battalion had been successfully carried out, its troubles began after the second objective had been consolidated. It had hardly had time to make the position secure, when the enemy's aircraft flying very low became unpleasantly attentive, and soon afterwards it was subjected to a very heavy shelling from the enemy's artillery. Lieutenant Tabor was shot in the ankle, and soon afterwards Second Lieutenant Stratford was wounded in the thigh. Captain Sir A. Napier was slightly wounded, but remained at duty. The total casualties in the Battalion were 33 killed, 123 wounded, 11 missing, 21 slightly wounded, total 188.

THE 3RD BATTALION

On October 7 the 3rd Battalion reached H Camp in Forest Area, and on the following day moved up towards its assembly positions. There had been heavy rain during the 7th, but on the 8th the weather improved. The attack of the 2nd Guards Brigade was to be undertaken by the 1st Battalion Scots Guards and the 2nd

Chapter XXV.
3rd Batt.
Oct. 1917.

Battalion Irish Guards, who were to seize the first two objectives, while the attack on the third objective was entrusted to the 3rd Battalion Grenadiers and 1st Battalion Coldstream.

The following officers of the 3rd Battalion took part in these operations :

Lieut.-Colonel A. F. A. N. Thorne, D.S.O.	Commanding Battalion.
Capt. the Hon. A. G. Agar-Robartes, M.C.	Adjutant.
Lieut. F. W. R. Greenhill	Intelligence Officer.
Capt. J. C. Craigie, M.C.	No. 1 Company.
Lieut. E. G. A. Fitzgerald	,, ,,
Lieut. E. W. Seymour	,, ,,
Capt. W. H. Beaumont-Nesbitt, M.C.	No. 2 Company.
2nd Lieut. W. H. S. Roper	,, ,,
2nd Lieut. J. Chapman	,, ,,
Lieut. J. C. D. Tetley	No. 3 Company.
Lieut. N. Thornhill	,, ,,
Lieut. the Hon. H. E. Eaton	,, ,,
Capt. G. F. R. Hirst	No. 4 Company.
Lieut. F. J. Heasman	,, ,,
Lieut. J. F. Worsley	,, ,,
Lieut. H. Dearden, R.A.M.C.	Medical Officer.
Capt. the Rev. S. Phillimore	Chaplain.

Patrols which had been sent out by the leading Battalion reported the ground in front to be wet and boggy, but passable. Lieut.-Colonel Thorne sent forward guides to make themselves thoroughly acquainted with the assembly position, so that they might lead the Battalion to its destination without delay. This comparatively simple task was not without danger, and when Second Lieutenant Greenhill, who was in charge of the guides, met the Battalion at Wood 15, his party

CROSSING OF THE BROEMBEEK

had already suffered six casualties. At 5.20 A.M. the attack commenced, and the leading Battalions started off preceded by a barrage. The Broembeek was crossed without difficulty, and the first objective was secured according to the scheduled time. The companies in support then passed through and captured the second objective. The 3rd Battalion Grenadiers and 1st Battalion Coldstream received instructions not to cross the Broembeek until the first objective had been secured. They accordingly waited until 7.30 A.M., and then advanced. On nearing the second objective the 3rd Battalion deployed with No. 3 Company under Lieutenant J. C. D. Tetley on the right, and No. 4 Company under Captain G. Hirst on the left. Nos. 1 and 2 Companies under Captain J. Craigie and Captain W. H. Beaumont-Nesbitt were in support. The moment had now arrived for the two rear Battalions to pass through the troops in front, and attack the third objective. There were, however, some very strong concrete posts to be disposed of before the third objective could be reached, and there seemed every prospect of desperate fighting. The 1st Battalion Coldstream had one particularly strong post to deal with, and by working round the flanks it succeeded in effecting its capture. Barring the way of the 3rd Battalion Grenadiers was a concrete block-house, the garrison of which no doubt thought it held an impregnable position. Lance-Sergeant Rhodes determined to silence the fire from this post, and most gallantly advanced towards it by himself. His bravery was rewarded in an astonishing manner, for the whole garrison

CHAPTER XXV.

3rd Batt. Oct. 1917.

of eight men surrendered to him under the impression that he was the leading man of a large party. For this conspicuous act of gallantry Sergeant Rhodes was recommended for the V.C., the award of which was published on November 27, the day on which he was mortally wounded in the attack on Fontaine in the Cambrai offensive.

Nor was this the only notable act of gallantry during the advance, for Lance-Sergeant Horgan and Lance-Corporal Unsworth, on reaching Suez Farm, succeeded in capturing two field-guns and fifteen prisoners. The Germans who took refuge in dug-outs were a constant trouble; in cases where they surrendered at once, they were simply made prisoners. In certain instances, however, when they imagined they were stronger than their captors, some of them tried to fight their way out. In this way three men of No. 4 Company found a dug-out full of Germans, and there seemed no reason why they should surrender. The leading men who emerged from the dug-out, finding their captors only numbered three, determined to fight, but were instantly killed, and the remainder, numbering fifteen, were made prisoners.

Thus the third objective was secured. Carrying parties with wire from No. 1 and No. 2 Companies came up, and consolidation was at once begun. Two machine-guns were also sent up to be placed at the strong posts east of Veldhoek Cemetery. In the afternoon the enemy was seen advancing down the Panama House—Faidherbe road, and they were dispersed by machine-gun fire.

CROSSING OF THE BROEMBEEK

All through the day the Chaplain, Capt. Phillimore, behaved with great gallantry, attending to the wounded and encouraging the men during the advance—quite oblivious of the shells and rifle-fire. When it was dusk the sad task of burying the dead had to be undertaken, and Capt. Phillimore stood up with his head uncovered, and read the service. Although the shells fell unpleasantly close to the burial-ground, which was in the open, he refused to shorten the service in any way, and when one of the men silently handed him a helmet, he merely shook his head, and continued to read the service as if there were no shells.

During the 10th the 3rd Battalion remained in the line they had captured. About 4.30 A.M. the Germans put down a heavy barrage on our line, but no infantry attack developed, and the remainder of the day was quiet. Before nightfall the Battalion established two strong posts on the road east of Faidherbe Cross-roads, and that night, relieved by the 4th Battalion Grenadier Guards, it retired to H Camp.

Lieutenant F. W. R. Greenhill and Lieutenant J. C. D. Tetley were killed, and Second Lieutenant W. H. S. Roper died of the wounds he received. Lieutenant N. Thornhill and Lieutenant E. G. A. Fitzgerald were wounded. Among other ranks there were 13 killed, 61 wounded, 3 missing, and 2 slightly wounded remained at duty.

During the attack the Battalion captured 2 field-guns, 4 machine-guns, 2 trench mortars, and 93 prisoners.

THE 1ST BATTALION

Chapter XXV.
1st Batt. Oct. 7–13. 1917.

Although the 1st Battalion took no part in the attack on October 9, it had a very strenuous time during the preparations. All the men worked every night for the five nights previous to the attack, and were employed in forming dumps for the attacking Brigades, and in helping to get the artillery into their forward positions in the Steenbeek Valley.

On the 9th the 1st and 4th Battalions Grenadiers and the 1st Battalion Welsh Guards were assembled in the neighbourhood of Wood 15. The following officers of the 1st Battalion took part in these operations :

Lieut.-Colonel M. E. Makgill-Crichton-Maitland, D.S.O.	Commanding Battalion.
Capt. P. J. S. Pearson-Gregory	Adjutant.
2nd Lieut. A. S. Chambers	Intelligence Officer.
Lieut. D. H. S. Riddiford	Transport Officer.
Capt. L. G. Fisher-Rowe, M.C.	King's Company.
Lieut. L. de J. Harvard	,, ,,
2nd Lieut. V. A. N. Wall	,, ,,
2nd Lieut. J. A. Lloyd	,, ,,
Capt. A. T. G. Rhodes	No. 2 Company.
Lieut. A. A. Moller	,, ,,
Lieut. L. G. Byng	,, ,,
2nd Lieut. E. G. Hawkesworth	,, ,,
2nd Lieut. R. Hall-Watt	,, ,,
Lieut. O. F. Stein	No. 3 Company.
Lieut. J. P. Bibby	,, ,,
Lieut. P. G. Simmons	,, ,,
2nd Lieut. F. H. Ennor	,, ,,
Lieut. J. F. Tindal-Atkinson	No. 4 Company.
2nd Lieut. C. C. Mays	,, ,,
Lieut. R. P. le P. Trench, M.C.	,, ,,
Capt. J. C. B. Grant, R.A.M.C.	Medical Officer.

CROSSING OF THE BROEMBEEK

The attack by De Crespigny's and Sergison-Brooke's Brigades was so successful that the services of Seymour's Brigade were not required. Owing to the strenuous work of the previous nights the men were exhausted, and would have been glad of some rest, but the bad weather, wet ground, and constant shelling made their position far from comfortable. The German prisoners taken were employed in carrying the wounded, but they were not sufficient for the purpose, and 100 men of the 1st Battalion were told off to assist. Had it not been for this impromptu assistance, the medical arrangements would have broken down very badly. On the night of the 10th a relief was carried out, which has an especial interest for the Regiment: by a curious chance the 2nd and 3rd Battalions of the Grenadiers were relieved in the line by the 1st and 4th Battalions respectively. The line occupied by De Crespigny's and Sergison-Brooke's Brigades was taken over by Seymour's Brigade, and the 1st Battalion Grenadiers placed all four Companies in the front trenches.

The attack of the 9th had carried the Guards Division to its final objective, but the troops on the right had not been so successful, with the result that Seymour's Brigade had taken over a salient more acute than a right angle, which made the general plan for a further attack rather awkward. On the evening of the 11th, Nos. 3 and 4 Companies moved up behind the King's and No. 2 Companies with two platoons of the 2nd Battalion Scots Guards, which went to Egypt House. These two platoons had been specially detailed to get in

CHAPTER XXV.

1st Batt.
Oct.
1917.

260 THE GRENADIER GUARDS

CHAPTER XXV.
1st Batt.
Oct. 1917.

touch with the 51st Brigade, which had met with so much opposition that it was unable to advance. During the night the enemy put down a heavy gas-shell barrage on the front line, and caused a large number of casualties. On the 12th a further attack was commenced, and the British barrage proved to be irregular and ragged, in marked contrast to the excellent barrages of July 31 and October 9. Under this barrage the 1st Battalion moved up to its objective, which it successfully captured. Lieutenant J. P. Bibby was killed as he advanced with No. 3 Company, and there were a good many casualties among other ranks. Unfortunately the Officer Commanding the two platoons of Scots Guards was killed, and Second Lieutenant L. G. Byng was sent to take his place.

Although the Battalions from the 51st Brigade reported themselves on their objectives, the contact patrols which were sent out failed to find any trace of them. It was afterwards found that this Brigade had reached its objective, passing over many Germans in doing so, and had swerved away too far to the right. Early in the morning the 1st Battalion reported a field-gun in action on the edge of the forest a few hundred yards in front of it. In response to an appeal for assistance, our artillery applied destructive fire to the spot indicated, and put down a box barrage to enable the patrols to go forward and destroy the gun, but owing to the hostile sniping this was impossible. On the night of the 12th the Battalion succeeded in clearing up the situation on the right, and getting in touch with the 51st

CROSSING OF THE BROEMBEEK 261

Brigade. The following day it was relieved by De Crespigny's Brigade, which now took over the line. During the relief Second Lieutenant R. Hall-Watt was killed, and Captain Rhodes was wounded, but remained at duty. The casualties among other ranks were 36 killed and 200 wounded or missing.

Chapter XXV.
1st Batt. Oct. 1917.

THE 4TH BATTALION

For two days previous to the 7th, the 4th Battalion had been working in the trenches in the front line and carrying up material to the dumps. On the night of the 6th a large fatigue party under Lieutenant Nash had worked for six hours with water and mud up to their waists, endeavouring to lay mat crossings over the marsh. The following day Lord Gort took round representatives of the 1st Guards Brigade, which was to use these mats during the attack, and showed them the positions of the bridges which had been made. Unfortunately in the early morning many of them had been destroyed, and Lieutenant Nash was again at work repairing them and relaying others. On the night of the 7th the 4th Battalion was relieved, and retired to Dulwich Camp near Bluet Farm. The following officers took part in the operations from the 9th to the 12th October:

4th Batt. Oct. 7-13.

Lieut.-Colonel Viscount Gort, D.S.O.,
  M.V.O., M.C. . . . . Commanding Officer.
Capt. G. C. Sloane-Stanley . . Adjutant.
Lieut. M. Chapman . . . Intelligence Officer.

CHAPTER XXV.
4th Batt.
Oct. 1917.

Capt. J. N. F. Pixley . .	. No. 1 Company.
2nd Lieut. E. H. Tuckwell . .	,, ,,
2nd Lieut. T. T. Pryce, M.C. .	. No. 2 Company.
2nd Lieut. R. C. Denman . .	,, ,,
2nd Lieut. H. W. Windeler . .	,, ,,
Capt. J. B. M. Burke . .	. No. 3 Company.
Lieut. C. S. Nash . . .	,, ,,
2nd Lieut. D. J. Knight . .	,, ,,
Lieut. H. H. Sloane-Stanley .	. No. 4 Company.
Lieut. E. R. D. Hoare . . .	,, ,,
Lieut. N. R. Abbey . . .	,, ,,
Capt. N. Grellier, M.C., R.A.M.C. .	Medical Officer.

On the 9th Seymour's Brigade was not called upon to fight, and after reaching Wood 15 remained in shell-holes and abandoned gun-pits. Lieutenant Ingleby, the acting Quartermaster, brought up hot soup in the morning, and bivouac sheets were given to the men to protect them from the rain which now came down heavily. On October 10 the 3rd Brigade was sent up to take over the whole line, and relieve the other two Guards Brigades. The 4th Battalion was to be in the centre, with the 1st Battalion Grenadiers on the right, the 1st Battalion Welsh Guards on the left, and the 2nd Battalion Scots Guards in reserve. Lieut.-Colonel Lord Gort and Lieut.-Colonel Maitland went up to ascertain the exact positions their Battalions were to take up, and as there seemed a good deal of uncertainty about the position on the right, the Brigade-Major suggested they should wait until the contact aeroplane had dropped its report. This would have entailed some delay, and the Commanding Officers decided to bring up their Battalions at once to Vee Bend. In order to

CROSSING OF THE BROEMBEEK 263

ensure the close co-operation of the 1st and 4th Battalions, it was agreed to have one Headquarters for both Battalions. On arrival in the front line, No. 3 Company under Captain Burke, and No. 2 under Second Lieutenant Pryce, were placed in the front line with the remainder in reserve. The relief was arduous, as the ground was a mass of shell-holes full of water, with the sides slipping and crumbling. On the 11th detailed orders for the attacks on the next day were issued, and the position of the enemy was carefully studied. In the morning German aircraft came over flying at 300 feet: the pilots were clearly visible leaning over the edge of their fuselages, and dropping Véry lights on to the trenches to indicate them to their artillery. They were received with a fusillade of Lewis-gun and rifle fire, and No. 3 Company succeeded in bringing one down in flames at the southern end of Houthulst Forest; but the enemy's artillery had received sufficient information to shell the front trenches with considerable accuracy, and shells began to fall in large numbers. That night a good deal of difficulty was experienced in bringing up the rations, for it was extremely dark and the mud on the sand-bags made it almost impossible to distinguish the marking. No. 4 Company under Lieutenant H. H. Sloane-Stanley were told off for this task, and worked very hard under great difficulties. Sergeant Billings of No. 3 Company, observing an enemy patrol approaching our lines, ran out and captured the officer and his orderly, from whom much valuable information and some maps were secured.

CHAPTER XXV.
4th Batt.
Oct.
1917.

At 5.25 A.M. on October 12 the attack was launched. The task allotted to Seymour's Brigade was small compared with that of the troops on the right, as the direction of the advance of the Division was half left. Nos. 2 and 3 Companies under Second Lieutenant Pryce and Captain Burke consolidated their positions on the new objective during the previous night, although No. 3 Company had to withdraw to its original line at daybreak, as it was in the direct line of the creeping barrage. The Welsh Guards on the left remained stationary while the forward movement was being made on the right, and No. 3 Company of the 4th Battalion had only to go about 100 yards, so that these units were in position before zero hour. The object of the attack was to bring the whole line to within 150 yards of Houthulst Forest. As soon as our barrage came down, two platoons of No. 3 under Lieutenant Nash advanced and captured their objective with comparative ease, while two platoons from No. 1 Company occupied the old front line in close support. Not long afterwards Lieutenant Pryce reported that his two platoons had also reached their destination. The whole advance had been attended with but few casualties, as the enemy offered very little opposition. While coming up to inspect his two front platoons, Captain Pixley was killed by snipers, who had been left behind when the enemy retired to harass the advance. Any movement immediately drew the fire of these snipers, and after some of them had been located and killed it was easier to move about. About 11.30 A.M. the

CROSSING OF THE BROEMBEEK

enemy's barrage died down, and as there were no signs of any counter-attack, the rest of the day was spent in consolidating the position and in attending to the wounded. Two patrols were sent out into the fringes of Houthulst Forest, and returned with reports of the enemy's defences and the condition of the ground, obtained from some prisoners they captured. Since it was clear that the enemy knew the range of the taped tracks, repeated hits having been registered on it, a party was detailed to lay out a new course on the 13th. The construction of this course was fully justified later by the absence of casualties when the Battalion was relieved. Including the two days in bivouacs on the east side of the canal, the Battalion had spent seven days in the open, exposed to the rain, and lying on waterlogged ground with little or no shelter.

The total casualties in the Battalion were 20 killed, 4 missing, and 64 wounded. On the night of the 13th the Battalion was relieved, and travelled by train from Boesinghe to Ondank Station, where it went into billets at De Wippe Corner.

CHAPTER XXVI

CAMBRAI AND GOUZEAUCOURT

Diary of the War, October, November, December 1917

SUCCESSFUL operations were carried out by Field-Marshal Sir Douglas Haig in front of the Passchendaele Ridge at the beginning of October, when a large number of prisoners were captured, and, in spite of repeated counter-attacks by the Germans, the British forced their way to Houthulst Forest. The French made a successful advance on the Aisne front across the Soissons—Laon road, and penetrated the German line in several places. At the beginning of November the Germans retreated from the Chemin des Dames, and were closely followed by the French.

Sir Julian Byng with the Third Army gained a remarkable victory in the direction of Cambrai, and penetrated the Siegfried line. Farther advances were made, until the whole of the Bourlon Wood fell into the hands of the British, but the Germans attempted an encircling movement, to cut off the troops in the salient that had been created, and forced back the British line at Gonnelieu and Bourlon. After some very heavy

CAMBRAI AND GOUZEAUCOURT

fighting Sir Julian Byng was able to bring up reinforcements, and restore the line.

In Italy the Austrians, reinforced by some German divisions, gained a decisive victory over the Italians, and advanced far into Italy. So serious was the situation that the Allied War Council decided to send British and French Divisions to the aid of the Italians. The Italians continued to retreat until they reached the Piave, and at one time Venice seemed threatened, but eventually the Italian resistance stiffened, and the Austrian invasion was checked.

In Palestine, after a series of brilliant operations, General Sir E. Allenby captured Jerusalem.

From Mesopotamia came the sad news of the death of General Sir Stanley Maude from cholera, and the appointment of General Sir W. R. Marshall as his successor.

CAMBRAI AND GOUZEAUCOURT

In November Sir Douglas Haig determined to take advantage of the concentration of the enemy's forces on other parts of the line, to carry out a surprise attack in the direction of Cambrai, and to penetrate as far as possible into the German lines, with a view to dislocate one of the enemy's nerve centres. In his despatch he makes it clear that the capture of Cambrai itself was a secondary consideration, and that his main object was to secure the right flank of the principal objective north-east of Bourlon.

Sir Julian Byng, to whom these operations were entrusted, received instructions to dispense with artillery preparation, and to depend entirely on the tanks, to cut through the enemy's wire. This was an entirely new departure. Hitherto it had been generally admitted by both sides that no infantry attack could possibly succeed, without an artillery preparation and a creeping barrage, and it remained to be seen whether the absence of all artillery support would be compensated for by the tanks, and by the undoubted advantage of attacking without giving the enemy any warning. With the utmost secrecy Sir Julian Byng assembled flotillas of tanks, and hid them in the woods.

The attack started on November 20, and succeeded beyond all expectations, for not only was the Siegfried line pierced to a depth of six miles, but over 10,000 prisoners and 142 guns were taken. The capture of Bourlon Wood was successfully effected, but the Germans soon recovered from their surprise, and commenced to bring up reinforcements, with the result that the Guards Division on attempting a farther advance on Fontaine found the enemy in great strength.

The ground that had been gained during the British advance formed an awkward salient about ten miles in width and six miles in depth, and the problem that confronted Sir Douglas Haig was whether to continue the advance or to withdraw. After weighing the various considerations involved, he came to the conclusion that it would be best to advance. On the enemy's side the Germans were at first rather staggered at finding that their impenetrable Siegfried line had been pierced, but Ludendorff determined to take

CAMBRAI AND GOUZEAUCOURT 269

advantage of the situation that had been created, and to strike on each side of the salient with a view to cutting off the troops in front.

On November 30, after a severe bombardment with gas shells, the Germans advanced under cover of the morning mist, and surprised our men in the trenches. From Bonavis to Gonnelieu, the Germans pushed through masses of men, and succeeded in capturing a large number of prisoners, although their attacks between Mœuvres and the Scheldt Canal were not so successful. The situation was extremely critical, and at one time it seemed that the enemy would succeed in cutting off all the British troops in the salient. They would undoubtedly have done so, had it not been for the gallant stand made by the Twenty-ninth Division at Masnières. This enabled Sir Julian Byng to bring up reinforcements, and the Guards Division was thrown in to stop the rush. The British troops retook the St. Quentin Ridge, and entered Gonnelieu and Gauche Wood; but meanwhile the position at Masnières had become precarious, and the Twenty-ninth Division was ordered to withdraw. Although the situation was saved, Sir Julian Byng saw that he must either retake Bonavis Ridge, or else withdraw to the Flesquières line. The latter course was considered best under the circumstances, and accordingly the shortening of the line commenced on December 4.

Divisional Account

After the successful operations in October the Guards Division had a month's rest. On

November 9 the move southward began, although the eventual destination was not known, and many days were spent in long marches. On the 11th Major-General Feilding was informed of the proposal to attack Cambrai, but was warned that the success of the whole operation depended on its being kept a profound secret. The Guards Division was to move by easy stages to that area, marching invariably by night, and the eventual attack was to depend on the result of the operations then in progress in Bourlon Wood. If they were successful, the Guards Division was to advance on Cambrai, but if not, the attack was to be altered to a raid on a large scale. Major-General Feilding confidentially informed his Brigadiers and Commanding Officers of the impending attack, but in order that some ostensible reason might be given for these continual marches, he told them to announce that the Division was on its way to relieve the French. It was, however, necessary to account for the order to leave the kits behind, as this was generally associated in the men's minds with an impending attack. It was consequently announced that, on account of the lack of accommodation in the part of the French line to which the Division was going, the kits must be stored. It was generally believed that these orders were also due to the transfer of large forces to Italy and the consequent dearth of transport.

It was not until the 23rd that the Guards Division reached the neighbourhood of Flesquières, and De Crespigny's and Seymour's Brigades were sent up to relieve two Brigades

CAMBRAI AND GOUZEAUCOURT 271

of the Fifty-first Division. This was a very long day for the men, involving a march of over fifteen miles across an unknown country in the dark, and it was far more difficult to find the way than it need have been, because the positions of the Brigade and Divisional Headquarters were incorrectly given by the Corps Staff. The cavalry, to be employed in certain eventualities, stood about in large numbers, and blocked the road, but eventually the relief was successfully accomplished. The Divisional front extended from the south-eastern outskirts of Cantaing to the north-eastern corner of Bourlon Wood, and was supported by four Brigades of R.F.A. and two of Guards Divisional Artillery.

CHAPTER XXVI.

Nov. 1917.

Although the situation remained unchanged during the 24th, the Fortieth Division, on the left, had some severe fighting in Bourlon Wood. The same night General Feilding placed the 2nd Battalion Scots Guards under the orders of General Ponsonby, commanding the Fortieth Division, and sent them up to reinforce General Crozier's 119th Brigade, which was hard pressed. This Battalion moved up to the south-east corner of Bourlon Wood, where it received orders to clear the wood of the enemy. This attack, which started at 2 P.M., had the effect of advancing the line some distance.

Nov. 24.

Meanwhile the 4th Battalion Grenadiers, which had taken the place of the 2nd Battalion Scots Guards, received orders on the 25th to move up in support of the Fortieth Division. This meant that it had to advance in full view of the Germans, who at once put down a heavy barrage

Nov. 25.

in front of it. With the utmost coolness and steadiness the 4th Battalion advanced through this barrage as if it was on parade, and earned special praise from General Ponsonby. Though the 4th Battalion moved up into close support in Bourlon Wood, its services were not needed, as the Fortieth Division had secured all its objectives.

Next day General Feilding held a conference of Brigadiers, and discussed in detail the plan of attack on Fontaine, which was to be carried out by General Sergison-Brooke's Brigade. The general scheme did not appear to offer much prospect of success, since the whole country between Bourlon Wood and Flesquières was overlooked by the enemy, whose guns were posted on the ridges, west of Cambrai, north of Bourlon Wood, and east of the Canal. The Germans would therefore be able not only to concentrate their fire on Fontaine but to sweep the back areas where our reserves would be massed. Major-General Feilding had already pointed out that, unless these ridges were captured, it would be quite impossible for any troops to remain in Fontaine. He had only six available Battalions, and the line was 3800 yards in length, so that it was expecting a great deal of half a division to attack a position so strongly held. The Higher Command, in spite of these weighty arguments, however, decided to attempt the experiment. The attack was to be undertaken by the 3rd Battalion Grenadiers, 1st Battalion Coldstream, and 2nd Battalion Irish Guards, while the 1st Battalion Scots Guards was to hold the right of the line.

CAMBRAI AND GOUZEAUCOURT 273

ATTACK ON FONTAINE

It was 6.20 on the morning of the 27th that the attack started. As the tanks were late in crossing the line, the infantry did not wait for them. Advancing with the 3rd Battalion Grenadiers on the right, the 1st Battalion Coldstream in the centre, and the 2nd Battalion Irish Guards on the left, the force at once came under heavy machine-gun fire. All the ground on the way to the first objective—approximately 1000 yards off—was covered with houses, which were practically untouched by shell-fire, and afforded cover to the enemy's machine-guns. Moreover, our artillery were not allowed to shell Cambrai. But in spite of innumerable difficulties the three Battalions went gallantly forward, and captured the first objective by 8.30 A.M.

The casualties, however, were very heavy, and so weakened the attackers, that they had not enough men properly to " mop up " the houses in the village and the dug-outs north of it. The tanks, which had been detailed to move round the outskirts of Fontaine, were knocked out almost at once, but one or two that later went through the village itself were of great assistance in clearing the streets. Everywhere the enemy were in large numbers, and though at one time over 1000 prisoners had been taken, only 600 eventually reached the Divisional cage, owing partly to the small numbers available for escort, and partly to the incomplete " mopping-up." Just the same difficulty confronted the 2nd Battalion Irish Guards, which had to go through Bourlon Wood, lost many prisoners in the thick undergrowth, and on reaching the northern edge of the wood, came in for a deluge of shells from the enemy's artillery.

When General Sergison-Brooke received the report that the first objective had been secured, and that the Battalions had been greatly weakened, he sent word to Lord Gort, in command of the 4th Battalion Grenadiers, to move forward in support. One company was to support the 3rd Battalion Grenadiers, and two others the 1st Battalion Coldstream, while the remaining company was to watch the left flank of the 2nd Irish Guards. At the same time he asked that the 1st Welsh Guards from General Seymour's Brigade might be lent to him. This was immediately done.

In the meantime the Germans had developed very strong counter-attacks against the Irish Guards in Bourlon Wood, and, finding there was a gap between that Battalion and the 1st Battalion Coldstream, endeavoured to drive in a wedge. In their endeavours to close this gap the Coldstream only succeeded in creating another gap between them and the Grenadiers. The result was that the Irish Guards at the north edge of Bourlon Wood were completely cut off, and there seemed every prospect of the 3rd Battalion Grenadiers in Fontaine and the 1st Battalion Coldstream on the left being cut off too. The 3rd Battalion Grenadiers' casualties amounted to well over half of its attacking strength, including nine officers out of twelve killed and wounded. It was now seen that the

CAMBRAI AND GOUZEAUCOURT 275

enemy had brought up large masses of troops, and were attacking vigorously on the whole front. General Sergison-Brooke therefore gave orders for all three Battalions to withdraw to the line from which they started.

Such a move was most disappointing to the men who had reached the first objective, but in the circumstances there seemed no other alternative. The enemy continued to throw in more men, and once more the fighting became very fierce, but though our depleted Battalions were unable to maintain their hold on Fontaine, the enemy found it equally impossible to advance or make any impression on the line. Under cover of darkness the 1st Battalion Grenadiers and the 1st Battalion Welsh Guards took over the line that evening, and Sergison-Brooke's Brigade withdrew to La Justice, while the 4th Battalion Grenadiers retired to Flesquières.

This was the first real failure the Guards Division had. In part it was due to the enemy having masses of men available for the counter-attack, but there was also a notable lack on our side of any reinforcements at the critical moment, which was attributed at the time to the faulty arrangements of the Corps Staff.

On hearing of the heavy casualties suffered by the Guards Division, the Twenty-seventh Corps sent up two Brigades of the Fifty-ninth Division, but they had a considerable distance to cover, and there was no hope of their reaching the line that night. Consequently they were sent to Ribecourt and Trescault, while De Crespigny's Brigade was moved from Ribecourt to Metz.

Fortunately, the night of the 27th was fairly quiet, and these movements were carried out without much difficulty.

A day without any incident worth recording followed, and on November 29 the Fifty-ninth Division took over the whole area. The Guards Division was disposed as follows : the Divisional Artillery at Flesquières, the Royal Engineers at Trescault, De Crespigny's Brigade at Metz, Sergison-Brooke's Brigade at Ribecourt, and Seymour's Brigade at Trescault. After a hard week in the line they were now to rest, and retire by easy stages to billets.

Suddenly a telegram arrived announcing that the Germans had broken through our line, and the whole Division was ordered to be ready to move at a moment's notice. Then came a stream of orders, conveying instructions for different Brigades to be placed under different Corps, that followed one another with bewildering rapidity, only to be countermanded the next moment. Finally the whole Division was placed under the Third Corps, and General Feilding motored off to get instructions.

Information was now received that the enemy were holding the line Villers Plouich—Gouzeaucourt, and as De Crespigny's Brigade was already marching on the latter place, orders were sent to divert Seymour's Brigade, which was moving south, and bring it up on the left of De Crespigny's forces.

Meanwhile General de Crespigny determined to ascertain for himself the exact situation in front of his Brigade, for the roads were all

CAMBRAI AND GOUZEAUCOURT 277

blocked with retiring troops, and all sorts of rumours had reached him. So off he rode at full gallop in the direction of the enemy. Having crossed the open, he came in view of Gouzeaucourt, and there saw the Germans making preparations for a farther advance. He quickly returned to his Brigade, and at once gave orders to attack. All the four Commanding Officers had also ridden ahead of their Battalions, to see for themselves what the ground was like; and so it came about that this Brigade, which a few hours before had been resting and preparing to retire, were now going forward to the attack, as if they had had plenty of notice. The advance of De Crespigny's Brigade in perfect formation through all the stragglers and despite the general disaster was a splendid and heartening sight, which restored confidence to all the army in that area.

GOUZEAUCOURT

The ground consisted of undulating downs gradually descending from Gouzeaucourt Wood, which occupied a commanding position, to the village of Gouzeaucourt, and thence rising more steeply towards Gauche Wood and Gonnelieu. One great disadvantage Major-General Feilding had to contend with was the total absence of artillery support. The guns had been left in the line at Flesquières, and it was impossible for them to reach the Guards Division until 7 o'clock that evening. The attack had therefore to be launched entirely unsupported by artillery, and had there been any guns there was no Artillery

Divisional Commander or Artillery Staff. When they did eventually come into action, they were too doubtful about the situation in front to be of any real assistance.

About noon the head of the Brigade reached Gouzeaucourt Wood, and as they arrived the Battalions formed up for attack. The 1st Battalion Irish Guards were on the left, with their right on the Metz—Gouzeaucourt road; the 3rd Battalion Coldstream in the centre, with their left on this road, and the 2nd Battalion Coldstream on the right; the 2nd Battalion Grenadiers were in reserve in Gouzeaucourt Wood. Each Battalion assumed artillery formation, with two companies in front and two in support, and was responsible for 500 yards of frontage. There was no time for written orders, and all instructions were given by word of mouth.

At 12.30 the attack was launched, and, as soon as the leading troops appeared on the crest of the hill, they came under heavy machine-gun fire. No very striking incident marked the initial stages of the attack, but when the leading Battalions came within 1000 yards of Gouzeaucourt they found a few men of the Royal Engineers and some remnants of the Twenty-ninth Division still holding on to a trench. Later on the 20th Hussars (dismounted) came up on the right of the 2nd Battalion Coldstream, and prolonged the line to the right. During the descent of the slope towards the village, the machine-gun fire became intense, but it never even checked the attacking Battalions, who swept on down the hill and up again to the far side of the village. When they

CAMBRAI AND GOUZEAUCOURT 279

reached the rise immediately east of the village, the shells from the enemy's artillery on St. Quentin's Ridge raked them at very close range, but in spite of this the whole objective, including the village, was captured by 1.30 P.M.

CHAPTER XXVI.

Nov. 1917.

General de Crespigny now found that his left flank was in the air, but the Cavalry Corps sent up a regiment to fill the gap, and touch was subsequently gained with the 4th Battalion Grenadiers in Seymour's Brigade. Soon after a cavalry regiment on the right came into action mounted, and made a gallant attempt to turn the enemy's left flank, but was stopped by wire and machine-gun fire. The tanks came up on the right, but directly they were seen by the enemy four of them were put out of action. With great promptitude the crews got their Lewis guns out and joined the 2nd Battalion Coldstream. It was now beginning to get dark, and the battle died down. During the day about 100 prisoners were captured, besides a number of machine-guns, and many British howitzers were recovered. Two supply trains were found at Gouzeaucourt station untouched.

While De Crespigny's Brigade was taking Gouzeaucourt, Seymour's Brigade, which had come into the field with equal rapidity, was ordered to prolong the line to the right. But this order was subsequently cancelled, and they were told instead to hold the line Gouzeaucourt — Villers Plouich. Moving off in artillery formation, they advanced between Gouzeaucourt Wood and Havrincourt Wood, and lined the railway line between Gouzeaucourt and Villers Plouich.

At this juncture General Feilding received orders to continue his advance, and attack the ridge running from Gonnelieu through Gauche Wood to Villers Hill. To General de Crespigny he entrusted the attack on Gauche Wood, and to General Lord Henry Seymour the capture of Gonnelieu. Lieut.-Colonel the Hon. Claud Willoughby, in charge of the tanks, had been kept at Divisional Headquarters in anticipation of an attack, and so only verbal orders for their assembly direct to him were needed. The tanks were to precede the infantry, while the Divisional artillery put down a heavy barrage. The Fifty-ninth Division were assigned to the left, and the Cavalry Division to the right. The whole attack was only to take place if the Twentieth Division failed, and it was not till 2.45 A.M. that the failure was announced.

Capture of Gauche Wood

The orders originally sent to the Division were to attack the line from Gonnelieu to Gauche Wood (exclusive) but Major-General Feilding quickly realised that until Gauche Wood was taken, there was small prospect of success for the attack on the left. When the cavalry did not appear on the left, he instructed General de Crespigny to make Gauche Wood inclusive.

In De Crespigny's Brigade the 2nd Battalion Grenadiers and the 3rd Battalion Coldstream on the right and left respectively started off. But the tanks which were to have operated on the right of the Brigade were late, as well as the

CAMBRAI AND GOUZEAUCOURT 281

cavalry that should have joined in the attack. After waiting ten minutes in vain for the tanks, Lieut.-Colonel Rasch attacked without them. The tanks detailed to the left of the Brigade arrived just in time, and were of the greatest possible assistance; in fact, it is doubtful whether the ridge could ever have been taken without their help. However, the 2nd Battalion Grenadiers reached the wood without any tanks to help them, apparently because the enemy's machine-guns were aimed too high.

Immediately the wood was reached two counter-attacks were launched by the enemy, but a company from the 2nd Battalion Grenadiers, which had gone out to protect the right flank of the Battalion, quickly disposed of them. After much fighting the whole wood was eventually cleared of the enemy, but the thickness of the trees gave the enemy's snipers a good opportunity of picking off our officers and N.C.O.'s, and the casualties among them were very heavy. When the tanks on the right came up, they were of little use in the wood, and as they appeared to attract the enemy's shells from all sides, they eventually retired. Although the cavalry on the right were over an hour late, when they did arrive they not only reinforced the men in the wood, but made the right flank of the Brigade quite secure. There was some difficulty in maintaining touch between the two Brigades, and a company of the 1st Battalion Irish Guards at one time had to be sent up to fill the gap. During this attack over 300 prisoners were captured, in addition to 3 field-guns and nearly

CHAPTER XXVI.

Dec. 1917.

100 machine-guns, which had been packed, ready for removal, near the railway-station.

ATTACK ON GONNELIEU

Seymour's Brigade meanwhile attempted the more difficult task of taking Gonnelieu and Quentin. There should have been a large number of tanks to help, but at the last moment only nine could be procured. Most of these arrived too late, but one that was working in conjunction with the Welsh Guards was of great assistance, and was largely responsible for clearing a trench held by machine-guns. The 1st Battalion Welsh Guards on the right and the 4th Battalion Grenadiers began the advance, but were at once met by heavy machine-gun fire—so intense was it that progress on the right was completely arrested, until a tank saved the situation.

It seemed almost impossible to take this village without the aid of artillery, as there were machine-guns bristling from every building, and since the Twentieth Division had failed there appeared to be but small hope of this second attempt succeeding. Yet so determined and persistent was the onslaught of the 4th Battalion Grenadiers that isolated parties managed to penetrate into the village. But this was not enough to silence the enemy's machine-guns, and soon it became clear that all we could do was to hold the line 200 yards from the western edge of the village. On the left of the line two Companies of the 1st Battalion Grenadiers were sent up to strengthen that flank.

CAMBRAI AND GOUZEAUCOURT 283

That night the position was as follows: the 1st Battalion Welsh Guards was established on the high ground on the right, in touch with De Crespigny's Brigade; the 4th Battalion Grenadiers, reinforced by two Companies of the 1st Battalion, held the line west of Gonnelieu, with its left in touch with the 2nd Battalion Scots Guards, who were covering Villers Plouich. Through the failure of the 183rd Brigade to arrive in time for the relief on the night of December 1, the men in the front line, who had had very heavy fighting, were obliged to remain where they were for another twenty-four hours. Next day the relief was carried out, and on the 3rd De Crespigny's Brigade took over the line.

Two bombing attacks were made by the enemy on the front line on the morning of the 5th, and at one time they gained a foothold in our trenches, but a prompt counter-attack by the 1st Battalion Irish Guards soon re-established the line. On that night De Crespigny's Brigade was relieved by the 26th Infantry Brigade.

The casualties in the Guards Division between November 25 and December 5 were:

	Officers.	O.R.
1st Guards Brigade (De Crespigny)	44	820
2nd Guards Brigade (Brooke)	40	1136
3rd Guards Brigade (Seymour)	34	928
Divisional Artillery	4	49
Royal Engineers	2	10
R.A.M.C.	1	19
4th Guards Machine-Gun Company	...	4
Total	125	2966

284 THE GRENADIER GUARDS

On December 5 Field-Marshal Sir Douglas Haig telegraphed :

> I desire to congratulate the Guards Division most warmly on their fine counter-attacks at Gouzeaucourt and Gonnelieu. The promptness of decision and rapidity of action displayed by them were successful in dealing with a difficult situation.

Lieut.-General Sir W. Pulteney sent the following message :

> The Corps Commander wishes to express to all ranks of the Guards Division his high appreciation of the prompt manner in which they turned out on 30th November, counter-attacked through a disorganised rabble, and retook Gouzeaucourt. The very fine attack which they subsequently carried out against Quentin Ridge and Gauche Wood, resulting in the capture of these important positions, was worthy of the highest traditions of the Guards.

THE 4TH BATTALION

On October 20 the 4th Battalion left the Houthulst Forest area, and went into billets at Le Marais, where the men were comfortably housed. There it remained until November 9, when the march to the south through Fiefs to Averdoingt was commenced. On November 2 Captain C. R. Britten, Lieut. L. R. Abel-Smith, and Lieut. the Hon. A. H. L. Hardinge joined. The village of Averdoingt proved too small for the whole Battalion, and one Company went to La Neuville Planquette, while another was billeted at the Le Haut Barlet Farm.

The transport had been very much reduced, owing, it was said, to the despatch of British

CAMBRAI AND GOUZEAUCOURT 285

Divisions to Italy, and an order was issued restricting the officer's kit to a minimum of 40 lb., including the valise. But, as the officers never saw their kit after November 23, these regulations made very little difference. Officers and men lived out in the open, exposed to rain and frost, without any change of uniform or underclothes.

On the 17th the march was continued through Ivergny, Bienvilliers-au-Bois to Achiet-le-Petit, which the Battalion reached on the 20th. There the news was received that the forward movement of the British Army had resulted in a considerable gain of territory, and that the Division was now to continue the advance. Lord Gort sent for the Company Commanders, and explained the details of the operations, which were to take place the following days, giving a sketch of the part to be played by the Guards Division. There was still some distance to go before our men reached the area of operations, and in order to avoid aerial observation the advance was continued by night. The whole Brigade moved in buses through Bapaume and Le Transloy to Rocquigny, and reached Baumetz-les-Cambrai on the 23rd.

The following officers took part in the operations of November 24-28 :

Lieut.-Colonel Viscount Gort, D.S.O.,
   M.V.O., M.C. . . . . Commanding Officer.
Capt. C. R. Gerard . . . Adjutant.
Capt. M. Chapman . . . Intelligence Officer.
2nd Lieut. N. A. Pearce . . Transport Officer.
Capt. H. H. Sloane-Stanley . . No. 1 Company.
Lieut. C. E. Irby . . . . ,, ,,
2nd Lieut. E. H. Tuckwell . . ,, ,,

CHAPTER XXVI.
4th Batt.
Nov.
1917.

Capt. C. R. Britten, M.C.   . . No. 2 Company.
2nd Lieut. R. C. Denman   . .   ,,   ,,
2nd Lieut. H. W. Windeler   . .   ,,   ,,
Lieut. C. S. Nash, M.C.   . . No. 3 Company.
2nd Lieut. F. R. Oliver   . .   ,,   ,,
2nd Lieut. G. W. Selby-Lowndes   .   ,,   ,,
Capt. G. H. T. Paton, M.C.   . . No. 4 Company.
Lieut. E. R. D. Hoare   . .   ,,   ,,
Lieut. L. R. Abel-Smith   . .   ,,   ,,
Capt. N. Grellier, M.C., R.A.M.C. . Medical Officer.

Nov. 23. The march to Flesquières was very trying, and the whole Brigade had some difficulty in finding the way in the dark. Owing to the constant checks and hesitation, which betrayed the uncertainty of the leaders as to the direction, there were brief halts, not long enough even to allow the men to sit down, then sudden rushes followed again by abrupt halts, and so on for several hours. As a bridge had been blown up by the enemy, the 4th Battalion was forced to go some distance out of its way through Graincourt, which was within 100 yards of the outpost line. Flesquières itself was occupied by the 1st Battalion Grenadiers, and the 4th Battalion was billeted just outside the village, in a portion of the famous Hindenburg line, which the Germans had considered impregnable!

Perfectly drained and dry underfoot, the trenches were 15 feet wide and 10 feet deep. The men's quarters were in dug-outs constructed with massive wooden beams and reinforced concrete, and were fitted with tiers of beds. The communication trenches were perfectly camouflaged with rabbit-wire and boughs, so strongly staked to the side that a man with full equipment could

CAMBRAI AND GOUZEAUCOURT 287

safely use the wire as a bridge. The belt of wire in front of the trenches was 100 yards wide in places, and seemed untouched by shell-fire. The effect of the attack by the tanks was clearly visible, for great rides had been made through the wire, and a number of bodies crushed out of all human semblance lay across the tracks, while groups of dead Germans, killed in the act of flight, lay scattered about between the trenches and the village. The trenches were full of German equipment, abandoned in the panic, and two valuable periscopic observation sets were found by the 4th Battalion, and forwarded to General Headquarters.

CHAPTER XXVI.

4th Batt. Nov. 1917.

The labour entailed in digging this stupendous work, which may fairly be compared in conception and execution to the great Chinese Wall, was clearly beyond the powers of any army actively engaged, however high might have been its discipline and capacity for work. But the problem of how this wonderful result had been achieved was solved when a notice-board was discovered on which was printed " For Russian Prisoners Only."

Bourlon Wood

On the morning of the 24th, a cold, wet day, with a gale blowing, a warning order arrived, instructing the 4th Battalion to move to the neighbourhood of Bourlon Wood. Later this order was cancelled, and the Battalion was told to take over from the 2nd Battalion Scots Guards the position north of Flesquières. It moved into

Nov. 24.

its new position that night, and by midnight the relief was complete. The Battalion Headquarters were in a dug-out, cut out of the solid chalk, and formed a good example of the comfort and luxury in which the Germans had been living. The former occupant of this palatial abode had provided himself with a wardrobe, looking-glass, and other luxuries, and had actually arranged a number of flowering shrubs in pots at the entrance to improve its appearance.

Early next day the 4th Battalion was placed under the orders of the 119th Infantry Brigade, and was sent up to relieve the 2nd Battalion Scots Guards in Bourlon Wood. The Fortieth Division were engaged in the difficult task of capturing Bourlon Wood, and both these Battalions had been lent to Major-General Ponsonby. While Lord Gort went off to Graincourt to report to his new Brigadier, Captain Chapman proceeded with the Intelligence Party to Anneux chapel, to reconnoitre the position to be occupied by the Battalion and the route it was to follow.

By now the Germans had begun to recover from the defeat inflicted on them, and were bringing up a number of guns to bear on our position. Bourlon Wood and Anneux chapel were subjected to a severe shelling, and the 119th Brigade suffered very heavy casualties. The Intelligence Party had been ordered by Colonel Benzie, commanding the forward area round Anneux chapel, to remain in the sunken roads, and were therefore protected from shell-fire; but, when they returned by the road which had been selected for the 4th Battalion to march by, they came in for

CAMBRAI AND GOUZEAUCOURT 289

a certain amount of shelling and lost 2 men, while Captain Chapman himself was slightly wounded. It seemed perfectly clear that, if a small party could be seen by the enemy from Fontaine, a whole battalion would necessarily offer a tempting target to the German artillery. Captain Chapman therefore decided to alter the route, and approach Anneux chapel by another road, leaving Graincourt on the right.

CHAPTER XXVI.

4th Batt. Nov. 1917.

Meanwhile the 4th Battalion, with No. 4 Company under Captain Paton leading, waited in the position held on the previous night, south of La Justice, along the southern edge of the Graincourt—Marcoing road, until the Intelligence Party returned, and then advanced by the new road that had been chosen. For the first 200 yards nothing happened, and then suddenly the enemy put down a heavy barrage across the line of advance. No doubt he imagined that his barrage would effectually prevent any troops coming up; in practice it proved a perfectly useless barrier, for the Battalion took not the slightest notice of it. There was about half a mile to be crossed, on which the shells continually fell, and the Battalion did not even check its pace.

Assuming artillery formation, it went straight through the barrage. Spouts of earth sprang up at the men's feet as if by magic, and the noise was deafening, but they plodded on. So steady was the behaviour of all ranks that General Ponsonby afterwards issued a special order of the day, stating that the 4th Battalion had come up to his support as steadily as if it had been on parade. It suffered 30 casualties, which, in view of the amount of shell-fire, may be considered astonishingly light.

The following graphic description of these two days was written by Captain M. Chapman in a sketch entitled " Intelligence," which he began, but which he never lived to finish.

" On the morning of the — the Battalion marched up a long wet *pavé* road in the direction of the gun-flashes and the Véry Lights, whilst the Battalion 'drums,' somewhere in the dark, played the tune that Grenadiers call their own, and the C.O. in silence watched his men file by. The test of discipline and training had begun. The figures of the men looked tall and grim, magnified by the shadows cast from the shrouded lanterns of the motor-lorries. The night was dark, and a driving rain soon soaked the tramping men. In an hour's time you could see by the light of a torch a mist rising from the soaked and perspiring humanity in front.

"A halt was called and men were detailed to pick up bivouac-sheets and petrol-tins of water. The already heavy-laden troops moved on again more slowly with their increased burden, along slippery wooden tracks laid across a field of mud. Another halt. An officer appeared, dripping with moisture, accompanied by guides who took charge of the companies and allotted them their area in which to bivouac.

"To-morrow was zero day, not for the 4th Battalion, but for some one else. If some one else failed, then the Grenadiers would have to put matters straight; that is to say, the Grenadiers

CAMBRAI AND GOUZEAUCOURT 291

were in reserve. The Intelligence Officer gave one last look at the inky darkness, and going down on hands and knees crawled into a long, low-arched dug-out. Sleeping men sprawled across the floor, while at the farther end a solitary candle burned. Picking his way across the recumbent figures he saw the Commanding Officer lying on his back, his head propped against a pack, silently smoking a cigarette and thinking. The Intelligence Officer lay down by his side, and, watching the Adjutant writing orders and speaking down a telephone, fell into a fitful sleep.

CHAPTER XXVI.

4th Batt. Nov. 1917.

"Zero hour for some one else left him cold, unmoved. The accustomed environment of war and great fatigue dull the sensibility of man. The steady roar of countless guns was a pleasing murmur as of rippling water in his sleepy brain.

"A ray of sunlight struggled through the narrow entrance of the dug-out, and the sleeping mass of humanity near the door stirred uneasily. The Intelligence Officer shivered, and, cautiously rising into a stooping posture, crawled out into the open air. The sun was trying to pierce a passage through the heavy ground-mist. The troops were cooking their breakfast and beating their chests with a flapping motion to restore the circulation in their half-frozen limbs.

"On a modern battlefield, lines of wooden 'duckboards' run like arteries across the trackless waste towards the front. Up the arteries flow fresh men, new blood, human forms complete; food to support life, ammunition to destroy it. Down the arteries flow ghosts of what yesterday were men, with tissues torn, and muscles rent;

gibbering prisoners and men who have been spared to be shattered another day.

"An artery passed the dug-out door. The Intelligence Officer observed the circulation to and from the battlefield, and speculated on the fate of the tide going up, watching the expression on the faces of the advancing and receding groups. The men lazily watched the passing tide, exchanging jokes with friends going either way. Prisoners alone excited interest, but not sufficient to make men move more than a few yards from where they stood.

"French gunners in a wood near by ran hotfoot to see each band of prisoners pass, but our men with British phlegm stayed where they stood, and eyed the foe with casual glance. The passing wounded drew no expression of pity from the onlookers, nor did the fate of the ingoing tide even raise a questioning expression on their faces. This was the last spot where selfishness still reigned supreme—the fringe of the battle. Death and danger were not sufficiently close to draw out the best in man; he behaved as he did in civil life—each man for himself and the devil take the hindmost.

"The men who marched up the endless ribbon to the front looked just like other men, and anxiety for their own safety left no trace in their expression. They might have been the crowd that streams through the factory gates in the early morning. The outgoing men were different. They hastened by and looked neither to the left nor right. They felt that fate had been too good to them and that it might change

CAMBRAI AND GOUZEAUCOURT 293

its mind and rend them if they loitered by the way. They had reached the fringe where the 'Ego' was whispering in their ears with insistent voice. They were alive; the others— they might be dead—what matter? They were alive.

"The wounded stared in front of them, except those in pain, and the prisoners looked cowed and miserable. The escorts walked with jaunty air, rifle slung, bayonets fixed, and exchanged jokes with all who would pay attention. The feeling of victory was still in their veins, for the slouching prisoners spurred their pride of race; were they not the symbol of all their friends 'up there' had done?

"The stretcher-bearers, intent on their work, passed the fringe of selfishness untouched. The bond of pain and suffering held them fast in unselfishness until the moment when they delivered their charge to the clearing-station in the rear. While other men hurried from the battlefield, these slowly and with aching arms and legs carried their burdens carefully. Human suffering must touch some special chord of self-sacrifice in man. Duty, discipline, and other self-taught virtues would never produce that careful studied plod of the stretcher-bearer under heavy shell-fire, or those deliberate halts to attend to their patients' needs.

"Thus the second day passed. The Grenadiers were not called upon, but sat in the pit and watched the puppets moving on and off the stage. The Intelligence Officer had the critic's box and made his notes. The night passed quietly and

CHAPTER XXVI.
4th Batt.
Nov. 1917.

slowly, the news filtered back that our friends in front had taken all their objectives and that all went well. The morning brought the fateful news that the 4th Battalion was under orders to take over the front line that night, and afterwards to attack. Every one was busy, even the Intelligence Officer, and the passing puppets moved unnoticed. The 4th Battalion prepared to leave the pit and occupy the stage.

"The third day passed quickly in preparation. At 4.30 in the afternoon the first platoon stepped on to the wooden pathway and moved up towards the front. The Intelligence Officer started last, with Battalion Headquarters, while the Commanding Officer and Adjutant and orderlies plodded off alone. The sun had set and it was growing dark. That ribbon of wood which led to the unknown had its advantages, for it gave a hard, though slippery, foothold; but, once you stepped upon it, you became its slave. The Path began to assume a sinister character, when ahead you saw it lead into a wood full of bursting shells. Then it took the form of an endless moving staircase, surely leading to destruction. The serpent of men moved into such a wood. The very name it bore was ominous. No one spoke. The Intelligence Officer noticed his throat was very dry. His heart pumped at the scream of each arriving shell. He continued to move forward as in a dream. At intervals he made way for stretcher cases. The flash of the bursting shells disclosed a row of gun-emplacements. Two gunners pinned under an overturned carriage screamed.

CAMBRAI AND GOUZEAUCOURT

"Still Battalion Headquarters moved on—out of the wood into the open—away from death to what seemed like security. An odd shell or two burst near the path, while others shrieked their way overhead, dealing death somewhere behind. The mind neglected the latter, focussing all attention on the former. The pathway crossed two streams. By now the darkness was complete. A snorting, sobbing noise came from somewhere in front, succeeded by a splashing sound. The path went by a dark and slimy pool, in which the head and ears of a bogged horse waggled this way and that pathetically. Then all was still. A man's figure could be dimly seen attempting to cut off the pack saddle before it was buried in the slough.

"The wooden track abruptly ended. A white tape feebly glimmered in the dark, hanging loosely between upright iron stakes, rifles driven muzzle down into the sodden soil, and portions of broken branches.

"The Intelligence Officer seized the tape and floundered slowly on. The men behind him breathed heavily, and in quiet tones cursed the water and the mud, the tape and the hand that laid it. Some one tripped. A halt was called. The obstruction proved to be a comrade, some flotsam from the men ahead. He was alive, warm, but inarticulate. A sergeant felt him over in the dark. Some one said, 'My Gawd, Sir, 'e's got it through the throat.' The Intelligence Officer spoke words of promise to the man and left him there. 'Outgoing troops would pick him up,' and other well-worn words of

CHAPTER XXVI.
4th Batt.
Nov. 1917.

comfort, although he knew they might not see him. He felt he was leaving him to die. This is war.

"The tape suddenly ended. Heaps of broken stone disclosed the close proximity of a concrete dug-out. A guide cautiously felt his way into the darkness and presently led the Intelligence Officer down some steps below the ground. At the foot of the steps hung a soaking blanket, behind which a light glimmered feebly. The Intelligence Officer cautiously pulled the blanket to one side, and blinked at the group inside. Two Commanding Officers and two Adjutants were talking. 'Handing over' was in process. The outgoing were clearly anxious to be gone; the incoming were anxious not to let them go without knowing what lay before them.

"A succession of officers and orderlies peered through the doorway, saluted and uttered the magic words, 'Relief complete, Sir,' and vanished into the outer darkness. Their strained expressions did not belie the full meaning of the sentence. The outgoing C.O. pushing back his chair with a scraping noise said, with a half-apologetic air, he would be off, and he and his satellites vanished. He had laid down his burden; the 4th Battalion had assumed it. His footsteps sounded light and care-free as they died away.

"All that night officers and men groped their way through mud and filth, visiting outposts, distributing rations, each bent on a mission involving the safety and comfort of the other. The Intelligence Officer felt that the atmosphere

CAMBRAI AND GOUZEAUCOURT 297

had changed. The Commanding Officer could have reclined on the German bed in the dug-out, his feet out of the six inches of liquid slush. Actually he spent his time going round the line, four hours of intense physical strain. Shells and bullets do not sound more pleasant because it is dark.

"The Transport Officer might have dumped the rations beyond the barrage and returned to the security of the horse-lines, and the warmth of his valise. As a matter of fact, he led his struggling animals up a broken, shattered road, through the barrage, round the trunks of fallen trees, and delivered his consignment at B.H.Q. The Adjutant might have said with reason that the ration parties had lost their way, that conditions were impossible, but the Intelligence Officer watched him supervise everything in person—in the open. Before dawn the front line was rationed—every post established, no chances taken. The Intelligence Officer saw it all and said : ' If this is war, some parts of it at least are good.'

"At dawn the next morning he arose and stood shivering in the cold mist. He visited his observation-post, and, watching trenches through his telescope as the sun slowly made its way through the haze, he smiled as he recognised well-known N.C.O.'s and men moving about in the nonchalant manner which all assume before the sniper starts his work, and when tired gunners take their rest. He knew that later he might search for hours and find no movement; all would be hiding in their shell-hole lairs.

CHAPTER XXVI.
4th Batt.
Nov.
1917.

"A distant hum reminding him of some gigantic insect, drew his attention from his work, and two aeroplanes appeared, flying very low. In a few minutes the moving figures vanished from the field of view of his telescope. The earth swallowed them up. Then commenced manœuvres that reminded him of sparrow-hawks quartering their haunting ground for prey. The droning insects flew back and forth. No movement was visible on the ground. A hooded head looked over the fuselage of each machine. The Iron Cross showed clearly on the wings. Then warning lights were dropped from each machine. Each light marked the position of a trench and seemed to say, 'Eat, drink, and be merry, for soon you will die.' The whole proceeding revolted the men watching from the O.P. They knew the full intent of it. Their imagination heard the scream of the shells which would surely fall where the lights had dropped. They felt for their friends out there. Discovered by their enemies, the hiding men used their weapons viciously. The rattle of machine-guns and rifles was mixed with the drone of the aeroplanes. The pilots knew their work was done. They turned to fly. One of them staggered in his course. The Intelligence Officer watched the machine crash in flames in a distant forest. The hiding men in their shell-holes sat down to wait for the punishment that they knew must come. The Intelligence men watched great spouts of earth rise skywards and listened to the rending crash that came slowly across the intervening space. They longed to help; instead they noted the time and place and entered the information in their Intelligence report.

"Zero was set for 5 A.M., this time a zero that concerned the 4th Battalion alone. The Commanding Officer and the Intelligence Officer moved forward through the darkness to an advanced position at three o'clock in the morning. Here the nerve centre of the 4th Battalion was established. Here would enter the news of battle. The Intelligence Officer established himself in a corner of the new dug-out. His carrier-pigeons made little noises to themselves, while the telephone operators tested and re-tested their lines. The Intelligence Officer's hand kept wandering to his watch. The Commanding Officer snored. His plans had been truly laid; interference now would be fatal. He was a well-trained soldier, and he slept.

"Five minutes before zero the Intelligence Officer woke the Commanding Officer, and both waited for the well-known throb of innumerable guns. One of them at least thought of his friends waiting to follow up the moving death. What were those others, his enemies, doing? Did they realise what hell would break upon them? Did they suspect the impending stroke?

"The blow fell to the minute. The dug-out rocked. A sheet of flame lit up the sky. A thousand devils seemed to be forging a red-hot band on the earth as far as the eye could see. Their countless hammer-strokes were merged into one loud growling, rumbling noise. Gradually the ear became accustomed to the sound and detected the sharp crack of answering bullets

CHAPTER XXVI.
4th Batt.
Nov. 1917.

and the rattle of machine-gun fire. Dawn was breaking and eyes were strained to pierce the half-light. Minutes seemed like hours.

"The first messenger arrived at the nerve centre. He brought good news. Others followed. All reported success. The Intelligence Officer took out one of his pigeons, attached a message to its leg, and released it. He noticed how clumsy his handling of the bird had become. The pigeon circled once and flew straight as an arrow in the right direction. This was dramatic, exciting, the cream of war. Then came the sordid side.

"The enemy artillery awoke. Great shells came hurtling through the sky.

"The shelling grew less. The machine-gun fire died away. The enemy was accepting the new situation. We had won; he had lost. Both sides prepared to settle down where they found themselves, too tired to prolong the struggle.

"The Commanding Officer was satisfied with the position. Emerging cautiously from its shelter, the party moved back to the original Battalion Headquarters. As they passed the trenches and the scooped-out holes in which the supports sheltered, inquiries were made as to casualties, and brave words spoken to cheer the exhausted men. The Intelligence Officer, ruminating on death, saw many signs of it. The true value of the body in which for a short period resides the soul of man was brought home to him. Three men crouched in a trench. Two were cooking; some conversation was in progress. The third man sat by their side and took no part. He seemed by his attitude to be thinking deeply, immersed in the solution of a problem. His face was turned away. The attitude was one of puzzled thought.

"The Intelligence Officer made inquiries as to how they had fared. Two of the men looked up; they gave him a friendly smile and told him all they knew. The other sat with his head bent, still studying that inscrutable problem. The Intelligence Officer noticed with a start the colour of his ears, how wax-like in appearance; then he knew in a flash—the man was dead. His comrades did not even explain the fact. They seemed to realise that the figure by their side no longer counted, that the soul and personality were fled, that there was nothing dreadful in the husk that sat there and still seemed one of them. War had taught them what a small thing the body really is, what a matter of indifference whether it is smashed or not. They had learned one thing at least—the proportionate value of the body and the soul.

"That night the 4th Battalion handed over its burden to some one else. It was due to be relieved. The Chaplain had arrived to see to it that the brave dead had decent burial. When it was possible, the Grenadiers always carried down their dead, so that in the future, grouped together, they would stand as a memorial of the cause they fought for, and indicate plainly to future generations how Grenadiers could fight and die —a monument to the power of discipline, self-sacrifice, and pride of race."

No. 1 Company under Captain Sloane-Stanley, No. 3 under Lieutenant Nash, and No. 4 under Captain Paton, dug themselves in with entrenching tools along the Anneux chapel—Mœuvres road, while No. 2, under Captain Britten, was placed in Anneux chapel itself. The shelling was very violent, and all the roads, by which supplies and supports had to move, were accurately and persistently shelled. The Brigadier, Lord Henry Seymour, came along, quite unconcerned and not even wearing a helmet, to see how these companies were getting on, and told them they might have to move up later into Bourlon Wood. When it got dark snow began to fall, and it became bitterly cold. The position of a lent battalion is by no means an enviable one, and soon orders and counter-orders from different authorities succeeded each other with amazing rapidity. Finally definite orders were sent to the Battalion to take up a position in Bourlon Wood, and at the same time it was placed under the orders of the 186th Brigade. While this move was being carried out, Lieutenant Nash was wounded in the leg and sent back to the dressing-station. In order to keep in touch with the 186th Brigade, Second Lieutenant Tuckwell was sent to Graincourt to act as liaison-officer to General Bradford, V.C.

Bourlon Wood, which covers about 100 acres, might well have been a typical English covert, with its tall trees interspersed with undergrowth about eight feet high. The line to be held consisted of a road running north and south, parallel to the front line. The ground was soaking wet, and

CAMBRAI AND GOUZEAUCOURT 303

the men had to force their way through the dripping leaves and lie out in the wood with no protection of any kind. Digging through the stubborn soil and soaking undergrowth was no easy matter with light entrenching tools, but they soon produced some sort of cover. The Fortieth Division, however, had succeeded in its attack, and so there was nothing for the 4th Battalion to do but to remain in the wood where it was. In the evening, much to the satisfaction of every one, it reverted to the command of the Guards Division. Lieutenant Ingleby, the acting Quartermaster, arrived at Battalion Headquarters at 11 that night, having guided the transport up to Anneux chapel through intense shelling, and reported that Second Lieutenant N. A. Pearce, the transport officer, who had shown great determination and pluck in his efforts to bring all that was wanted up to the men in the trenches, had been killed by a shell. Major-General Feilding received the following message from Major-General Ponsonby :

CHAPTER XXVI.
4th Batt. Nov. 1917.

> I wish to express on behalf of my Division my sincere thanks for the support given us on the 24th and 25th by the Battalions of the Guards Division placed at my disposal for the defence of Bourlon Wood, namely the 2nd Battalion Scots Guards and 4th Battalion Grenadier Guards.
>
> I should like to bring to your notice particularly the 2nd Battalion Scots Guards, who throughout the period prevented the enemy from breaking through the right flank of the position, and assisted in repelling at least two of the enemy's counter-attacks. I enclose extracts from the report of the Brigadier-General commanding the 119th Infantry Brigade :

CHAPTER XXVI.
4th Batt.
Nov.
1917.

"The 2nd Battalion Scots Guards reinforced the firing line, which had become very thin, early in the morning of November 25, and remained in action until they came under the orders of the 186th Infantry Brigade on the night of 26-27th November. All ranks behaved with the utmost gallantry, and assisted to repel at least two German counter-attacks in addition to continual enemy pressure. They inspired all with great confidence.

"The 4th Battalion Grenadier Guards came under my command in the afternoon of the 25th inst. To reach a position of readiness it had to cross the open in artillery formation for a great distance under enemy observation, and were heavily shelled in so doing. The men were as steady as if on parade. To the above-mentioned units I wish to express my gratitude."

Nov. 26.

The next day passed quietly, and the company commanders were able to go in turn to Battalion Headquarters to have some rest. In the evening snow fell heavily, and the men had a cold and uncomfortable night. The 4th Battalion was again to be lent to another brigade, that of General Sergison-Brooke, who received orders to attack Fontaine. It was not actually wanted for the attack, but merely to form a defensive line, on which the assaulting waves could fall back in case of failure.

The enemy put down a heavy barrage on the whole line that night, and Lord Gort sent Captain Chapman to inquire from the 2nd Battalion Irish Guards what was happening, but it proved to be merely the outcome of nervousness on the part of the Germans, and no attack developed. The Battalion moved off at 5.30 A.M., to take up new positions facing east instead of north, at very short notice; and, as the night was very dark and wet and the enemy was so close, the advance into position required some care. In order to prevent any confusion in the jumping-off line, the Battalion was told to occupy a position immediately in rear of the line, and to move up in the line only when the attack had actually started.

ATTACK ON FONTAINE

In a drizzle of rain, and under an intense enemy barrage, the attack of Sergison-Brooke's Brigade started at 6.30 in the morning of the 27th. It reached its objective, but the cost was so great, that the survivors found it impossible to maintain the position they had so dearly gained, without reinforcements. So weak were the attacking battalions, that they were in danger of being overwhelmed by counter-attacks. While the 4th Battalion was waiting for orders about 10 A.M., the German counter-attacks began to develop, and fire from the left became very heavy. No. 2 Company under Captain Britten was sent off to secure the left flank of the Division, which seemed to be in a dangerously weak condition. As they came up Second Lieutenant Windeler was killed by a sniper, and Captain Britten himself was wounded in the arm by a rifle bullet. Soon afterwards Second Lieutenant Oliver, who was now in command of No. 3 Company, was severely wounded in the chest, arm, and foot, while going out to bring in a wounded Irish Guardsman. The casualties among other ranks were proportionately heavy.

CHAPTER XXVI.
4th Batt.
Nov. 1917.

A warning order arrived from Brigadier-General Sergison-Brooke at 10.30 A.M., preparing the Battalion to supply two companies for the support of the 3rd Battalion Grenadiers and 1st Battalion Coldstream, but it seemed doubtful whether a couple of companies, or even four, would be of any use in the circumstances. Captain Gerard, the Adjutant, reported that he had heard from Captain Paton that already the 2nd Guards Brigade was falling back to the original line.

Lord Gort went off at once with Captain Chapman to the headquarters of the 3rd Battalion, and discussed the new situation with Colonel Thorne. They decided that it would be inadvisable, in view of the enemy's strength, and the absence of any appreciable reserves on our side, to renew the attack, and so use up the 4th Battalion with small chance of success. Orders were accordingly issued for the original line now held by the 4th Battalion to become the line of resistance, under the command of Captain Paton and Captain Sloane-Stanley. That night the 4th Battalion was relieved, and returned to the Hindenburg line at Flesquières.

Nov. 28.

On the 28th it marched to Trescault, and pitched a camp on the open ground between the Trescault—Metz road and Havrincourt Wood. The enemy's aircraft left them no peace, and so the tents were struck the next morning, and pitched again in Havrincourt Wood. The undergrowth was thick, and the cutting of it took some time, but when the camp was finished it proved snug and sheltered.

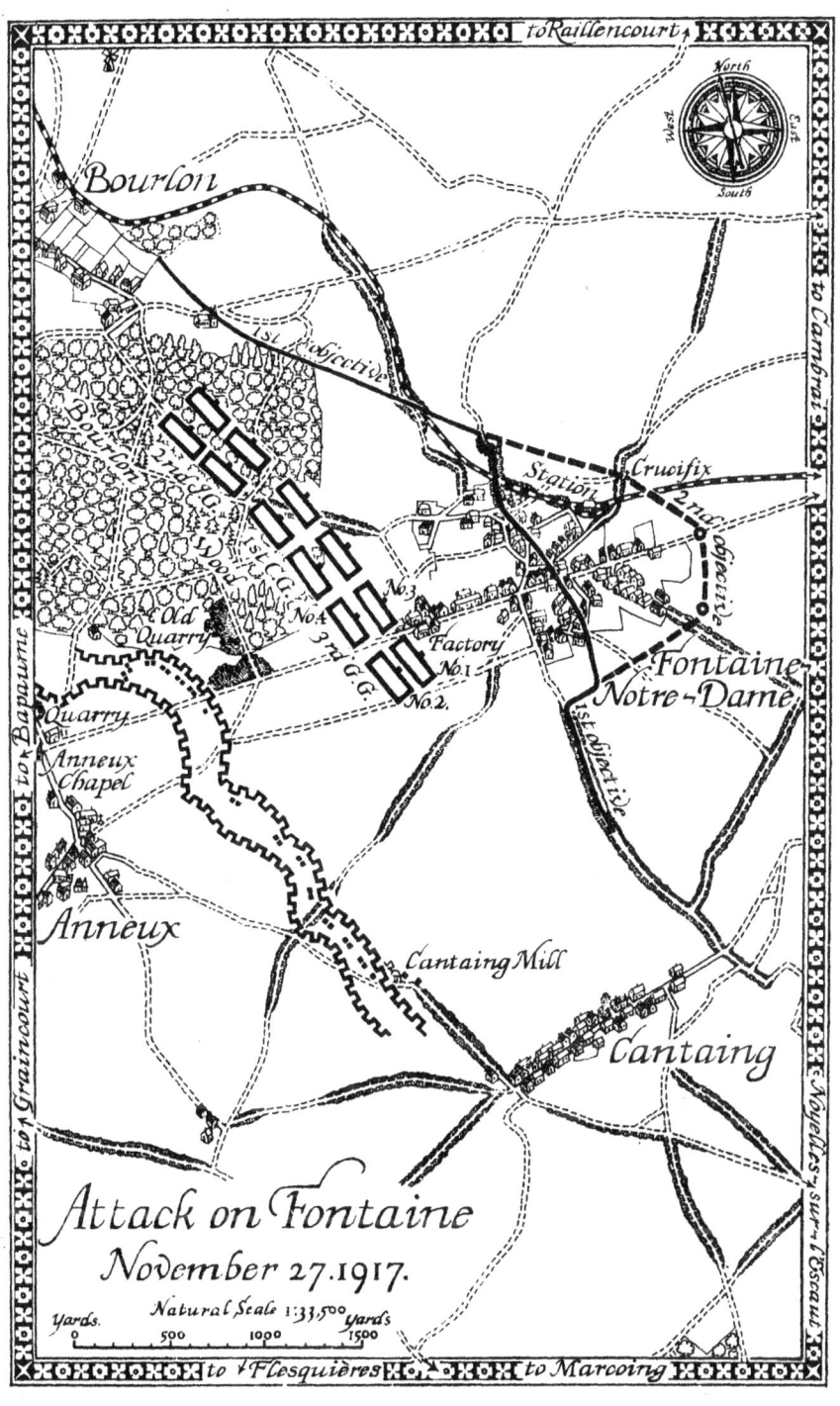

CAMBRAI AND GOUZEAUCOURT 307

The officers had just finished breakfast on the 30th, and were about to inspect their companies, when the news arrived that the Germans had broken through the line near Gonnelieu. It was said that the enemy had been seen marching in fours through Gouzeaucourt. Immediately orders were given for the Battalion to be ready to start at a moment's notice. Although the men had expected a quiet day, and were quite unprepared, so perfect were the organisation and discipline that in half an hour's time the Battalion was ready to move off.

Lord Gort's orders were to concentrate on Metz, and accordingly the Battalion moved off in that direction. The road was full of transport moving in the opposite direction, and with it ran a stream of men looking strangely unlike British soldiers, with no rifles or equipment—wounded and unwounded with incoherent stories, officers half-undressed, gunners with breech-blocks in their hands, all with a hunted look. Some high-explosive shells came streaming over, and pitched not far from the road. Lord Henry Seymour with his commanding officers rode on ahead to try and glean some information, while the four battalions of his Brigade marched through Metz, past the beetroot factory and on to the open ground beyond, where they lay down and waited.

Attack on Gonnelieu

About 2.30 P.M. the whole Brigade, in artillery formation, moved off in the direction of Gouzeaucourt, and in the meantime the attack of De

CHAPTER XXVI.
4th Batt.
Nov.
1917.

Crespigny's Brigade had been completely successful and required no reinforcements. The direction of the march was consequently slightly changed. The 4th Battalion crossed the Trescault—Gouzeaucourt road, where, thanks to Lieutenant Ingleby, the cookers arrived, and the men were provided with hot food. That night General Walker, commanding the 16th Brigade of the Sixth Division, held a conference at the 4th Battalion Headquarters. His object was to ensure that the 4th Battalion understood his scheme of attack, for if his brigade failed it would have to carry out his plan. The hurried manner in which the attack was planned, and the obviously scanty information on which the plan was based, seemed to indicate that it was not likely to succeed. At 1 A.M. a warning order was issued to the effect that Seymour's Brigade would assault Gonnelieu, if the attack of the 16th Brigade failed. Lord Gort thereupon wrote out his orders with the very meagre information at his disposal.

To have to select a definite objective after dark made things very difficult, since the final disposition depended upon the attack of the 16th Brigade, and whatever happened an indefinite front line would be the result. If the 16th Brigade succeeded, Seymour's Brigade would simply relieve it, but if it failed the attack would have to be attempted a second time. These considerations alone made it necessary to work out alternative schemes. Lord Henry Seymour fortunately prepared a detailed plan for the worst event, and fully realised that his Brigade

CAMBRAI AND GOUZEAUCOURT

was to be employed in a manner generally accepted as impossible, except in a great emergency, involving the advance of infantry, unsupported by artillery, across the open against an enemy occupying trenches, and houses bristling with machine-guns.

The following officers took part in the attack on Gonnelieu :

Lieut.-Colonel Viscount Gort, D.S.O., M.V.O., M.C.	Commanding Officer.
Major W. S. Pilcher, D.S.O.	2nd in Command.
Capt. C. R. Gerard	Adjutant.
Capt. M. Chapman	Intelligence Officer.
Capt. H. H. Sloane-Stanley	No. 1 Company.
Lieut. C. E. Irby	,, ,,
2nd Lieut. J. M. Chitty	,, ,,
2nd Lieut. B. J. Hubbard, M.C.	No. 2 Company.
2nd Lieut. R. C. Denman	,, ,,
2nd Lieut. D. E. A. Horne	,, ,,
Capt. J. B. M. Burke, M.C.	No. 3 Company.
Lieut. the Hon. A. H. L. Hardinge	,, ,,
Lieut. L. R. Abel-Smith	,, ,,
Capt. G. H. T. Paton, M.C.	No. 4 Company.
Lieut. B. C. Layton	,, ,,
2nd Lieut. J. J. M. Veitch	,, ,,

When the news of the failure of the 16th Brigade's attack reached Lord Gort, he at once started off with the Battalion, and crossed the Villers Plouich road. On reaching the railway the companies extended, and dug themselves in. There they waited in the dark for zero hour.

The order of battle for Seymour's Brigade was as follows : The 1st Battalion Welsh Guards on the right and the 4th Battalion Grenadiers on the left were to undertake the attack. The 1st Battalion Grenadiers was in support on the

Chapter XXVI.
4th Batt.
Nov. 1917.

310   THE GRENADIER GUARDS

CHAPTER XXVI.
4th Batt.
Nov. 1917.

left, and had to protect the left flank as the attack advanced, while the 2nd Battalion Scots Guards had already occupied the high ground about Villers Plouich. In the 4th Battalion No. 2 Company under Second Lieutenant Hubbard on the right and No. 3 under Captain Burke on the left formed the first line. No. 4 Company under Captain Paton was in support, and No. 1 under Captain Sloane-Stanley formed the reserve. Captain Chapman was sent forward to establish a forward Battalion Headquarters.

Dec. 1.

Without any artillery preparation the attack started at 6.30 A.M. It was still fairly dark, but the Germans could see enough to use their machine-guns with considerable accuracy. The line of advance was over open ground, up a gentle slope leading to Gonnelieu, and there was no cover or protection of any kind for the attackers. On came the leading companies of the 4th Battalion in perfect order. The men never wavered for an instant, though they knew that they were to be sacrificed to save the situation. They all understood that the rules of modern warfare were to be defied, and that instead of following a creeping barrage they were to advance across the open, with not even a preliminary bombardment. Though they knew this, they never faltered.

The enemy's machine-gun fire when it broke over them was terrible, like a driving hailstorm, but the pace was never checked for a moment. Especially on the right the fire was terrific, and No. 2 Company, which had gone rather too far in that direction, suffered heavy losses: one

CAMBRAI AND GOUZEAUCOURT 311

platoon was practically wiped out. Second Lieutenant Hubbard himself was killed, and Second Lieutenant Denman was mortally wounded, gallantly attempting to silence a German machine-gun, while Second Lieutenant Horne was also wounded. No. 3 Company under Captain Burke maintained its direction, and had few casualties until it came up close to the village. On reaching a road running in the direction of Vacquerie, it had to pause for a moment to allow No. 4 to come up before continuing its advance. Second Lieutenant Veitch had his thigh smashed by a bullet, and fell back into a shell-hole. Almost simultaneously a man shot through the head fell on the top of him, and being too weak to move the dying man, for twelve hours he remained in this cramped position.

The left of the line met with less resistance than the right, and so got far in advance. No. 3 Company dashed forward into the outskirts of Gonnelieu, but the village seemed almost impregnable against infantry unsupported by tanks or artillery. A small enclosure sheltered by ruined buildings was the only protected spot, the ground all round it was swept by machine-gun fire, and of course the shrubs and rank grass were no cover at all. Captain Burke dashed in on the left, and penetrated into the eastern outskirts of Gonnelieu, while Lieutenant Hardinge with a few men got round to the north of the village, and brought up a Lewis gun to a position in the cemetery. This had a most disconcerting effect on the enemy, for it threatened his right flank, and enfiladed the troops opposing Nos. 2 and 4 Companies.

The Germans quickly grasped the fact that this movement on Lieutenant Hardinge's part required immediate action. They managed to press back the troops on the left of the Brigade, with a view of enfilading the cemetery. With great ingenuity they worked round with their machine-guns, and soon Lieutenant Hardinge's position became untenable. All his men were killed or wounded with the exception of Sergeant Hull. Then the gun jammed. There was now nothing to be done but to get back as best he could, and being luckily only slightly wounded, he was able to make his way back, accompanied by Sergeant H. Hull.

Meanwhile Lieutenant L. Abel-Smith and Sergeant Williams went down a line of huts to the right, to see if an advance could be made in that direction, but were met with a withering fire from the right flank. With two platoons they therefore advanced a short distance down the centre of the village, but the enemy's machine-gun fire was so fierce that the ground over which they crawled was plastered with bullets. Some men, who were creeping along behind a wall, were killed by bullets which pierced the brickwork, and Lieutenant L. Abel-Smith himself was wounded.

This most gallant attempt on the part of No. 3 Company to capture the village resulted in such heavy losses that it was obvious it would have to retire. A German counter-attack as it was attempting to consolidate its position settled the matter. A certain number of men managed

CAMBRAI AND GOUZEAUCOURT 313

to get back, but most of them were killed or taken prisoners, including Captain Burke himself, who died fighting to the last. The same fate befell Second Lieutenant Chitty, who, with a party of No. 1 Company, had succeeded in entering the village.

Captain Paton with No. 4 Company had the difficult task of deciding what he should do, on reaching the trench in front of Gonnelieu. No. 3 had gone on into the outskirts, and there was no sign of the Welsh Guards on his right. It was obvious that his best plan would be to hold the trench until the others came up into line, so that at least those who had gone on would have a strong supporting line to retire to. But there was a mixed medley of men on his left, who seemed to be wavering in the face of the counter-attack. Captain Paton thereupon leaped out of his trench, and ran across the open, with machine-gun bullets ploughing up the ground all round him. With almost reckless bravery he went from trench to trench in full sight of the German machine-gunners, encouraging these groups of men from various regiments. At first he seemed to have almost a charmed life, and his splendid example inspirited all who saw him. The situation was saved, and he fell soon afterwards mortally wounded. For this conspicuous act of gallantry he was posthumously awarded the Victoria Cross. Captain Gerard, the Adjutant, who came up to obtain information for Lord Gort, found that owing to Captain Paton's efforts the left flank was secure.

It was now clear that without considerable

CHAPTER XXVI.
4th Batt.
Dec. 1917.

reinforcements and unlimited sacrifices the village could not be taken. The enemy's machine-guns were too strong. The Germans were counter-attacking, and were able to overpower any parties that had gained a footing in the village. Only one of the fourteen tanks that had been expected appeared, and, although it was undoubtedly a great help to the Welsh Guards, it was quite inadequate by itself. The Brigade on the left and the Welsh Guards on the right had been held up, so that even had the Battalion taken the village they would not have been able to hold it. A German officer captured that day stated that his battalion had attacked from behind Gonnelieu at 6 A.M., and as our attack started at 6.30 they had been completely disorganised by our advance, which they imagined was a counter-attack delivered with amazing rapidity.

Captain Sloane-Stanley, who had come up with No. 1 Company, determined to consolidate the trench immediately in front of Gonnelieu, so that it might be held with what remained of the attacking Companies. Lieutenant Irby of the same Company held a block in the trench against persistent bombing attacks, and eventually knocked out a German machine-gun by counter-bombing. Lord Gort himself now came up to see exactly how matters stood, and walked about, as he always did on such occasions, with an absolute disregard for all danger. It was not long, however, before he was severely wounded; the only wonder was that he had not been hit before. There were many acts of individual bravery, and perhaps the gallantry displayed by Sergeants

Canham and Buckle was one of the most conspicuous. At one time, when the enemy were advancing dangerously near our line, these two sergeants left their trench, and charged. The Germans, imagining that these two were only the foremost of a large party, fled in confusion.

Major Pilcher, who now assumed command of the 4th Battalion, was confronted with a very difficult situation. The sadly depleted ranks of the Battalion were holding the trench in front of Gonnelieu, and there were only three officers left —Captain H. Sloane-Stanley, Lieutenant Layton, and Lieutenant Irby. The tactical position was hazardous in the extreme, for both flanks were in the air and dangerously large gaps in the line seemed to invite a German attack. When the troops on the left retired, Major Pilcher called on the 1st Battalion Grenadiers to send up one Company to his assistance, and Captain Rhodes was sent to form a defensive flank. Later, when further assistance was required, two more Companies under Captain Spence and Captain Lawford advanced down the sunken road, and prolonged the line to the left. This timely assistance undoubtedly saved the left flank of the 4th Battalion, and enabled it to maintain its position.

The line now formed a salient in front of Gonnelieu; the apex being held by the 4th Battalion with some men of the Northants Labour Battalion. On the left was the 1st Battalion Grenadiers, which formed a defensive flank, while the Welsh Guards écheloned back to the right. This position was maintained until December 3, when the 4th Battalion was relieved by the 2nd Battalion Scots Guards, which latter had been due the night before. Owing to the delay the already exhausted officers and men had to spend a further twenty-four hours in the trenches, exposed to a hard frost. It was only through almost superhuman efforts that they received their rations on the morning of the 2nd, as the failure to relieve them had upset all arrangements for supply.

On the night of the 3rd they marched back, and bivouacked in the open on some ground north of Gouzeaucourt Wood, where they remained ready, in case their services should be required.

When the Guards Division left the area of operations near Gouzeaucourt, the 4th Battalion proceeded to Etricourt, where they entrained for Laherliere. Thence they marched to Gouy-en-Artois, and were placed in comfortable billets in a château. On December 11 they proceeded to Dainville, where they remained till the end of the month training. The weather became very cold and misty, and later there was a good deal of snow. On the 23rd the following officers joined the Battalion: Lieutenant F. C. Lyon, the Hon. C. C. S. Rodney, Second Lieutenant B. R. Osborne, Second Lieutenant R. D. Richardson, and Second Lieutenant C. J. Dawson-Greene.

THE 1ST BATTALION

After the operations at Bixschoote in October, the 1st Battalion remained in billets at Zudroue, near Watten. During this period the following

CAMBRAI AND GOUZEAUCOURT 317

officers joined the Battalion: Lieutenant I. C. Gascoigne, Second Lieutenant D. B. Topham, Lieutenant R. D. Lawford, Second Lieutenant A. H. Forbes, Second Lieutenant C. Cruttenden, and Lieutenant H. G. Wiggins. Captain H. H. Castle, R.A.M.C., also arrived to take the place of Captain P. H. Wells, R.A.M.C. While the Battalion was at Zudroue, the Colonel of the Regiment, Field-Marshal H.R.H. the Duke of Connaught, paid them a visit.

On November 9 the move south began, and the 1st Battalion marched to Enquin-les-Mines, continuing its march on the following day to Fabain Palfart, and then on to Foolinricametz. Second Lieutenant S. J. Hargreaves joined from the base on the 15th. The march was continued on the 17th through Ivergny Pommier to Achiet-le-Petit, where the men had twenty-four hours' rest. The greatest secrecy was preserved, and no orders were issued to the Company Commanders till the last moment, though from the great concentration of troops it seemed clear that some big move was impending. The 1st Battalion was brought up in buses to Beaumetz-les-Cambrai, and from there it marched with the rest of Seymour's Brigade to Flesquières. Though two Battalions of the Brigade were sent up to support the Fortieth Division, which was taking Bourlon Wood, the 1st Battalion did not take part in these operations. On the night of the 27th the 1st Battalion Grenadiers and the 1st Battalion Welsh Guards, assisted by two Companies from the 2nd Battalion Coldstream Guards, relieved the 2nd Guards Brigade in the

CHAPTER XXVI.

1st Batt.
Nov.
1917.

front line. The following officers took part in these operations:

1st Batt.
Nov. 1917.

Lieut.-Colonel M. E. Makgill-Crichton-Maitland, D.S.O.	Commanding Officer.
Capt. L. G. Fisher-Rowe, M.C.	Second in Command.
Lieut. W. H. Lovell, M.C.	Acting Adjutant.
Lieut. L. de J. Harvard	King's Company.
Lieut. J. A. Lloyd	,, ,,
2nd Lieut. J. H. Frere	,, ,,
Capt. A. T. G. Rhodes	No. 2 Company.
2nd Lieut. L. G. Byng	,, ,,
2nd Lieut. E. G. Hawkesworth	,, ,,
2nd Lieut. W. U. Timmis	,, ,,
Capt. P. M. Spence, M.C.	No. 3 Company.
Lieut. H. G. Wiggins	,, ,,
Lieut. S. J. Hargreaves	,, ,,
2nd Lieut. C. Cruttenden	,, ,,
Capt. R. D. Lawford	No. 4 Company.
Lieut. the Hon. P. P. Cary	,, ,,
2nd Lieut. C. C. Mays	,, ,,
Lieut. N. G. Chamberlain	,, ,,
Capt. H. H. Castle, R.A.M.C.	Medical Officer.

Conditions were favourable for carrying out the relief, and the next day passed without incident, although the enemy continued to shell the valley south of Bourlon Wood. On the evening of the 28th the 3rd Guards Brigade, having been relieved by the Fifty-ninth Division, marched to the reserve trenches south-west of Ribecourt. Next day it proceeded to Havrincourt Wood. A camp was pitched, and to make way for the tents it was necessary to clear away the undergrowth, which so delayed matters that it was not till 10 P.M. that every one had settled down.

Nov. 30. Barely had the officers finished breakfast on

CAMBRAI AND GOUZEAUCOURT 319

the morning of the 30th, when rumours reached them that the Germans had broken through the line. At first no one believed this possible, and, as the camp was quite five miles from our front line, a further report that the Germans were not far off was received with incredulity. But soon small parties of men were seen coming over the hill, as well as gunners and horses without guns. By degrees these isolated parties became a mob, and the road was blocked by a torrent of transport and men. A few shells pitched not far from the camp, and confirmed the news of the approach of the Germans. At the same time there arrived a warning order to be ready to move at a moment's notice, and soon the whole camp was filled with bustle and excitement.

The first warning said that Seymour's Brigade was to be ready to take up a defensive position on the ridge of Havrincourt Wood. This was cancelled later, and the Brigade was told to concentrate at a point near Metz. As soon as the order was confirmed, the 1st Battalion moved off to join the rest of the Brigade on the Trescault—Metz road. The march was trying, as the road was blocked with traffic, all moving in the opposite direction. At some points the Brigade encountered as many as three limbers abreast. Sometimes, therefore, the troops had to go in single file through a mass of vehicles and men, and then to double so as to keep touch with those in front. Being on a hill, the road was clearly visible for miles, and the Germans soon started hammering it with high-explosive shells, which added to the general confusion. It requires a very highly disciplined force to move quickly against such a stream as this was, but the men never checked their pace for a moment. Spades and shovels were drawn in Metz, and the whole Brigade was soon ready to advance in artillery formation. The 1st Battalion followed the Welsh Guards across country in the direction of Gouzeaucourt and Villers Plouich. Brigadier-General Lord Henry Seymour rode on in front with his Staff.

Attack on Gonnelieu

The position taken up by the Brigade was just under the crest of the ridge, running north from Gouzeaucourt Wood, and the 1st Battalion bivouacked for the night within half a mile of the camp in Havrincourt Wood, where the stores and transport had remained. As the night was bitterly cold, one blanket per man and the officers' trench kits were fetched, and eventually, when the cookers came up, tea and porridge was given out to the men.

At 4 A.M., after the Company Commanders had returned from reconnoitring, orders were issued for the 1st Battalion to move by Companies in artillery formation, and take up a line on the railway between Gouzeaucourt on the right and Villers Plouich on the left. By 9 A.M. the Companies were in position: No. 2, under Captain Rhodes, on the right and in touch with the 4th Battalion Grenadiers; No. 3, under Captain Spence, in the centre; No. 4, under Captain Lawford, on the left; and the King's Company, under Lieutenant Harvard, in reserve.

CAMBRAI AND GOUZEAUCOURT 321

Both the railway and a sunken road which ran parallel with it were shelled incessantly by the enemy, while machine-gun bullets also swept down the line from the direction of Gonnelieu. The 4th Battalion Grenadiers and the 1st Battalion Welsh Guards were ordered to undertake the attack, while the 1st Battalion was to be in support, and guard the left flank as the advance progressed. At 6.20 A.M. the attack began, and a rather feeble bombardment was continued for ten minutes by three Brigades of R.F.A. Twenty-two tanks had been allotted to the Division, eight of which were to co-operate with Seymour's Brigade.

Lieut.-Colonel Maitland summoned the four Company Commanders to Battalion Headquarters, and they started off just as the Germans were putting down a heavy barrage on the railway. As they made their way along the embankment, shells were pitching among the men, and causing groups of casualties. As soon as any reinforcements were wanted, Captain Rhodes was to take his Company up the sunken road from Gouzeaucourt to Gonnelieu. No. 3 and No. 4 Companies were to advance across the open, so as to be near at hand when called upon. The Company Commanders scrambled back to their Companies, and explained the general idea to their Platoon Commanders as far as time would permit. It was a trying time for the men, who had to sit still as mere targets for the German gunners, and watch their comrades again and again being blown to pieces. They felt that even an advance under machine-gun fire would have been preferable.

As soon as the attack started, the 1st Battalion advanced under a hail of bullets, although there was no artillery fire, and many men fell at once. The 4th Battalion Grenadiers, which it supported, was at first so successful that it outstripped the troops on the left, and consequently had that flank in the air. Lord Henry Seymour sent orders to the 1st Battalion to secure the high ground to the north of Gonnelieu, hoping that by this means it would not only secure the left flank of the 4th Battalion, but also materially assist it to hold the village. The 1st Battalion had therefore to advance half left, and after going about 600 yards it was joined by men of various regiments.

Complete success attended the first part of the attack, and the three leading Companies, by a free use of the bayonet, captured the first German trench they reached. It was then necessary to "mop up," and clear all possible hiding-places where any Germans might be lurking. Apparently the enemy had been taken unawares, and there were traces everywhere of surprise and precipitate flight. One German officer was caught while changing his clothes, and had nothing on but a shirt. The men stood up, and fired their rifles from the shoulder at the retreating Germans, and the Lewis gunners did their work well. A large number of the enemy were killed, and 110 prisoners were taken. No. 3 Company, under Captain Spence, was on the right, in touch with the 4th Battalion, and No. 4, under Captain

CAMBRAI AND GOUZEAUCOURT 323

Lawford, on the left, in touch with the 2nd Battalion Scots Guards. No. 2, under Captain Rhodes, in the centre, had the most difficult task, as it had continually to swing round to keep up with the Companies on either flank.

Having succeeded so well with the first trench, the 1st Battalion continued its advance until it arrived at a well-wired trench north of Gonnelieu. The three leading Companies managed to get through gaps in the wire, and push on, but when they topped the ridge they were met with a terrific machine-gun fire, which staggered them, and caused many casualties. It seemed madness to advance in the open against well-posted machine-guns, and orders were therefore given to withdraw to the trench they had already gained. In the meantime five tanks were seen advancing up to the ridge south of Gonnelieu; three of them were put out of action before they reached the village, and none were able to enter the village itself. Captain Spence, finding that his Company had run short of ammunition, sent back a small party to fetch some from Battalion Headquarters.

During the last advance Lieutenant Chamberlain, who had gone on too far, had been either cut off or killed, and half of No. 2 Company, having gone astray, was nowhere to be seen. The whole line in fact had been bent to a semicircle, and needed reorganising. Lieutenant Wiggins was sent by Captain Spence to get touch with No. 2, which should have been on his right, and, after hunting about for some time, reported that he could find no trace of this half-

Company. At the same time Second Lieutenant Cruttenden went off to find Lieutenant Chamberlain, and after a fruitless search was shot through the lungs by a sniper. By degrees every one got into his right place, and the missing half of No. 2 Company was retrieved by Captain Rhodes.

As soon as it became dark, began the difficult task of collecting the wounded and getting them down to the dressing-station. The stretcher-bearers worked indefatigably all night, and were assisted by any men who could be spared. Another search-party, under Sergeant Porter, went out to find Lieutenant Chamberlain, but was no more successful than the first.

Next day the Battalion remained in the same position, but two platoons were sent off to reinforce the line held by the 4th Battalion. That night the 1st Battalion was relieved, partly by the 2nd Battalion Scots Guards, and partly by a battalion of the 183rd Brigade, and was sent off to relieve the Welsh Guards. As the 2nd Battalion Scots Guards did not arrive till dawn, Nos. 3 and 4 Companies had to hold on all night. There was a rumour that Seymour's Brigade would continue the attack on Gonnelieu the next day, but nothing came of it. On December 3 the whole position was severely shelled, and there were several casualties, including Lieutenant Bevan, who was wounded.

In the evening the Battalion was relieved, and retired to Gouzeaucourt, where it remained in reserve. On the 6th it moved to Etricourt, where Second Lieutenant F. H. Ennor and Second Lieutenant R. C. Bruce arrived, and on the 11th

CAMBRAI AND GOUZEAUCOURT 325

it retired to Arras, where it remained till the end of the month. Second Lieutenant A. Forbes and Second Lieutenant V. A. N. Wall rejoined from the Reinforcement Battalion on the 16th.

THE 2ND BATTALION

For the rest of October the 2nd Battalion remained at Tournehem in the area between St. Omer and Calais, carrying out training of all kinds. Lieutenant O. Martin Smith and Lieutenant S. T. S. Clarke arrived on the 18th.

On November 11 the Battalion with the rest of De Crespigny's Brigade started their march south, through Herbelle, Lairs, and La Thieulloye. A Divisional Reinforcement Battalion was now formed. This was a new idea, which had gradually come to be adopted, whenever an attack was impending, and which had been rendered necessary by the large numbers of all ranks who were left behind whenever offensive operations were undertaken. Companies at that time neither attacked nor went into the line with a greater average strength than 32 other ranks per platoon and 3 officers per Company, and the Reinforcement Battalion was designed to take charge of the remainder. Though some such scheme was doubtless necessary, its application inevitably proved chaotic, for a hurriedly improvised Battalion Staff administered by the A. and Q. branches, who were themselves always at their busiest time, when the Reinforcement Battalion came into existence, hardly made an ideal administrative machine.

CHAPTER XXVI.
2nd Batt.
Nov. 1917.

From the Battalion point of view the result was desperate. All ranks returning from leave were usually detained at the Reinforcement Battalion, so that it was never known from day to day what officers, N.C.O.'s, and men would be available for duty, nor was it possible to obtain appropriate substitutes to fill deficiencies caused by sickness.

On the 13th there was a Divisional Conference, which was attended by the Brigadiers and Commanding Officers, when Major-General Fielding outlined the future operations. After four days spent at La Thieulloye the Battalion marched to Manin, and on the 18th went into camp between Blaireville and Hendecourt. There the Commanding Officer held a conference, at which he explained the scope and intention of the forthcoming operations. On the 19th the Battalion marched by night from Blaireville, through Hamelincourt and Ervillers, to a tented camp at Gomiecourt. A full moon lit the road, and the Battalion was in great spirits, all the companies singing on the march, and all ranks feeling the suppressed excitement which precedes an attack. The road passed through an area which the Battalion was to know very well four months later, when it was called upon to stem the German onslaught.

After two nights in this camp the Battalion proceeded in buses to huts near Barastre, where it was quartered in very comfortable billets. It was nearly dawn by the time the troops settled down, as the journey had been slow and laborious owing to the congestion on the roads, which, though

CAMBRAI AND GOUZEAUCOURT 327

deserted by day, were crowded with men and vehicles from dark to dawn.

November 23rd was one of the most remarkable days in the Battalion's experience. Starting from camp near Barastre in the dark at 5.30 A.M., it marched through Velu to a field on the western outskirts of Doignies, which was reached about 9.30 A.M. Here the men drew bivouac-sheets, and set to work to make provision for the night, having been told that no move would be undertaken that day, whilst the Commanding Officer and most of the Company Commanders went out to reconnoitre various routes. Early in the afternoon an order was received that the Battalion would be required to move at short notice, and that it would relieve a Battalion in the line that night. Marching orders were issued, and bivouac-sheets returned. Shortly after 7 P.M. an order was received that the Battalion was to march off immediately; it was not known what Battalion was to be relieved, nor where it was, but it was said that definite orders would be received at the Canal du Nord. General de Crespigny had gone off to reconnoitre the forward area, and had not returned.

The whole of De Crespigny's Brigade and part of Seymour's Brigade were found to be on the same track, and as it was already congested by the passage in both directions of ammunition limbers, ambulances, and traffic of every description, progress was slow and wearisome. During the course of the march, the Lewis-gun limbers, which had started with the Battalion, but had become slightly separated in the press of the traffic, were diverted by a Staff Officer. The Battalion Headquarters were not informed of this, and consequently it was not until some time after their departure that the absence of the guns became known. On reaching the Canal crossing at Lock 7 the Battalion halted, and the men fell out on the side of the road to snatch a few minutes' sleep, while Captain A. Penn, the Adjutant, rode forward to meet Lieutenant-Colonel Follett, who was commanding the Brigade in the temporary absence of General de Crespigny. From Colonel Follett it was learnt that the Brigade to be relieved was in the neighbourhood of Cantaing. Lieut.-Colonel Rasch thereupon rode forward to find the outgoing Battalion, to arrange for guides, and to borrow Lewis guns, while the Battalion wearily followed the road through Graincourt. The men who were not required to take part in the operations were diverted from the main body, and sent off under Lieutenant Drummond and Lieutenant Layland-Barratt, to find their way to Ribecourt. The march was undisturbed, and the night quiet, save on the hill crowned by Bourlon Wood, which all night was intermittently shelled.

Near Brigade Headquarters at La Justice Farm, north of Orival Wood, the Battalion met guides from the 9th Battalion Royal Scots (152nd Brigade), which was holding the first line on the eastern outskirts of Cantaing. Thanks to the admirable arrangements made by this Battalion, which had been heavily engaged for some days past, the remainder of the relief passed off without difficulty. Just before daylight the

CAMBRAI AND GOUZEAUCOURT

Battalion completed a relief, which the Royal Scots at any rate believed to be impossible of achievement, in view of the demands it made on the endurance of the men, who had been on the move almost unceasingly for twenty-four hours.

Chapter XXVI.
2nd Batt. Nov. 1917.

When once the relief was complete, the tour passed without incident, except that Lieutenant Alexander was wounded in the hand, whilst throwing from the slit he was occupying an enemy grenade, which had fallen unexploded among his men.

No. 2 Company was on the right, stretching towards Bois Neuf, and in touch with the 8th Battalion Bedfordshire Regiment; No. 4 on the left held a line of posts just east of the Cantaing—Fontaine road, facing La Folie Wood, and in touch with the 1st Battalion Irish Guards, which stretched towards Bourlon Wood; No. 1 was in support, and No. 3 in reserve. Everywhere there were signs of the rapidity with which the British attack had swept the enemy from his trenches, and derelict and charred tanks, scattered in all directions, bore evidence of the stubborn resistance with which our advance had been met. The country was open and undulating, and the spires of Cambrai were distinctly visible in the clear wintry light. On the 26th the Battalion was relieved, and marched back in a blinding snowstorm to Ribecourt, passing the Battalions of the 2nd Guards Brigade, on their way to carry out the attack on Fontaine-Notre-Dame. The night spent at Ribecourt was one of the most miserable passed by the Battalion. Soaked by the snowstorm, through which they had marched from Cantaing, and sodden with mud from the line, the men, whose blankets and greatcoats had been stored when the advance began, found no accommodation but a few leaky shelters in the Hindenburg Line. All the dug-outs with any possibilities of comfort had already been occupied by the swarm of troops following the advance. In the afternoon of the 28th, orders were received to march to billets in Metz, and thither the Battalion went in the evening, finding on its arrival rather cramped but quite comfortable quarters.

The Capture of Gouzeaucourt

At daybreak on 30th November the sound of a heavy bombardment on a wide front made it clear that the enemy was undertaking a counter-attack. At the same time a long-range gun began to drop shells into Metz, where the Battalion was resting, causing casualties to the troops billeted there. The village street was quickly choked with a miscellaneous rabble of soldiers of every kind, all streaming back in hopeless confusion, and spreading rumours of a break-through by the enemy. Soon after 9 A.M. a message was received from General de Crespigny that the Third Corps was being heavily attacked at Gonnelieu, about four miles away, and ordering the Battalion to move at short notice. At 10.30 Lieut.-Colonel Rasch was told to march the Battalion towards Gouzeaucourt, and to clear Metz by 12.25 P.M. He handed over the command of the Battalion to Captain Harcourt-Vernon, and

CAMBRAI AND GOUZEAUCOURT

rode off to the Brigade Headquarters to get as much information as possible.

The following officers took part in these operations:

Lieut.-Colonel G. E. C. Rasch, D.S.O.	Commanding Officer.
Capt. G. C. FitzH. Harcourt-Vernon	Second in Command.
Capt. A. H. Penn	Adjutant.
Lieut. J. C. Cornforth, M.C.	No. 1 Company.
2nd Lieut. P. A. A. Harbord, M.C.	,, ,,
2nd Lieut. S. H. Pearson	,, ,,
Lieut. F. A. M. Browning	No. 2 Company.
Lieut. F. H. G. Layland-Barratt, M.C.	,, ,,
2nd Lieut. F. H. J. Drummond, M.C.	,, ,,
Lieut. A. W. Acland, M.C.	No. 3 Company.
Lieut. F. A. Magnay	,, ,,
Lieut. R. Y. T. Kendal	,, ,,
Lieut. G. R. Westmacott	No. 4 Company.
Lieut. W. H. S. Dent	,, ,,
Lieut. F. P. Loftus	,, ,,
Capt. J. A. Andrews, M.C.	Medical Officer.

Half a mile from Metz, Lieut.-Colonel Rasch and the Company Commanders, who had preceded the Battalion, rejoined, with the news that De Crespigny's Brigade was to advance immediately towards Gouzeaucourt, which was reported to be in the hands of the Germans: the 1st Battalion Irish Guards on the north of the Gouzeaucourt—Metz road, the 3rd Battalion Coldstream in the centre, and the 2nd Battalion Coldstream on the right; the 2nd Battalion Grenadiers in Brigade support.

The whole countryside was by this time dotted with men retiring, and the A.P.M. at the Metz cross-roads was busily engaged in dealing with stragglers; throughout the advance of the

332 THE GRENADIER GUARDS

CHAPTER XXVI.
2nd Batt.
Nov. 1917.

Brigade no trace was seen of any defending infantry. On clearing the village, the Battalion assumed artillery formation, and advanced to Gouzeaucourt Wood, a low scrubby plantation crowning the ridge which bisects the ground lying between Metz and Gouzeaucourt. Here the Battalion waited full of anxious curiosity. Shelling caused a few casualties, but the protection of the rising ground sheltered it from the rifle and machine-gun fire, directed at the leading battalions, which were now advancing towards Gouzeaucourt village. The capture of Gouzeaucourt was a fine achievement carried out with wonderful precision. So successful was it that the Battalion was never required: by nightfall the village had been completely cleared of the enemy, and all British stores had been recovered. When it was known that the Battalion was not likely to be called upon until the next day, cookers were brought up, and provision for the cold night was made as far as possible.

CAPTURE OF GAUCHE WOOD

Dec. 1.

At 2.30 A.M. General de Crespigny received orders to attack and capture Gauche Wood, in co-operation with Seymour's Brigade on the left, and the cavalry on the right. The objective of the Battalion was the eastern edge of Gauche Wood, and the 3rd Battalion Coldstream was to be on the left. This wood was oblong in shape, and measured approximately 700 by 300 yards; its nearest corner was about 1200 yards from the line which the Brigade had taken up the

CAMBRAI AND GOUZEAUCOURT 333

CHAPTER XXVI.
2nd Batt.
Dec. 1917.

night before. Orders were written and explained to the Company Commanders. The Battalion was to form up behind a sunken road on the eastern outskirts of Gouzeaucourt village, which then constituted the front line. Twenty tanks were allotted to the Brigade, but as there seemed grave doubt as to whether they would be able to reach their rendezvous at so short notice, companies were ordered not to wait for them.

In the 2nd Battalion the attack was undertaken by No. 1 Company under Lieutenant Cornforth on the right, and No. 3 under Lieutenant Acland on the left, each in two lines of two platoons, followed at a distance of 250 yards by No. 4 under Lieutenant Westmacott, and No. 2 under Lieutenant Browning, in similar formation. Lieut.-Colonel Rasch went on ahead with the Company Commanders to reconnoitre the forming-up ground, whilst the Battalion followed after breakfast, and picked up tools on the way. At 6.30 the artillery support, which was most attenuated, opened and searched the wood and the ravine behind it. No tanks had yet put in an appearance, and, after giving them ten minutes' grace, the attack was launched without them.

The enemy retaliated with a heavy barrage, most of which fortunately fell behind the advancing troops, but the machine-gun fire made it doubtful whether any one would ever reach the wood. When the attack opened, all four companies advanced at a great pace over the intervening grass land, which rose in a gentle slope up to the wood. It is difficult to understand why,

Chapter XXVI.
2nd Batt.
Dec. 1917.

with the machine-guns posted at the edge of the wood, the enemy did not wipe out the whole Battalion. Ignoring all regulations about short rushes, both officers and men went straight for the wood as fast as they could. They instinctively felt that the only chance was to cover the mile of naked slope in the shortest possible time. In all probability the German machine-gunners in the half-light of the morning became flurried, at seeing this formidable attack sweeping over the ground, for, although the fire was very hot, the bullets passed over the men's heads, and it was not until they had nearly reached the wood that casualties occurred. Here the fringe of German machine-guns, established at the edge of the wood, began to take heavy toll, and then began perhaps the fiercest fighting of all. When the leading companies reached the wood, it became a struggle of man to man. But the Germans soon found that with the bayonet they were no match for the Grenadiers. Back into the wood they were forced, and then down into a hollow in the centre of it. Their machine-guns were all captured, and, although some fought stubbornly, most of them were driven slowly up the incline on the far side into the corner of the wood. Second Lieutenant Pearson was killed as he went through the wood, and Second Lieutenant Harbord, whilst most gallantly rushing a machine-gun, received wounds from which he died later in the day. Lieutenants Cornforth, Drummond, Dent, Kendal, Acland, and Magnay were all wounded, and the Battalion lost many valuable N.C.O.'s.

CAMBRAI AND GOUZEAUCOURT 335

This left Lieutenant Browning and Lieutenant Westmacott responsible for the whole Battalion front, and to them the success of the attack was largely due. Between them they reorganised and controlled the whole line, making their dispositions with great skill. On reaching the wood, Lieutenant Westmacott faced part of his company to the right flank, to guard against a counter-attack from the south. Hardly had he done so when about seventy Germans appeared; they were met with steady rifle-fire from the wood, and wavered for a moment, uncertain as to what they should do, but they finally made for the wood. Our fire, however, was too steady for them, and accounted for all but a handful of men, who were taken prisoners. Soon afterwards another party of sixty appeared from the same direction, but they also were met with so well-directed a fire that they were staggered, whereupon the men of No. 4 Company charged them with the bayonet.

Lieutenant Westmacott now decided that he must push his men farther forward on the right flank of the wood, so as to command the valley, which lay between the wood and the village of Villers Guislain. He had just moved forward his company, and prolonged the right with two platoons of No. 2 Company, when some dismounted cavalry, consisting of the 18th Bengal Lancers and a detachment of the 7th Dragoon Guards, appeared from the same direction as the enemy attacks. Their orders had not enabled them to attack simultaneously with the 2nd Battalion, and it was in all probability this delayed advance that precipitated the two unfruitful attempts of the enemy to gain the wood. Their arrival was of the greatest value, and at Lieutenant Westmacott's suggestion they proceeded to reinforce the other companies, which were meanwhile fighting their way through the wood. Several tanks had by now put in an appearance, although the majority had been knocked out before they reached the wood, by a most accurate shell-fire directed by a low-flying aeroplane. The lack of any particular trench for the surviving tanks to attack made their fire ineffectual, and their presence seemed to attract the shells of all the German batteries in the neighbourhood, causing many casualties in the Battalion.

Lieutenant Layland-Barratt, who had been assisting Lieutenant Browning to reorganise the companies in the wood, was wounded by a splinter of a shell, and had to retire to a dressing-station. This left only Lieutenant Browning in the wood, and Lieutenant Westmacott and Lieutenant Loftus outside.

Lieut.-Colonel Rasch went up to the line, and organised a readjustment of the companies. Lieut.-Colonel E. C. Corbyn, commanding the 18th Bengal Lancers, was asked to withdraw his men to the centre of the wood so as to form a reserve, and dig a support line on some commanding ground in the wood. The dash and fighting spirit of all ranks of this regiment, and the help and experience which Colonel Corbyn gave at that critical moment, made the greatest impression on the Battalion, and enabled the Grenadiers to realise how great a loss his regiment suffered, when he was killed by a shell later in the afternoon.

In a letter describing this attack an officer of the 18th Bengal Lancers wrote:

We then occupied the captured trench sandwiched in between the Grenadiers and Coldstream. . . . I have now seen His Majesty's Guards in action and fought alongside of them, and I take off my hat to them. They can die like gentlemen, without a groan. Four of our men were carrying a Guardsman who appeared to be suffering considerably. I asked him who he was, and he instinctively straightened himself as best he could and said, " A Grenadier," his tone implying how proud he was to be one, and, what I also thought, " how magnificent they were."

The comradeship between the two regiments was later marked by the presentation of a Grenadier Bugle, with an inscription, which the Battalion gave to the 18th Bengal Lancers. Subsequently the Lancers presented the 2nd Battalion with a silver statuette of a mounted Bengal Lancer, on the plinth of which was the following inscription: "To Lieut.-Colonel G. E. C. Rasch, D.S.O., and Officers of the 2nd Battalion Grenadier Guards, as a memento of Gauche Wood."

On the return of Lieut.-Colonel Rasch, Captain Harcourt-Vernon went up to the line, taking with him some ammunition and also a company of the 2nd Battalion Coldstream, under Captain H. Brierley, M.C., which had been sent to prolong the right flank, still dangerously in the air. In the afternoon a party of Strathcona's Horse began an attack, and made very little headway. Half a squadron came into the wood, but was withdrawn later to link up the right of the Brigade line with the remainder of Strathcona's Horse.

338 THE GRENADIER GUARDS

Chapter XXVI.
2nd Batt.
Dec. 1917.

Shelling continued almost without cessation during the rest of the day, but no further enemy action developed, and about 10 P.M., in heavy rain, the Battalion began to be relieved by the Deccan and Poona Horse and one company of the 3rd Battalion Grenadiers, under Captain Ridley, and marched back to bivouacs in Gouzeaucourt Wood. There it remained until December 5, when the Guards Division was relieved, and retired out of the area of operations. The casualties in the Battalion were 153 killed, wounded, and missing; among the twelve Company Officers who went into action, one was killed, one died of wounds, and seven were wounded. The percentage of N.C.O.'s killed was also very high, including many first-rate sergeants. Three field-guns and twelve machine-guns, in addition to many prisoners, were captured in this attack. The Battalion proceeded by train to Beaumetz, and went into billets at Berneville, where it remained until the end of the month.

The following officers joined during December: Second Lieutenant F. J. Langley, Lieutenant G. B. Wilson, Second Lieutenant R. T. Sharpe, Second Lieutenant C. C. T. Giles, and Second Lieutenant S. C. K. George.

The 3rd Battalion

3rd Batt.

During the last ten days of October and the first week of November, the 3rd Battalion was in good billets at Moule. During that time, Lieutenant G. W. Godman, Second Lieutenant G. H. R. Hoare, and Second Lieutenant E. C. Long

CAMBRAI AND GOUZEAUCOURT

arrived. On the 21st the Battalion was inspected by the Duke of Connaught, and lined both sides of the Calais—St. Omer road. On the 25th the whole Guards Division was inspected by the Commander-in-Chief, Field-Marshal Sir Douglas Haig.

On November 10 the march south began, and the 3rd Battalion proceeded to Enquingatte. On the following days it marched through Heuchin, Hernicourt, Houvin, Bailleulval, Courcelles-le-Comte, Beulencourt, and Le Bacquiere to Ribecourt, which it reached after a fortnight's hard marching. There the men had twenty-four hours' rest, during which they managed to collect a considerable amount of salvage, and on the 26th they quietly took over the line, round the south-east edge of Bourlon Wood, opposite the village of Fontaine-Notre-Dame, from the 3rd Battalion Coldstream. That evening Sergison-Brooke's Brigade received orders to attack a front, extending from the village of Fontaine-Notre-Dame to a point about 1000 yards east of the centre of Bourlon village—that is to say, a front of about 3500 yards. The intention to attack Fontaine was only decided upon at the last moment after much discussion, and even General Sergison-Brooke himself knew nothing of it till the afternoon of the 26th. The orders reached the 3rd Battalion only as it was on its way up to relieve the 3rd Battalion Coldstream.

ATTACK ON FONTAINE

The first objective, which was to be the main line of resistance, ran through the road junction at the east end of Fontaine to the northern edge of Bourlon Wood. The second objective was the station and the eastern outskirts of Fontaine, which was to become the outpost line. The 3rd Battalion Grenadiers was to be on the right, the 1st Battalion Coldstream in the centre, and the 2nd Battalion Irish Guards on the left. The first objective of the 3rd Battalion was half-way through the village, including the church on the right, after which it was to push its outposts on to the road leading from Fontaine to La Folie Wood.

As soon as Colonel Thorne received his orders, he rode off, and collected the Company Commanders, as the Battalion was moving through Flesquières. Detailed orders were dictated, and the maps were carefully marked. Two hours later the Company Commanders overtook their companies, and the relief began. No. 1 and No. 3 Companies, under Lieutenant Bowes-Lyon and Second Lieutenant G. Hoare, were to form the first line, with No. 2 and No. 4, under Captain Beaumont-Nesbitt and Captain Hughes, in support.

The following officers took part in the attack:

Lieut.-Colonel A. F. A. N. Thorne,
    D.S.O. . . . . . Commanding Officer.
Capt. E. D. Ridley, M.C. . . Second in Command.
2nd Lieut. C. C. Carstairs . . Intelligence Officer.
Lieut. G. P. Bowes-Lyon . . No. 1 Company.
2nd Lieut. H. St. C. Cooper . . ,, ,,
2nd Lieut. E. C. Long . . . ,, ,,
Capt. W. H. Beaumont-Nesbitt, M.C. No. 2 Company.
Lieut. J. F. Worsley . . . ,, ,,
2nd Lieut. C. B. Hollins . . ,, ,,

2nd Lieut. G. H. R. Hoare	. No. 3 Company.	
2nd Lieut. A. C. Knollys	. ,, ,,	
2nd Lieut. W. B. Ball	. ,, ,,	
Capt. J. S. Hughes	. No. 4 Company.	
2nd Lieut. C. W. Carrington	. ,, ,,	
2nd Lieut. Sir J. L. Hanham, Bart.	,, ,,	
Lieut. H. Dearden, R.A.M.C.	. Medical Officer.	
Capt. the Rev: S. Phillimore	. Chaplain.	

The night was bitterly cold, with snow and sleet soon after midnight. At 5.30 A.M. Colonel Thorne, accompanied by the Intelligence Officer, Lieutenant Carstairs, went round the line and found all the companies ready for the attack, which started at 6.20, after a very short and light artillery preparation. It was practically dark, and as the sleet had turned to a steady drizzle of rain it was difficult to see more than a few yards ahead. The tanks were late, but it was decided not to wait for them, and the signal to advance was given. Directly the 3rd Battalion left its trenches, it was met by a heavy machine-gun fire from a small house 200 yards to its right front, as well as from the line of trenches, just east and south of Fontaine, and began to suffer casualties. On reaching the German line, the wire was found to be uncut, and this, combined with the absence of the tanks, nearly ruined the success of the whole movement.

In spite of these difficulties, however, Nos. 1 and 3 Companies got through the wire, and captured the trench, but their losses were very heavy. It was asking a good deal of a battalion to advance against a number of machine-guns, with strands of uncut wire intervening, and it was truly a marvellous performance to take the

Chapter XXVI.
3rd Batt.
Nov. 1917.

enemy's trench under such conditions. Actually Lieutenant Bowes-Lyon with No. 1 Company managed not only to penetrate the wire, but to seize the machine-guns in the small house.

Second Lieutenant G. Hoare, who was on the left with No. 3 Company, was wounded in the face by a bullet, as he arrived at the enemy's wire, and Second Lieutenant A. C. Knollys took over command. This company was more fortunate than the others, for after it had penetrated the enemy's wire and was entering Fontaine, the tanks came up, and enabled it to secure the first objective without much trouble or many casualties. The difficulty was the mass of isolated houses, which were admirably suited for defence, and which provided good cover for the enemy's machine-guns. The first house on the north side of the road held up the advance, until Second Lieutenant Carrington with some of No. 4 Company came up in support of No. 3, and seized the house, together with all its occupants. On the south side of the road the enfilade machine-gun fire was terrific, and before the men could reach the shelter of any house, Captain Beaumont-Nesbitt was killed. The two companies in support now came up, and the Battalion continued from this moment to fight practically as two half-battalions. No. 1 and No. 2 Companies suffered most, and all the officers and most of the N.C.O.'s were killed or wounded. In the village it became a difficult matter to distinguish between the houses held by the enemy and those occupied by our men, and thus several parties were cut off.

CAMBRAI AND GOUZEAUCOURT 343

After some very fierce fighting the Germans were slowly driven back all along the line. Lieutenant Bowes-Lyon, who had gallantly rushed on, was killed, and Lieutenant Worsley shared the same fate. The remaining officers of these two companies were all wounded: Second Lieutenant Hollins through the foot, Second Lieutenant Cooper through the arm, and Second Lieutenant Long in the face and arm. A dozen men of one party, without an officer, fought their way through to the church, where they joined up with some men of No. 3 Company.

The first objective was now secured, although the price paid had been heavy, and the village had to be mopped up. Here was another difficulty: the companies were so weak that they could not even find enough men to escort the prisoners they had taken. Then the ammunition began to run short, and the supply of bombs became alarmingly low. The enemy remained in possession of two derelict tanks, captured in an earlier attack, and from the trenches just south of the village were able to keep up a harassing fire. Captain Hughes, when he came up with No. 4 Company, determined to push on, but could find no signs of No. 2 Company in the labyrinth of houses. He divided his company into two parties, one of which he himself led to attack the trench on the Cambrai road, while the other, under Second Lieutenant Carrington, was ordered to secure the Station road as far as the Crucifix. Both parties secured their objectives, and began to consolidate their position.

It was shortly afterwards discovered that the

right flank of No. 3 Company was in the air. At the time nothing was known of the failure of No. 1 and No. 2 Companies to carry their objective, and in anticipation of their arrival a defensive flank of a sergeant and twelve men with a Lewis gun was formed. The valley to the south of the village was filled with the enemy, and under the wall of the churchyard there was a deep dug-out full of Germans, one of whom was so placed at the entrance that he could not be seen. Every time a bomb was thrown from round the corner he fired at the thrower's hand, and managed to kill one man and wound another. As no phosphorous bombs were available, a guard was placed over the entrance, and the dug-out was left for future treatment.

But it was beginning to dawn on the remaining officers of the 3rd Battalion that all was not well, since not only did no reinforcements arrive, but the troops on the left seemed to be in great difficulties. Colonel Thorne went round, and told all the parties he saw to hold on where they were, until reinforcements came up, but the men were being shot at from houses in all directions. A determined counter-attack by the Germans, who seemed to be in some force, drove back Captain Hughes's platoons, and Second Lieutenant Sir J. Hanham was wounded, but the tables were soon turned when the tanks came up, and poured a terrific fire into the retreating enemy. Captain Hughes, who had dealt successfully with a very complicated operation, was now wounded, and Second Lieutenant Carrington took command of No. 4 Company.

The situation had begun to look very precarious. The houses in the village, most of which were undamaged, might easily mask the advance of considerable numbers of the enemy, and the men did not know how long they could hold on to their position, without being cut off. Although the tanks had done wonders in clearing the streets, as well as the trenches along the embankment, they were of very little assistance in the village itself, where so many houses were still untouched by artillery fire. The enemy's shells, which never ceased to fall, combined with the snipers' bullets, made the position anything but pleasant.

Two companies from the 4th Battalion were ordered up, but the situation demanded more drastic measures, and before these small reinforcements even started, the enemy made very heavy counter-attacks, first from the railway-cutting north-east of Bourlon Wood, on the left flank of the 1st Battalion Coldstream, then against the junction of the 1st Battalion Coldstream and 3rd Battalion Grenadiers, while a third took place round the southern edge of the village. Colonel Thorne decided to hold the village with three centres of resistance, one from the cross-roads in the centre of the village to the south corner of the village beyond the church, under Second Lieutenant Knollys, the second at the cross-roads in the centre of the village, under Lieutenant Mackay of the Machine-Gun Guards, with two machine-guns, and the third on the left from the cross-roads to the right flank of the 1st Battalion Coldstream, under Second Lieutenant Ball. At the same time Lieutenant Carstairs was sent up with six men, to get touch with Lieutenant Carrington, who with thirty men was stubbornly holding on to the position he had gained.

These measures would have been very effective if it had been merely a matter of clinging on till reinforcements arrived, but as these depleted companies could not expect to hold their own for long unsupported, Colonel Thorne determined to go back himself, and press for more troops to be sent up. It now appeared that there was a gap of nearly 500 yards between the 3rd Battalion Grenadiers and 1st Battalion Coldstream, and that the enemy were creeping through. But so intent were they on cutting off the Coldstream that they did not appear to notice the Grenadiers, with the result that they were heavily enfiladed. They retired precipitately, but their retirement was only momentary, for in a short time they returned with two machine-guns. At the same time Germans were reported to be advancing from the north in large numbers, while the counter-attack against the Irish Guards was developing with renewed vigour.

The position of the 3rd Battalion was now perilous in the extreme. They were outflanked, and the enemy in front was visibly increasing in numbers. Lieutenant Mackay with the centre party was forced to retire before a large number of the enemy, and his withdrawal rendered the position of both Second Lieutenant Knollys and Second Lieutenant Ball untenable. Quite apart from the danger of being cut off, these platoons were not nearly strong enough to resist any attack in large numbers.

Thus No. 4 Company, under Second Lieutenant Carrington, was practically cut off, with the enemy already behind it. It had held on under the impression that another brigade would come to its support, but found itself in danger of being surrounded. So the men faced about and fought their way back to the original line. No attempt was made to hold the old German front trench, for it was without a field of fire on the east, and the wire was all on the wrong side, while it could be raked by fire from the buildings on the western end of the village at a range of about fifty yards.

This, as already remarked, was one of the only failures in which the Guards Division took part. This splendid Brigade had been practically decimated, and no advance had been made. The first objective had been taken, and in some places even the second objective was reached, but all the work was wasted, owing to the failure of the higher command to bring up any reinforcements.

The casualties were: Three officers killed and six wounded; while among other ranks the total casualties were 270.

On the 28th the 3rd Battalion Grenadiers, 1st Battalion Coldstream, and 2nd Battalion Irish Guards were relieved by three battalions of Seymour's Brigade, and remained in support in La Justice area. That night the Guards Division was relieved by the Fifty-ninth Division, and withdrew to Trescault, Metz-en-Couture, and Bertincourt.

CHAPTER XXVI.
3rd Batt.
Nov. 29.
1917.

Dec.

On the 29th Sergison-Brooke's Brigade moved from Trescault to Bertincourt. There they remained until the dramatic news arrived that the Germans had broken through our line, when it moved to Gouzeaucourt Wood, where it bivouacked in the open, but its services were not required. On December 1, when De Crespigny's and Seymour's Brigades attacked Gauche Wood and Gonnelieu, it was in reserve, and that evening it relieved De Crespigny's Brigade in the front line and occupied chalk trenches, in part of Gauche Wood, and in bitterly cold weather, with no coats or blankets, until December 4. During those four days there was the usual amount of shelling, but no attack was made by either side. On the night of December 1 the Germans brought up teams of horses to remove two field-guns, which had been abandoned within twenty yards of the trenches by Villers Guislain, occupied by No. 3 Company, but were driven off by rifle and revolver fire. On December 4 the 2nd Brigade was relieved by the 1st and 2nd South African Regiments, and retired from the area of operations with the rest of the Guards Division. On the 7th the Battalion moved to Simencourt, where it remained till the end of December. The following officers joined during December: Second Lieutenant W. A. Pembroke, Captain N. C. Tufnell, Lieutenant C. H. Bedford, Lieutenant W. Champneys, Second Lieutenant E. J. Bunbury.

CHAPTER XXVII

JANUARY, FEBRUARY, MARCH 1918

Diary of the War

ALTHOUGH fighting went on all down the line, and constant raids were made, no operations on a large scale were carried out by either side during the first two months of the year. In March the great German attack on the Third and Fourth British Armies commenced. The British positions were penetrated in several places, and a large number of prisoners were claimed. This initial success was quickly followed by other victories, and the territory which had been gained during the last year was lost by the British. Towards the end of March the German rush was checked, but not until they had nearly reached Amiens.

In Russia peace was signed with the Germans, and hostilities ceased on the Eastern front.

In Italy attacks on a small scale continued, but no large operations were attempted.

In Palestine General Allenby continued his advance north of Jerusalem, and in Mesopotamia General Marshall defeated the Turkish Army at Khan Baghdadre.

THE 1st BATTALION

January 1 to March 31, 1918

The officers of the 1st Battalion were as follows :

Lieut.-Colonel M. E. Makgill-Crichton-Maitland, D.S.O.	Commanding Officer.
Major Viscount Lascelles	Second in Command.
Capt. P. J. S. Pearson-Gregory, M.C.	Adjutant.
Lieut. W. H. Lovell, M.C.	Lewis Gun Officer.
2nd Lieut. L. G. Byng	Transport Officer.
Capt. J. Teece, M.C.	Quartermaster.
Lieut. L. de J. Harvard	King's Company.
Lieut. J. A. Lloyd	,, ,,
2nd Lieut. R. C. Bruce	,, ,,
Lieut. A. A. Moller, M.C.	No. 2 Company.
2nd Lieut. W. U. Timmis	,, ,,
2nd Lieut. E. G. Hawkesworth	,, ,,
2nd Lieut. V. A. N. Wall	,, ,,
Lieut. O. F. Stein	No. 3 Company.
Lieut. P. G. Simmons, M.C.	,, ,,
2nd Lieut. F. H. Ennor	,, ,,
2nd Lieut. S. J. Hargreaves	,, ,,
Capt. R. D. Lawford	No. 4 Company.
Lieut. R. P. le P. Trench, M.C.	,, ,,
Lieut. J. F. Tindal-Atkinson	,, ,,
2nd Lieut. C. C. Mays	,, ,,
Capt. H. H. Castle, R.A.M.C.	Medical Officer.

The 1st Battalion left its billets north of the Scarpe, and went by train to Fampoux, where it relieved the 12th Battalion Highland Light Infantry in the line, with three companies in the front trench and one in reserve. On the 5th it was relieved by the 4th Battalion Grenadiers, and retired into Brigade Reserve for four days. On returning to the front trenches on the 9th, a hostile patrol was observed approaching our lines,

JANUARY TO MARCH 1918

and was easily dispersed. One German appeared without any arms or equipment, and on being challenged gave himself up: he turned out to be a miserable specimen belonging to the 236th Prussian Infantry Regiment. On the 13th the 1st Battalion again went into reserve, and on the 16th retired to Arras. During the days spent in the trenches, one man had been killed and several wounded. Lieutenant H. B. Vernon, Second Lieutenant J. H. Frere, Lieutenant R. Echlin, and Second Lieutenant J. R. Nicholson joined the Battalion, and Major Lord Lascelles left to go through a Commanding Officers' course at Aldershot. On the 25th the 1st Battalion again went into the line, relieving the 1st Battalion Irish Guards just south of the River Scarpe. On the 29th the enemy put down a considerable barrage, lasting half an hour, of all calibres, including trench mortars, on the front line where No. 2 Company under Captain Rhodes was posted, and made an attempt to raid the posts in two places under cover of the barrage. They were, however, repulsed, and never succeeded in entering our trenches. A patrol, that subsequently went out, found two dead and two wounded Germans belonging to the Twenty-fourth Divisional Sturm-Truppen, and ascertained from one of the wounded men that the raiders had numbered fifty, but had been prevented from advancing any farther on account of their barrage shooting short. The casualties in No. 2 Company were two killed and nine wounded, mostly by shell-fire.

The 1st Battalion remained in the line until

February 3, when it was relieved by the 1st Battalion Welsh Guards, and retired into billets at Arras. After four days' rest, it returned to the line for three days, and then proceeded to Gordon Camp, where it remained until the 14th. It spent three more days in the trenches, and on the 18th made a move to Baudimont Barracks. Captain Pearson-Gregory left, to join the Headquarters of the 3rd Guards Brigade, and in his absence Lieutenant Lovell was appointed acting Adjutant. Lieutenant Gascoigne and Second Lieutenant Ames rejoined the Battalion, and Lieutenant Ennor and Lieutenant Moller left to take up Staff appointments. After four days in the support trenches, the Battalion went up into the line on the 27th. During the various periods spent in the front trenches, there had been a few casualties, but on the whole the Battalion suffered very little loss during the month.

On March 8 Viscount Gort took over command of the Battalion from Lieut.-Colonel Maitland. A strong German offensive was now daily expected, and the Battalion was consequently reduced to fighting strength, the surplus men being sent to the Guards Divisional Reinforcement Battalion. But although the enemy's working-parties could be distinctly heard, nothing in the nature of an attack from the enemy took place during the first fortnight in March. The artillery on both sides was very active, and never ceased sending over shells. On March 15 the 1st Battalion retired to Gordon Camp, and remained always on the alert, so that it could be

JANUARY TO MARCH 1918

available at three-quarters of an hour's notice. Advantage was taken of a week's rest to have football matches, boxing contests, and musical entertainments in the evening, after the day's training had been done. This undoubtedly freshened up the men, and helped them to forget the monotony of trench life. On the 20th Captain Greville came from the 4th Battalion to take up the duties of second in command. On the 21st Major-General Feilding sent for the Battalion Commanders, and expounded his views on the various rôles in a counter-attack, which the Division might be called upon to play. It was of course impossible to issue any definite orders, since everything depended on where and in what strength the Germans contemplated making their attack.

CHAPTER XXVII.

1st Batt. March 1918.

OFFICERS WHO TOOK PART IN THE OPERATIONS AT THE END OF MARCH 1918

Lieut.-Colonel J. S. S. P. Viscount Gort, D.S.O., M.V.O., M.C.	Commanding Battalion.
Capt. R. D. Lawford, M.C.	Act.-Second in Command.
Lieut. the Hon. P. P. Cary	Act.-Adjutant.
2nd Lieut. E. G. Hawkesworth	Intelligence Officer.
Lieut. J. A. Lloyd	King's Company.
2nd Lieut. R. C. Bruce	,, ,,
2nd Lieut. A. Ames	,, ,,
Lieut. L. de J. Harvard	No. 2 Company.
2nd Lieut. J. H. Frere	,, ,,
Capt. O. F. Stein	No. 3 Company.
2nd Lieut. W. A. Fleet	,, ,,
Lieut. the Hon. T. G. P. Corbett	,, ,,
2nd Lieut. C. C. Mays	No. 4 Company.

2nd Lieut. G. E. A. A. Fitz-George Hamilton	. .	No. 4 Company.
Lieut. R. F. W. Echlin .	.	Transport Officer.
Capt. and Q.M. J. Teece, M.C.		Quartermaster.
1st Lieut. C. A. Forgety, U.S.M.O.R.C. .	. .	Medical Officer.

On the 22nd Brigadier-General Lord Henry Seymour took with him in buses the Commanding Officers of Battalions as well as the Company Commanders, to reconnoitre the ground round Henin. As soon as Lord Gort returned, the Battalion was ordered to move at half an hour's notice in buses to the Mercatel area. At 6 P.M. it reached its destination, and went into billets in some Nissen huts in the neighbourhood of that village. Immediately on arrival Lord Gort took the Company Commanders with him, to reconnoitre the 3rd system to the north-east of Boiry Becquerelle, and on the 23rd the Battalion went up into the front line with the King's Company under Lieutenant Lloyd on the right, No. 2 under Lieutenant Harvard in the centre, and No. 3 under Captain Stein on the left, while No. 4 under Lieutenant Mays remained in reserve. Patrols were at once sent out along the whole front, but discovered nothing, although a number of the enemy had been seen assembling in the sunken roads leading to Henin.

Mar. 24. On the morning of the 24th the Germans commenced an attack across the front of the Battalion, and were caught by enfilade fire from Captain Stein's Company, which inflicted heavy losses on them as they advanced. The troops employed by the enemy seemed to have been well trained in the new method of attack, and men were dribbled forward to their assembly positions, where they deployed into waves for the attack, but when they came under our machine-gun, Lewis-gun, and rifle fire, they soon began to bunch in groups. It seemed as if the enemy's troops had started with the intention of carrying out the operation at the double for the whole 3000 yards. In order even to attempt this, they must have undergone a considerable training to reach the standard of physical fitness necessary for such an attack. Round discs were used to maintain the correct direction, and the flanks of the attack were marked by flags. In other respects they appeared to have evolved no new ideas in minor tactics, and the absence of any covering fire during the advance was most noticeable. Light machine-guns followed up in rear of the assault, and only came into action to cover the retirement of the defeated "Sturm-Truppen."

On the 25th patrols were again pushed out, and, although the enemy could be seen moving about on the Croiselles—Henin road, the day passed quietly. That night, in accordance with verbal instructions received over the telephone, the 1st Battalion withdrew to the Army line, commencing the evacuation of the front trenches at 11.30 P.M. Although the orders for this retirement were originally received at 2.20 P.M., they were subsequently cancelled, and it was not until 1.30 A.M. that the retirement was carried out after verbal orders over the telephone had been received. The only incident that occurred during this withdrawal was the approach of an enemy patrol towards the rearguard platoon of the King's company, which at once opened fire on them. The hostile patrol scattered, and the retirement was carried out without further molestation. Lord Gort kept two platoons from No. 4 Company in their position, to ensure that no troops of the Guards Division had been left east of the Arras—Bapaume road. He also telephoned to the officer commanding the Royal Scots Fusiliers, and satisfied himself that this regiment was conforming with his movements before he withdrew the rearguard.

The new sector occupied by the 1st Battalion was to the north-east of Boisieux-St.-Marc, and was held by Lieutenant Lloyd's, Lieutenant Harvard's, and Captain Stein's Companies, each having two platoons in close support in shell slits. The 2nd Battalion Scots Guards was on the right, and the Royal Scots Fusiliers on the left.

Mar. 26. One and a half hours before dawn the next day outpost patrols, consisting of picked shots, were pushed forward by each Company in the line, so that any attempt on the part of the enemy to occupy Boiry Becquerelle might be instantly reported. At 7.30 one patrol sent back the information that the Germans could be seen, advancing in large numbers in artillery formation, and covered by a screen of scouts. The enemy's aircraft had been busy since the preceding day, in flying over this area, while the German artillery continued to shell the western end of Boiry Becquerelles and the Arras—Bapaume road with 5·9 howitzers. These combined efforts of the

JANUARY TO MARCH 1918 357

enemy's artillery and aircraft seemed to suggest that, in the opinion of the Germans, the Guards Division would be compelled, by the situation farther north, to withdraw. Orders for a farther withdrawal of Seymour's Brigade were issued, and were cancelled that evening, as the enemy made no signs of any further attack.

<small>CHAPTER XXVII.

1st Batt. March 1918.</small>

The enemy put down a heavy and accurate barrage on our front line, in the morning of the 27th, which lasted about an hour; in the afternoon it died down, and no infantry attack developed. That night the 1st Battalion was relieved by the 1st Battalion Welsh Guards, and went into support until the night of the 29th. During the relief Lieutenant J. R. Nicholson and Lieutenant W. U. Timmis were wounded.

<small>March 27–29.</small>

On returning to the front trenches, it found the enemy's machine-guns very active. At dawn patrols were sent out 300 yards in front of the line, and no movement on the part of the enemy was reported. Everything was quiet until 8 A.M., when the German artillery put down a heavy barrage on our front trenches. This bombardment was supplemented by Minenwerfer, and was directed more especially against certain points, which the enemy evidently considered of tactical value. The barrage increased in intensity later, and extended to the back area. Shells fell with considerable accuracy on the front trenches, and the whole Battalion had a terrible time. But the Germans, with characteristic thoroughness, were not content with this: they thickened up their barrage with machine-gun fire, and sent fourteen aeroplanes to drop

<small>Mar. 30.</small>

358   THE GRENADIER GUARDS

<small>Chapter XXVII.
1st Batt.
March 1918.</small>
bombs behind the trenches. They not unnaturally thought that, after three hours of a bombardment of this kind, no one could possibly remain to resist their infantry attack, but in this they were mistaken. The 1st Battalion remained unmoved. Shattered, covered with earth, deafened by the constant explosions, dazed by the spectacle of maimed and mutilated men, the Grenadiers hung grimly on to their line, though in some places the trenches were completely obliterated.

Amongst the casualties at this time were Lieutenant Harvard, who was killed by a Minenwerfer, and Second Lieutenant Mays, who was mortally wounded by machine-gun bullets.

At 10.45 A.M. the enemy's barrage lifted, and was replaced by an intense machine-gun fire, which swept the parapets. Under cover of this the enemy's attack developed, and dense masses of men could be seen advancing. Under the impression that the bombardment had accounted for most of the Battalion, and had so demoralised the survivors as to render them incapable of resistance, the Germans determined to turn the flank of Seymour's Brigade, and marched up the sunken road in close formation. They apparently thought that by sheer weight of numbers they could gain their object, and when they came in sight they were met with a withering fire which completely staggered them. To their dismay they found that not only was the 1st Battalion waiting for them, but that the men were shooting coolly and accurately, in spite of the shelling to which they had been subjected. The attack was stopped, and although the Germans suffered heavily in their ineffectual attempts to reach our trench, they never succeeded even in reaching the wire, except at one point opposite No. 2 Company. When they approached by the sunken road in dense masses, one of their companies was sent round the south-western edge of the road to carry out a flanking movement, and about fifty men succeeded in entering into the front trench, occupied by No. 2 Company. Captain Stein immediately organised a counter-attack, and in order to cut off any Germans who might escape, sent Lieutenant Corbett with a party to a position on the sunken road, where they could fire on the Germans as they were ejected from the trench. Meanwhile he himself led a bombing attack down the trench towards the sunken road. This manœuvre was completely successful, and was undertaken with so much rapidity and daring that the Germans were not only quickly ejected, but fell an easy prey to Lieutenant Corbett's party, as they attempted to escape down the sunken road. On returning to the trenches, Lieutenant Corbett was buried by a Minenwerfer, and had his leg smashed. The German attack had been a costly failure, and, in spite of the three hours' bombardment and the masses of men employed, not even a dent had been made in the line. From a wounded prisoner who was taken the next day it was ascertained that the Germans had employed two regiments (the 452nd and 453rd) in this attack, each having one battalion in the front line, while a third regiment was to exploit the attack if

360 THE GRENADIER GUARDS

CHAPTER XXVII.
1st Batt. March 1918.

successful. Although the infantry attack was effectually arrested, the enemy maintained a heavy machine-gun and rifle fire until it was dark, probably with the intention of preventing patrols following them up, and also to enable them to clear their wounded.

The casualties in the 1st Battalion were remarkably small, amounting to 80, with two officers killed and one wounded. The men were all dead beat after these strenuous days in the trenches, and they had to remain for another twenty-four hours in the front line. Lieutenant Vernon came up to command No. 4 Company, and Second Lieutenant Webber joined No. 3

Mar. 31. Company. The next day passed uneventfully except for a certain amount of shelling. Captain Malcolm was sent up to take command of the King's Company.

THE 2ND BATTALION

January 1 to March 31, 1918

2nd Batt. Jan.

ROLL OF OFFICERS OF THE 2ND BATTALION AT THE BEGINNING OF JANUARY

Lieut.-Colonel G. E. C. Rasch, D.S.O.	Commanding Officer.
Major the Hon. W. R. Bailey, D.S.O.	Second in Command.
Capt. A. H. Penn	Adjutant.
Hon. Capt. W. E. Acraman, M.C.	Quartermaster.
Lieut. G. G. M. Vereker, M.C.	Transport Officer.
Capt. F. A. M. Browning, D.S.O.	No. 1 Company.
Lieut. M. H. Ponsonby	,, ,,
Lieut. G. B. Wilson	,, ,,
2nd Lieut. R. G. Briscoe, M.C.	,, ,,
2nd Lieut. C. C. T. Giles	,, ,,

JANUARY TO MARCH 1918

Capt. C. N. Newton, M.C.	No. 2 Company.	
Lieut. the Hon. F. H. Manners, M.C.	,,	,,
Lieut. O. Martin Smith	,,	,,
2nd Lieut. R. H. R. Palmer	,,	,,
2nd Lieut. H. B. G. Morgan	,,	,,
2nd Lieut. S. C. K. George	,,	,,
Capt. G. R. Westmacott, D.S.O.	No. 3 Company.	
Lieut. S. T. S. Clarke	,,	,,
2nd Lieut. H. White	,,	,,
2nd Lieut. F. J. Langley	,,	,,
2nd Lieut. R. T. Sharpe	,,	,,
Capt. G. C. FitzH. Harcourt-Vernon, D.S.O.	No. 4 Company.	
Lieut. R. A. W. Bicknell, M.C.	,,	,,
Lieut. F. P. Loftus	,,	,,
2nd Lieut. G. H. Hanning	,,	,,
2nd Lieut. H. M. Chapman	,,	,,
Capt. J. A. Andrews, M.C., R.A.M.C.	Medical Officer.	
Lieut. H. M. Long	U.S. Army Medical Staff.	

CHAPTER XXVII.

2nd Batt. Jan. 1918.

On January 1 the 2nd Battalion marched from Berneville to Arras, and went into good billets in Levis Barracks. Second Lieutenant J. S. Carter and Second Lieutenant the Hon. S. A. S. Montagu arrived on the 8th. On the 9th the Battalion went into the line for a tour of sixteen days, spending alternately four days in the front trenches and four days in support. The frontage allotted to the Battalion was astride the River Scarpe, with one company in the village of Roeux on the north side, and the remaining three companies on the south side of the river. In many ways the line was convenient, for there was a light railway as well as a canal, which facilitated the bringing up of troops and rations to within a mile of the line. There were also cook-houses, where hot meals could be cooked, and conveyed thence in hot food containers to the line. Above all, there was a continuous line of communication throughout the Battalion area; on the other hand, the trenches had been neglected, and in places were unrevetted. During the first four days spent in the front line nothing of importance occurred, although there were a few casualties caused by shell-fire. Colonel Lord Ardee assumed command of the 1st Guards Brigade, replacing Colonel Follett, who had been in command while Brigadier-General de Crespigny was on leave. Rain fell almost unceasingly during the four days spent in support, and the trenches became so impassable that the men had to work day and night to make them habitable. On the 17th Lieut.-Colonel Rasch went on a month's leave, and Major the Hon. W. Bailey took over the command with Captain Harcourt-Vernon as second in command. The four days in the front line from the 17th to the 21st were unusually quiet, and the Germans confined themselves to spasmodic bombardments by trench mortars at dusk and at dawn. On the 19th the Corps Commander, Lieut.-General Sir Charles Fergusson (an old Grenadier), visited the Battalion. During the following days spent in support, there was a heavy bombardment with gas-shells, and when the next tour of duty in the front line came, the railway was subjected to heavy shelling. Several gas-shells fell among Nos. 2 and 4 Companies, which were waiting to entrain, but owing to good gas discipline the casualties were slight, the chief injuries being caused to men who were splashed with liquid from the exploding shells.

JANUARY TO MARCH 1918

Several men had to be sent to hospital suffering from the effects of gas, and Lieutenant M. H. Ponsonby was sent home for the same reason.

Owing to the formation of the 4th Guards Brigade in the Thirty-first Division, the Guards Divisional frontage was readjusted, and each Brigade, now consisting of only three battalions, had one battalion in the front line, one in support, and one in reserve, the latter usually in Arras. The 2nd Battalion was in support from the 2nd to the 5th, and was chiefly employed on fatigues, digging out forward trenches, and carrying up wire and duckboards. On the 6th it moved into the front line, when it had a few casualties. After four days in reserve at Arras it returned to the support line, and was again occupied in improving and strengthening the trenches. On the 14th Second Lieutenant A. P. J. M. P. de Lisle joined from the Reinforcement Battalion. Rumours of a coming German offensive reached the Division, and Staff Officers came from all directions, while new trenches in unexpected places sprang up every night. On the 22nd the Battalion went into reserve, and spent the following days resting in Gordon Camp.

On March 6 a raid was carried out by the 2nd Battalion. While it was in the support line, Major Bailey had been told that the Battalion would be required to carry out a raid when it went up into the front line, as the Intelligence Branch of the Headquarters Staff was anxious to obtain information with regard to the coming German offensive. The place selected for the raid was opposite the extreme left of the Battalion

CHAPTER XXVII.

2nd Batt. March 1918.

frontage, and had been chosen partly because the aeroplane photographs showed that the enemy was thinner there than elsewhere, and partly on account of some rising ground on the left which would give partial protection from machine-gun fire. In the original scheme a silent raid by twenty-four men under Lieutenant Palmer was proposed, but this was altered later to a raid on a larger scale with an artillery and trench mortar barrage. In addition to the twenty-four men from No. 2 Company, eight volunteers from the other three companies were called for, and the whole party proceeded to Gordon Camp under Lieutenant Clarke, with Captain Browning, who was an old hand at raids, to supervise their training. Meanwhile a great deal of valuable reconnaissance and preparation was carried out from the front line by Captain O. M. Smith, commanding No. 2 Company. Unfortunately during the few days before the raid the visibility was good, and therefore unfavourable for such operations, since the greater part of the wire-cutting had to be postponed until the day before the raid took place. In order to deceive the enemy as to the actual place selected for the raid, wire-cutting was carried out at different places along the whole Divisional frontage.

The night of the raid proved to be fine and bright. The raiders were brought up from Gordon Camp in buses, and, after an issue of rum at advanced Battalion Headquarters, formed up on a tape in No Man's Land about 150 yards from the enemy's trench (the total distance between the opposing trench lines being 240 yards). At zero hour, 2.40 A.M., our artillery put down a barrage on the German front trenches for one minute, and then lifted it on to the support trenches, where it was maintained during the raid. At the same time two separate barrages were dropped on either flank, while suspected saps, machine-guns, and communication trenches had a standing barrage of Newton trench mortars and howitzers directed on them. The raiders were divided into three parties : the right and left parties, each consisting of a sergeant and eight men, entered the enemy trench simultaneously and immediately wheeled outwards. The centre party, consisting of Lieutenant Clarke himself, a sergeant, two stretcher-bearers, and five men, remained at the point of entry. The orders were that the raid was not to last more than twenty minutes, and the raiders were to withdraw as soon as a prisoner had been captured. In order to confuse the enemy great quantities of coloured lights were sent up along the whole Divisional front. The enemy were completely taken by surprise, although, as subsequent examination of the prisoners proved, they had been warned of the possibility of a raid. The right and left parties had not gone far before they came upon several small shelters containing Germans. These were at once bombed and two prisoners were quickly captured. At the same time a machine-gun mounted on the parapet was taken, and the team bayoneted. The gun itself was carried back to our lines by Private Marshal of No. 1 Company. Lieutenant Clarke at once ordered a withdrawal, as the object of the raid had been accomplished, and the whole party returned safely with its two prisoners and machine-gun, having been away for only twelve minutes. Somewhat later the enemy retaliated with machine-guns, trench mortars, and artillery, but caused no casualties, and finally the shelling on both sides died down completely. The prisoners were identified as belonging to the 10th Imperial Bavarian Regiment; one was a machine-gunner and the other an orderly. A certain amount of useful information was elicited, but their knowledge was naturally only local.

With the exception of this raid, nothing of importance occurred at the beginning of March, until on the 12th Second Lieutenant G. H. Hanning and Second Lieutenant H. M. Chapman were both wounded by the same shell. Fortunately they were close to a dressing-station, and were in the doctor's hands within ten minutes. On the 13th an attack was expected, and our artillery fired continual bursts of harassing fire which brought retaliation from the Germans, during which one sergeant and three men were wounded. The four days from the 14th to the 18th were spent in the line, but proved uneventful, and on the 20th the 2nd Battalion retired to Arras. Next day rumours of a successful German offensive on a large front reached the Battalion, but nothing definite was known. Shells fell in Arras, causing many casualties, and the town began to be cleared of its inhabitants. On the 22nd Lieutenant P. V. Pelly and fifty men who had been transferred from the Household Battalion joined from the Reinforcement Battalion.

JANUARY TO MARCH 1918

Further disquieting rumours with regard to the German advance were repeated from mouth to mouth, and became so exaggerated that drastic and often unnecessary measures were taken to prevent any stores from falling into the hands of the Germans.

On the 24th preparations were made to relieve the 1st Battalion Scots Guards in the Army line, from St. Leger running north towards Henin, but in the afternoon these instructions were cancelled. It appeared that the enemy had taken Gomiecourt, and was advancing towards Courcelles. Lieut.-Colonel Rasch received orders to take up an outpost line on the high ground south-west of Boiry, and went off at once with the Company Commanders, to reconnoitre the ground and settle the boundaries.

The following officers accompanied the Battalion:

Lieut.-Colonel G. E. C. Rasch, D.S.O.	Commanding Officer.
Capt. G. C. FitzH. Harcourt-Vernon, D.S.O.	Act.-Second in Command.
Capt. A. H. Penn	Adjutant.
Capt. F. A. M. Browning, D.S.O.	No. 1 Company.
2nd Lieut. H. B. G. Morgan	,, ,,
2nd Lieut. J. S. Carter	,, ,,
Capt. O. Martin Smith	No. 2 Company.
2nd Lieut. S. C. K. George	,, ,,
2nd Lieut. A. P. J. M. P. de Lisle	,, ,,
Lieut. S. T. S. Clarke, M.C.	No. 3 Company.
2nd Lieut. F. J. Langley	,, ,,
2nd Lieut. the Hon. S. A. S. Montagu	,, ,,
Capt. G. B. Wilson	No. 4 Company.

Chapter XXVII.
2nd Batt.
March 1918.

Lieut. J. H. Jacob	. .	No. 4 Company.
Lieut. D. Harvey .	. .	,, ,,
Capt. W. H. Lister, D.S.O., M.C., R.A.M.C. .	. .	Medical Officer.

Mar. 26. All four companies were placed in the front line and told to find their own supports, but two platoons of No. 1 Company were kept in Battalion reserve. The line of resistance was just on the forward crest of a slope. Patrols were at once sent out, and reported the presence of several units of the Thirty-first Division, still holding the line in front of the Battalion. In the early morning troops were observed moving southward across the front, and these proved to be units of the Thirty-first Division, who had received their orders too late to withdraw under cover of the darkness. Later in the morning the 2nd Guards Brigade appeared on the right with orders to dig a line, in continuation of that held by the 2nd Battalion, and to cover the retirement of the rest of the Thirty-first Division. The remainder of the Guards Division had had to conform to the retirement on the right, by withdrawing during the night to a line which prolonged to the left the new position taken up by the 2nd Battalion, so that at daybreak all four Guards Brigades were in line between Boisieux - St. - Marc and Ayette. During the morning several battalions of the Thirty-first Division passed through the line on the left of the Battalion, and retired to the rear. All the time the enemy were following close behind, and about 7 P.M. Captain Martin Smith reported that 100 Germans could be seen advancing on the crest of a hill in front. They

JANUARY TO MARCH 1918

were preceded by machine-guns, which at once opened fire on our advanced posts, causing a few casualties. This advance on the part of the enemy was, however, soon arrested by Lewis-gun and rifle fire, and for the moment no action developed. As soon as it was dark, patrols were pushed out, and the trench line was wired. At 11.30 P.M. that night orders were issued for De Crespigny's Brigade to relieve Sergison-Brooke's Brigade, the relief to be complete by 4.30 A.M. The 2nd Battalion relieved the 1st Battalion Coldstream astride the Arras-Albert railway, with Nos. 1 and 2 Companies under Captain Browning and Captain Martin Smith on the east side, and Nos. 3 and 4 under Lieutenant Clarke and Captain Wilson on the west side of the railway line. The new position was difficult to hold, for, not only did it include three sunken roads and a railway, but it was also overlooked from the outskirts of Moyenneville and from high ground all along the front, where a number of deserted huts could give cover to snipers and machine-guns. During the night it was found necessary to throw back the right of the line towards the supporting battalion, which had to send up men to fill the gap made on the right by the withdrawal of the Thirty-first Division.

Soon after dawn on the 27th the German infantry appeared, and evidently intended to continue their advance. The whole method of attack seemed to have been altered by the Germans. No longer did they advance in close formation, and offer easy targets to their opponents. They copied our methods, running forward by twos and threes, until a sufficiently strong line of men had been built up for an assault, and all the time feeling for a weak place in the British line. This new method was difficult to counter in many ways, for not only was there no target for our artillery but it entailed a great expenditure of ammunition often with little result. On this occasion, however, the new German tactics were not attended with any success, for the men of the 2nd Battalion began shooting steadily and thinning out the enemy's ranks with great accuracy. The firing was soon universal down the whole line, and the Germans found it impossible to make any headway against the storm of bullets. All four companies had a great deal of shooting, but especially No. 1 under Captain Browning, since it was afforded an opportunity of enfilading the Germans, as they advanced across its front. All the time the enemy's shells fell on the trenches, and No. 4 Company under Captain Wilson suffered severely. Lieutenant D. Harvey was killed by a shell, and Captain Wilson was badly wounded. About the same time Second Lieutenant de Lisle in No. 2 Company was also wounded. Under the storm of shells and bullets the men found time to bring down one of the enemy's aeroplanes which had ventured down too low. The German attack did not progress in this part of the line, and the chief thrust drifted farther to the south opposite the 3rd Battalion Grenadiers and the 4th Guards Brigade. Second Lieutenant Montagu was sent from No. 3 to No. 4 Company, the latter having lost two officers.

The next morning No. 4 Company reported that its patrols had discovered the enemy lining up within 100 yards of its trench; this news was at once telephoned to our artillery, which soon dispersed them with a wonderfully accurate fire. During the morning No. 1 and No. 2 Companies were heavily shelled, and under cover of this barrage and of machine-gun fire, parties of the enemy made continual efforts to penetrate the line, but never even succeeded in reaching the wire. The Germans had direct observation on the whole of our line, and their shooting was consequently very accurate. On the other hand, their abortive attacks over the open cost them dearly, and their losses must have been very heavy. In the 2nd Battalion that day there were 22 killed and 42 wounded, among whom was Lieutenant J. H. Jacob.

The following day was quieter, as the main German attack was made farther south, and advantage was taken of this lull in the offensive to relieve some of the officers in the front line. Major the Hon. W. R. Bailey went up to take the place of Lieut.-Colonel Rasch, and Lieutenant Acland, Lieutenant Manners, Lieutenant Lubbock, Second Lieutenant Sharpe, and Second Lieutenant Pelly replaced Captain Martin Smith, Second Lieutenant Carter, and Second Lieutenant Montagu, who went down to the first line transport for a rest. Forty other ranks were also relieved every night in the same way.

After two hours' very heavy shelling on the 30th, the Germans made two very determined attacks on the Divisional front, but were repulsed with heavy losses. These attacks were not directed against the portion of the line occupied by the 2nd Battalion, which was not therefore engaged. Later on, however, the enemy launched two faint-hearted attacks on the Battalion, one up the railway, and the other west of the railway, and about a dozen Germans succeeded in getting a foothold in a post held by No. 3 Company, from which most of the occupants had been blown by shell-fire. They were promptly ejected, and the post was re-established. Lieutenant Manners and Second Lieutenant Langley were wounded, and the total casualties that day were 10 killed and 35 wounded. In the evening Lieutenant Palmer was sent up to relieve Lieutenant Clarke.

After a quiet day in the line on the 31st the 2nd Battalion was relieved by part of the 1st Battalion Irish Guards and 2nd Battalion Coldstream Guards, and went into Brigade Reserve, Nos. 2 and 4 Companies in huts near Boiry St. Martin, and the remainder of the Battalion in a camp between Heudecourt and Blairville.

THE 3RD BATTALION

January 1 to March 31, 1918

ROLL OF OFFICERS OF THE 3RD BATTALION AT THE BEGINNING OF JANUARY

Lieut.-Colonel A. F. A. N. Thorne, D.S.O.	Commanding Officer.
Major R. H. V. Cavendish, M.V.O.	Second in Command.
Capt. the Hon. A. G. Agar-Robartes, M.C.	Adjutant.

Lieut. C. H. Bedford	Intelligence Officer.
Lieut. E. W. Seymour	Assistant Adjutant.
Lieut. F. J. Heasman	Transport Officer.
Lieut. R. W. Parker	Quartermaster.
Lieut. E. G. A. Fitzgerald	No. 1 Company.
Lieut. W. Champneys	,, ,,
2nd Lieut. E. D. Tate	,, ,,
2nd Lieut. P. J. M. Ellison	,, ,,
Capt. L. Holbech	No. 2 Company.
Lieut. A. H. S. Adair	,, ,,
2nd Lieut. G. A. I. Dury	,, ,,
2nd Lieut. W. A. Pembroke	,, ,,
2nd Lieut. P. Durbin	,, ,,
Capt. N. C. Tufnell	No. 3 Company.
Lieut. A. C. Knollys, M.C.	,, ,,
Lieut. G. W. Godman	,, ,,
2nd Lieut. W. B. Ball	,, ,,
Capt. C. W. Carrington, D.S.O.	No. 4 Company.
2nd Lieut. F. S. V. Donnison	,, ,,
2nd Lieut. C. L. F. Boughey	,, ,,
2nd Lieut. E. J. Bunbury	,, ,,
2nd Lieut. N. C. Bennett	,, ,,
Lieut. H. C. Fish, U.S.R.	Medical Officer.
Capt. the Rev. S. Phillimore, M.C.	Chaplain.

The 3rd Battalion went into the line near Fampoux from the 2nd to the 4th, placing No. 2 Company under Captain Holbech and No. 4 under Captain Carrington south of the River Scarpe, with No. 3 under Captain Tufnell north of the river, and No. 1 under Lieutenant Fitzgerald in reserve. The front line was held by posts which were in good order, but it was bitterly cold, and there was snow on the ground. After two days in support the Battalion retired to Arras for eight days. On the 14th Lieut.-Colonel Thorne, in the absence on leave of the Brigadier, took command of the Brigade, and Major Cavendish commanded the Battalion. On the 17th the Battalion returned to the trenches. A thaw having now set in, the trenches became mere drains, and required a great deal of work to keep them habitable. The four days subsequently spent in support were made unpleasant by the gas-shells, with which the Germans searched the back area.

After four more days in reserve the Battalion returned to the trenches on February 1, when it came in for a severe bombardment with gas-shells, which caused 104 casualties; most of these occurred while the gas-shell holes were being filled in, as it had not been realised before that there was any danger of gas-poisoning while the men performed this work, and masks were therefore not worn. After the usual four days in support and four days in reserve, the Battalion began another tour of duty in the front trenches on the 15th. Patrols went out every night under Lieutenant Bedford or Second Lieutenant Durbin, to ascertain the effect of our trench mortar fire on the enemy's wire, in view of a raid being undertaken. After four more days in reserve the Battalion again retired to Arras.

The same routine was followed during the first three weeks in March, and the days spent in the front line proved uneventful. Rumours of a German offensive movement became more persistent every day, and it was perfectly clear that in the course of the next week the enemy would commence their great attack. Every possible precaution was therefore taken, and the

JANUARY TO MARCH 1918

men in the front line were always looking out for any sign of hostile movement. The German attack actually began at dawn on the 21st, when the 3rd Battalion was in reserve at Arras. The companies were marching off to do their training, when several shells fell in the town, causing four casualties in No. 1 Company. Orders were then received that there was to be as little movement as possible in the town, so that training was confined to musketry and gas drill carried out in the barrack-rooms. At 5.30 on the same evening the Battalion was ordered to move at once to the Mercatel area. There it remained the next day, ready to move at a moment's notice, and the Company Commanders took advantage of this pause to reconnoitre the third system of trenches, in front of Neuville Vitasse and north of Henin-sur-Cojeul. Meanwhile Brigadier-General Sergison-Brooke had been gassed, and the command of the Brigade had devolved on Lieut.-Colonel Follett.

OFFICERS WHO TOOK PART IN THE OPERATIONS AT THE END OF MARCH 1918

Lieut.-Colonel A. F. A. N. Thorne, D.S.O.	Commanding Battalion.
Capt. the Hon. A. G. Agar-Robartes, M.C.	Adjutant.
Lieut. E. W. Seymour	Assistant Adjutant.
Lieut. E. G. A. Fitzgerald	Intelligence Officer.
Capt. R. W. Parker	No. 1 Company.
2nd Lieut. E. D. Tate	,, ,,
2nd Lieut. P. J. M. Ellison	,, ,,
Capt. L. Holbech	No. 2 Company.
Lieut. G. A. I. Dury	,, ,,
2nd Lieut. W. A. Pembroke	,, ,,

Lieut. G. F. Pauling, M.C.	.	No. 3 Company.
Lieut. A. C. Knollys, M.C.	.	,, ,,
Lieut. E. N. de Geijer	. .	,, ,,
2nd Lieut. P. Durbin	. .	,, ,,
Capt. C. W. Carrington, D.S.O.	.	No. 4 Company.
Lieut. W. G. Orriss	. .	,, ,,
2nd Lieut. N. C. Bennett	. .	,, ,,
2nd Lieut. R. Van T. Ranney	.	,, ,,
Lieutenant H. C. Fish, U.S.R.	.	Medical Officer.

At 3 A.M. on the 23rd Lieut.-Colonel Thorne received verbal orders to bring up the Battalion at once, and to relieve the remnants of the 93rd Brigade in the line, but on reaching Boyelles he found that this Brigade had only just taken over the line and required no relief. He therefore withdrew the front companies, Nos. 1 and 4, and placed them in the support trenches, occupied by the West Yorkshire Regiment, which consequently had to retire into reserve. This manœuvre was carried out under heavy shelling, during which Lieutenant Seymour was wounded. That evening No. 2 Company under Captain Holbech and No. 3 under Lieutenant Pauling went up into the front trenches, the remainder of the Battalion being in support. The next day these two companies moved back from the railway cutting, which was being heavily shelled, and occupied the support trenches. The Germans could be seen advancing by twos and threes with the object of forming a sufficiently strong line to attack, but they were scattered by our rifle fire before they could complete the assembly. At night patrols were sent out to obtain identifications but were not successful, since the enemy had had time to remove their dead and wounded.

It was reported that Ervillers had been taken by the Germans; and there seemed every probability that the line held by the Guards Division would have to be withdrawn. A retirement to the Adinfer line being shortly expected, one officer per company was sent back to reconnoitre these trenches. There was little doubt that the Germans were massing their men in front of the line held by the 3rd Battalion, and Lieutenant Pauling reported that they were dug in not fifty yards away, dressed in pack order. The men were quite confident in their ability to stop any advance on the enemy's part, but it was essential that the Guards Division should conform to the movements of the other troops in the line. At 10 P.M. orders were received cancelling all previous ones, and instructing the Battalion to retire to a new line not yet dug. The withdrawal was carried out without hurry, companies retiring at half-hour intervals, and the Lewis-gun sections remaining till the end. The new trench line, composed of slits only, was at once begun, and was completed by the next morning. During the withdrawal Lieutenant Pauling and Second Lieutenant Durbin were killed by the same shell. They were both first-rate officers who could be ill spared, the former having already gained the Military Cross.

Nothing of importance occurred during the 26th, although the Germans were seen in large parties in Hamelincourt and Moyenneville. All day shells continued to fall, but no infantry attack developed.

On the 27th the 3rd Battalion was relieved by

CHAPTER XXVII.
3rd Batt.
March 1918.

the 2nd Battalion Coldstream Guards, and went into Divisional support, where it took up a position in an old German line on the ridge just south of Boiry St. Rictude with all four companies in the line. At 11 A.M. the East Yorkshire Regiment, which was in the front line, was attacked by Germans in mass formation, but held its ground. The enemy, however, was able to creep round in rear and cut it off. This movement placed the 2nd Battalion Irish Guards, on the right, in a perilous position, and forced it to retire. All the time the German artillery shelled the back area, and particularly the valley in which the 3rd Battalion Headquarters was situated. As the East Yorkshire Regiment also retired, the trenches held by the Battalion became the front line. The Germans now determined to pursue their success, and advanced with confidence towards No. 2 Company, but were met with an accurate and steady fire from the Lewis and machine guns, which staggered them and decimated their ranks. The fighting became general all along the line, but although the Germans fought with great courage they were unable to make any impression on the Battalion frontage. The casualties among our officers were very high, Captain Parker and Second Lieutenant Van Ranney receiving severe wounds from which they never recovered. Captain Carrington, Lieutenant Knollys, Second Lieutenant Bennett, Second Lieutenant Tate, and Lieutenant Fish, the American Medical Officer, were wounded. Among other ranks the casualties were 30 killed, 90 wounded, and 4 missing. The attack

JANUARY TO MARCH 1918

now drifted down towards the right, where the 4th Guards Brigade was posted, and the German troops opposed to the 3rd Battalion did not appear to be anxious to renew their attack. That night a somewhat complicated relief took place. Nos. 3 and 4 Companies were relieved by two companies of the 13th Battalion of the York and Lancaster Regiment; No. 3 passing into support, and No. 4 relieving another company of the York and Lancaster Regiment which prolonged the line to the right, and took the place of No. 2 Company. Just before dawn No. 3 Company moved up to get touch with the 2nd Battalion Coldstream Guards, and placed three platoons in the front line with one in support. All these moves were successfully accomplished by daybreak.

Although the Germans had lost very heavily in their attack on the 27th, they had not abandoned the idea of forcing back that part of the line. Early the next morning a heavy barrage was put down by the enemy on our trenches, and soon afterwards a force of about 200 Germans attacked No. 4 Company and the 13th Battalion York and Lancaster Regiment in four waves. So determined was this attack that the Germans succeeded in getting into the posts in the front line. Lieutenant Fitzgerald, who was in command of No. 4 Company, quickly organised a counter-attack from the support platoon of the York and Lancaster Regiment, and, having launched this, organised a second counter-attack from the platoon in support of his own Company, which he led himself. These counter-attacks

380 THE GRENADIER GUARDS

Chapter XXVII.
3rd Batt. March 1918.

were completely successful, and ejected the enemy, who made haste to retire some 400 yards. In order to ensure the stopping of the German attack, should it succeed, Captain Holbech had in the meantime made a strong point in rear of No. 4 Company. Another bombardment by the enemy seemed to indicate the imminence of a further attack, but the evening passed off quietly, the shelling being merely the fringe of the barrage, put down by the enemy farther to the right. There were further casualties among the officers: Lieutenant Orriss was mortally wounded, and Second Lieutenant Ellison was also wounded.

March 29–31.

The 3rd Battalion was then relieved by the 1st Battalion Scots Guards, and went into Brigade Reserve. No. 3 Company remained in slits along the ridge during the day of the 29th, but was withdrawn at night. On the 30th the 3rd Battalion returned to the front line, but except for a certain amount of shelling nothing of importance took place.

The 4th Battalion

January 1 to March 31, 1918

4th Batt. Jan.

At the beginning of 1918 the officers of the 4th Battalion were as follows:

Lieut.-Colonel W. S. Pilcher, D.S.O.	Commanding Officer.
Major C. F. A. Walker, M.C.	Second in Command.
Capt. C. R. Gerard, D.S.O.	Adjutant.
Capt. M. Chapman, M.C.	Intelligence Officer.
Lieut. I. H. Ingelby	Act.-Quartermaster.
2nd Lieut. G. W. Selby-Lowndes	Transport Officer.
Capt. H. H. Sloane-Stanley, M.C.	No. 1 Company.

Lieut. E. R. D. Hoare	No. 1 Company.	
Lieut. C. E. Irby, M.C.	,, ,,	
Lieut. E. H. Tuckwell, M.C.	,, ,,	
2nd Lieut. R. B. Osborne	,, ,,	
Capt. C. E. Benson, D.S.O.	No. 2 Company.	
Lieut. the Hon. C. C. S. Rodney	,, ,,	
2nd Lieut. T. T. Pryce, M.C.	,, ,,	
2nd Lieut. R. L. Murray-Lawes	,, ,,	
Capt. G. C. Sloane-Stanley	No. 3 Company.	
Lieut. the Hon. A. H. L. Hardinge, M.C.	,, ,,	
2nd Lieut. D. J. Knight	,, ,,	
2nd Lieut. C. J. Dawson-Greene	,, ,,	
Capt. B. C. Layton	No. 4 Company.	
Lieut. F. C. Lyon	,, ,,	
Lieut. N. R. Abbey	,, ,,	
2nd Lieut. G. R. Green	,, ,,	
2nd Lieut. R. D. Richardson	,, ,,	
Captain N. Grellier, M.C., R.A.M.C.	Medical Officer.	

On January 1 the 4th Battalion went by train to Athies, and moved into the support line with three Companies near Northumberland Lane, and one Company attached to the 1st Battalion Grenadier Guards. Lieut.-Colonel Pilcher was at the time on leave, and the Battalion was commanded by Major Walker. On the 5th three Companies were moved up into the front trenches with one Company in reserve. On the following day Company Sergeant-Major W. Stretton, Lance-Sergeant C. Hatton, and Lance-Corporal W. Long, all non-commissioned officers of great gallantry and experience, were killed by a Grenatenwerfer, while Captain Layton of the same Company was wounded. There was a hard frost followed by a heavy fall of snow, and a German mistaking his way in the snowstorm

382 THE GRENADIER GUARDS

CHAPTER XXVII.
4th Batt.
Jan. 1918.

walked into our lines, and was taken prisoner. On the 9th the 4th Battalion was relieved by the 1st Battalion, and retired into the support line, where it remained till the 13th.

A thaw now began and caused much damage to the trenches in many places, especially where they were not revetted. The following officers joined the Battalion: Lieutenant T. W. Minchin, D.S.O., Lieutenant M. D. Thomas, Second Lieutenant M. P. B. Wrixon, and Second Lieutenant R. M. Meikle. The four days spent in the front line from the 13th to the 17th were a time of hard frost, followed by a thaw, which made the trenches almost impassable. The enemy sent over a large number of gas-shells, but thanks to the masks there were no casualties. The Battalion was relieved by the 3rd Battalion Grenadier Guards, and marched to Fampoux, where it entrained for Arras. There it was placed in billets in the prison, with Battalion Headquarters in the Rue Gaugières. On the 25th it was sent up as support Battalion to the right sector, and came in for a heavy bombardment of gas-shells. The trenches were now in a deplorable condition, and constant fatigue parties had to be supplied for their improvement.

Feb.

On the night of February 2 a successful raid was carried out by Seymour's Brigade, and four prisoners were captured, but with this exception there was little activity in the front line, and the work of repairing the trenches was proceeded with unmolested. On the 5th the Battalion again retired to Arras for a week's rest, and occupied its old billets. The Battalion transport,

JANUARY TO MARCH 1918 383

inspected by the Brigadier, was reported to be the best in the whole Division, and Second Lieutenant Selby-Lowndes, the transport officer, received great credit for its high state of efficiency.

CHAPTER XXVII.

4th Batt. Feb. 1918.

A decrease in the supply of men for the Army made it necessary to reduce the fighting strength of divisions, and it was therefore decided to reduce each brigade in the Army by one battalion. A new Brigade, consisting of the 4th Battalion Grenadier Guards, 3rd Battalion Coldstream Guards, and 2nd Battalion Irish Guards, was therefore formed and placed under the command of Brigadier-General Lord Ardee. It was with much regret that these Battalions had to leave the Guards Division, in which they had fought for so long. Major-General Feilding sent the following message to Lieut.-Colonel Pilcher:

> I cannot tell you how sad I am that your Battalion should have to leave my Division. Throughout the time that the Battalion has been under my command it has maintained the great traditions of the Brigade of Guards.
>
> Formed as it was during the war, it was able at once to take its place equal in efficiency and smartness to any Battalion in the Division. It has been a great grief to me that I have not been able to be present to bid you farewell and thank all ranks for their services, and wish you all good luck in the future.

END OF VOL. II

Printed by R. & R. CLARK, LIMITED, *Edinburgh.*

www.ingramcontent.com/pod-product-compliance
Lightning Source LLC
Chambersburg PA
CBHW061926220426
43662CB00012B/1820